WOODWORKER'S
30 BEST PROJECTS

No. 3021
$23.95

WOODWORKER'S
30 BEST PROJECTS

THE EDITORS OF
WOODWORKER MAGAZINE

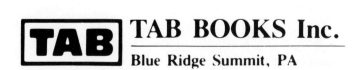 TAB BOOKS Inc.

Blue Ridge Summit, PA

FIRST EDITION

FIRST PRINTING

Library of Congress Cataloging in Publication Data

Woodworker's 30 best projects / by the editors of Woodworker magazine.
    p.   cm.
   Includes index.
   ISBN 0-8306-0421-9   ISBN 0-8306-9321-1 (pbk.)
   1. Woodwork. I. Woodworker (New York, N.Y. : 1980) II. Title:
Woodworker's thirty best projects.
TT185.W659 1988   88-15688
684.1′04—dc19   CIP

Contents

Introduction

THIS BOOK CONTAINS AN ASSORTMENT OF fine furniture projects for the advanced woodworker. They have been collected by the editors of *Woodworker* Magazine and represent the work of various craftsmen, chief among them John Capotosto. We at TAB BOOKS are proud to bring you this collection and are sure you will find *30 Best Projects* to be a source of enjoyment, not only in doing the work you love, but in using the projects in your home as well.

Most of the materials in this book are available at your local lumberyard. Some of the more unusual items—the carvings, clock mechanisms, spindles, finials, and appliques—are also available from Armor Products, P.O. Box 445, East Northport, NY 11731.

Antique Desk

YOU COULD PAY hundreds of dollars for a ready-made secretary-desk like this one—or you can build it in your home workshop for about one-tenth the price.

The economy trick is largely in the gold-antiqued finish, which conceals surface flaws so completely you can use board-grade or even secondhand lumber in the construction. All finishing materials, even the cloth pads for blending and texturing, are supplied in a nationally available kit.

To begin, round up as much scrap board and used lumber as you can to fill out the items specified in the Materials List. Edge-trim and sand all the old lumber. You need not get it smooth, just free of rough fibers. Squeegee a spackling compound over any pits; the antiquing process will hide this filler completely.

Cut the sides, tops, and bottoms of the upper and lower units, making certain the ends are square. The backs may be plywood or tongue-and-groove, although it's a good idea to use plywood for the back of the lower unit to ensure rigidity because the weight of the upper unit rests on it.

Use an original corner of the plywood panel for one of the cabinet corners and you'll square it immediately. Fasten all lumber-to-lumber joints with 8d finishing nails. Sink the heads and spackle them flush. If you are using 1¼-inch plywood for the back, install it with 1-inch brads. Try a gap-filler glue such as casein or aliphatic resin to reinforce the joints.

To prepare doors, rim the lower doors with 1- × -2 stock on all sides, except where the hinges will go. There, install 1- × -3 wood to allow the door to overlap the cabinet side.

Make the upper doors from stock screen frame. Recess an inside edge of the stock ¼ × ¾ inch and cut the horizontal

1

and vertical frame pieces. Lay out the mitered framing and attach with corrugated fasteners.

Instead of screening, cut ¾-inch welded wire mesh on the diagonal to fit the rabbeted area of each top door. A few shots from your staple gun will anchor the mesh, then run casein or aliphatic glue along the channels to lock it firmly all around. The diagonal position is not only decorative, but also braces the doors.

There's a simple trick to shaping the rounded upper portion of the doors. Merely cut a circle from scrap plywood and then use the cut-off sections in the doors. Fasten the plywood fillets in place at upper corners against the wire mesh, using 6d finishing nails through their tapered ends

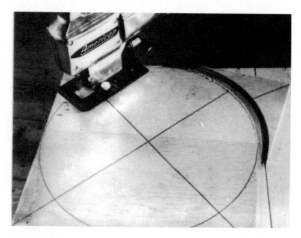

Fig. 1-1. Make both sections at the same time to make sure they will match in width. Favor plywood for the back of the lower unit; tongue-and-groove boards work well for the upper half.

Fig. 1-2. For stiffness, strengthen the lower corners of the upper doors with corner plates. Corrugated fasteners reinforced by curved sections will hold the miters at the upper corners.

Fig. 1-3. Here is an easy way to get curved sections for rounding the door tops. Cut a circle from a square equal to the diameter needed. Two cut corners combine to make a top.

Fig. 1-4. Use spackling compound to fill in every crack and seam that remains after gluing and nailing each curved section in place. The final finish will hide any touch-up work.

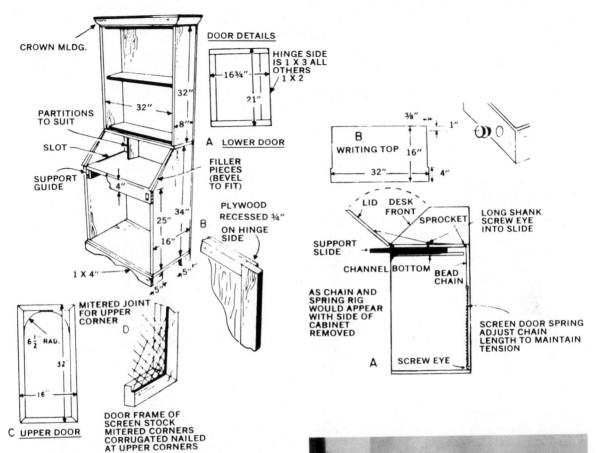

CROWN MLDG.

DOOR DETAILS

HINGE SIDE
IS 1 X 3 ALL
OTHERS
1 X 2

16¾"

32"

32"

21"

8"

PARTITIONS
TO SUIT

A LOWER DOOR

SLOT

FILLER
PIECES
(BEVEL
TO FIT)

SUPPORT
GUIDE

4"

PLYWOOD
RECESSED ¾"
ON HINGE
SIDE

34"

25"

B

16"

1 X 4"

5"

5"

B WRITING TOP

⅜"

1"

16"

32"

4"

LID DESK
FRONT

SPROCKET

LONG SHANK
SCREW EYE
INTO SLIDE

SUPPORT
SLIDE

CHANNEL BOTTOM BEAD
CHAIN

AS CHAIN AND
SPRING RIG
WOULD APPEAR
WITH SIDE OF
CABINET
REMOVED

SCREEN DOOR SPRING
ADJUST CHAIN
LENGTH TO MAINTAIN
TENSION

A SCREW EYE

MITERED JOINT
FOR UPPER
CORNER

D

6½" RAD.

32"

16"

C UPPER DOOR

DOOR FRAME OF
SCREEN STOCK
MITERED CORNERS
CORRUGATED NAILED
AT UPPER CORNERS

Fig. 1-5. Rim the lower doors with 1-×-2 stock on all sides except where the hinges will be placed. There, install 1-×-3 stock, which allows the door to overlap the cabinet side.

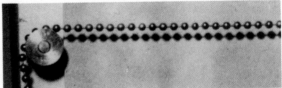

Fig. 1-6. A bead chain operates the writing lid's supports. It runs over standard bead-chain sprockets located at the rear of slots in the writing top; it connects the lid side, and spring.

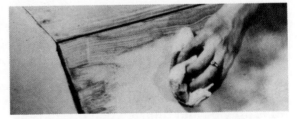

Fig. 1-7. After you apply base paint, brush on the gold antique, and then wipe it off the central panel areas. A gold luster remains; it's more prominent around the rims.

MATERIALS LIST

Purpose	Size	Description	Quantity
Top unit and rear writing surface	1″ × 8″ × 32″	Used or scrap wood	4
Bottom unit sides	1″ × 8″ × 34″	Used or scrap wood	4
Top and bottom of lower unit, and desk lid	1″ × 8″ × 33½″	Used or scrap wood	5
Door panels, lower unit	1″ × 8″ × 21″	Used or scrap wood	4
Base front and cross member above lower doors	1″ × 4″ × 33½″	Used or scrap wood	2
Base side	1″ × 4″ × 24″	Used or scrap wood	1
Lid support channels	1″ × 4″ × 16″	Used or scrap wood	2
Lower door rim	1″ × 4″ × 17½″	Used or scrap wood	2
Lower door rim	1″ × 2″ × 16¾″	Used or scrap wood	4
Lower door rim	1″ × 2″ × 17½″	Used or scrap wood	2
Vertical frame, upper doors	1″ × 2″ × 32″	Used or scrap wood	2
Horizontal frame, upper doors	1″ × 2″ × 16″	Used or scrap wood	4
Lid support slides	1″ × 2″ × 16″	Used or scrap wood	2
Bottom unit back	¼″ × 33½″ × 35½″	Plywood	1
Upper unit back	¼″ × 33½″ × 32	Plywood	1
Upper door top corners	½″ × 13¾″ × 14¼″	Plywood	1
Top unit	5″ × 5′	Crown molding	1
Upper door grilles	36″	Welded mesh	2 yds.
Lid support side returns		Screen door springs	2
Lid support side extensions	⅝″	Bead chain sprockets	2
Lid support side extensions	⅛″ × 60″	Bead chain	1

Note: Also need 6d and 8d finishing nails, 1″ brads, screweyes, casein or aliphatic resin glue, spackling compound, hardware and antiquing kit.

and glue along the edges. Conceal the seams with a spackling compound. Use corner plates to stiff the doors at their lower corners, and corrugated fasteners at the upper ones.

Desk lid supports slide out automatically through front guide holes when the lid is opened and return when it is closed. Two long screen door springs connected to these slides by a chain provide the loco-motion, doing away with any carefully fitted metal levers.

After installing the channel bottom in the lower section and cutting and fitting the writing top, insert the support slides and check them for proper fit. Attach a long-shank screw eye on the top of each slide about 4 inches from the inside end and on one side so that it will ride along the recessed side of the writing top. Install a standard ⅝-inch-diameter bead chain sprocket on each recessed edge of the writing top about 1 inch in from the end.

Now, attach ⅛-inch bead chain to the inside of the lid 4 inches from the hinge, using a small staple or screw eye. Feed the chain through the long-shank screw eye on the slide, pass it over the chain sprocket and down in back to the screen-door spring. Clinch the screw eye over the chain to lock it. With the lid closed, attach the chain to the spring with moderate tension.

As you open the desk lid, the screw eye will slide forward in its slot and the chain should slide the support until it is fully extended. Close the lid and the slide should retract out of sight. If any adjustment is needed, increase or decrease the spring tension. Once the tension is set correctly, cut off excess chain and hook up the other slide in the same manner.

You can place shelves in both upper and lower units to suit your needs. If you reinforce the shelves with glue and hold them with 6d finishing nails driven through the sides, you will not need to use cleats for normal loading.

Applying a finish to a cabinet built with wood would appear to present a tedious and expensive finishing problem. The secretary-desk, however, was transformed into a fine piece of furniture with materials obtained in an antiquing kit.

If you wish to do the job as we did it, choose white as a base color. Stir the base paint and apply, after making sure the surface is clean and dry. Some of the used lumber might already have paint on it. You can go over this if you first sand off the gloss.

One coat of paint is usually enough.

If the wood is badly blemished, add a second coat. Let it dry before you start antiquing.

Brush on antique gold after the base paint has dried overnight. It's not a gilt and not intended to cover like one. The base color will be partially visible through it. While the brushed-on gold is still wet, gently wipe the central area of the panel so the outer rim area will have a heavier coat. A subtle gold luster will still remain over the whole area.

Work only one panel at a time. Use the cloth pads from the kit to create any effect you want, using a patting or swirling motion and a light touch to blend out the gold and eliminate any brush marks. Stir the gold frequently while you work to keep the gold metallic particles dispersed through it.

If you prefer a wavy or stippled pattern, use the pads to create it. There is no set style for antiquing. The finest examples represent the preference of the craftsman who produced them, so use your own ideas. You can take plenty of time to work because the gold dries slowly, and you can add more after the first coat dries. Let it deposit in the crevices of moldings for emphasis.

Don't aim for a straight-lined mass-production look. The beauty of an authentic antiqued finish is in its individuality.

Apply the vinyl liquid laminate after the gold has dried overnight. This is the crystal-clear coating that makes your antiquing job completely scrubbable and prevents wet glasses from leaving rings on it. One coat is enough, but if you want a higher luster you can add another coat after the first one has dried overnight.

Breakfront China Cabinet

PLEASE YOUR WIFE by building this elegant piece of furniture to display her fine china. Made of birch lumber core, it has the appearance of a very expensive piece, but it can be built for relatively little cost. Featured are a curved molded pediment, raised panels, glass shelves, and ample storage space in the base. The glass shelves are easily removable for washing, and they allow light to penetrate and thus brighten up the chinaware.

The cabinet is designed to be made in two separate sections, thus making construction easier. Make the lower part first. Cut the sections to size, then rabbet the rear edges to accommodate the back panel and assemble using glue and finishing nails.

Use nails only where they will be hidden by moldings; otherwise use dowels, as in the doors. The one exception is the use of brads to attach the moldings.

The rabbeting can be done by one of several methods. The shaper, jointer, or router are fine. Another tool often used for rabbeting is the table saw. If you use the saw, make the vertical cut first. Because you are working with lumber core birch, it is not necessary to hide the edges. Simply sand them smooth.

Add the base pieces next. Cut them so the front piece overlaps the sides. Use grooved dowels to join the pieces. You'll need clamps for this operation. If you use plain dowels, crimp the edges with a pair

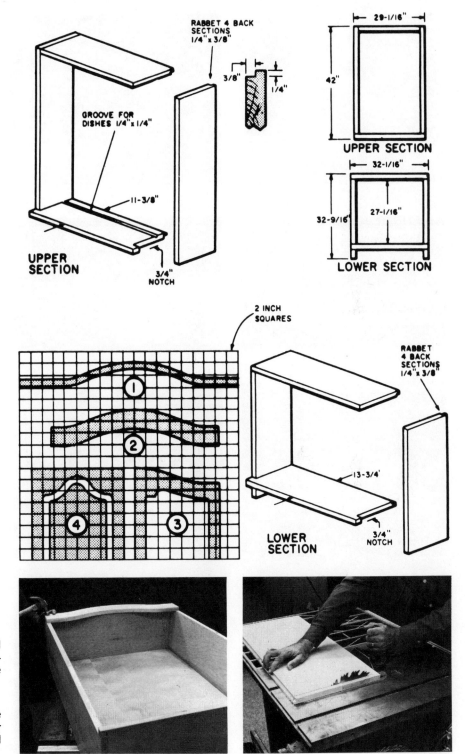

RABBET 4 BACK
SECTIONS
1/4" x 3/8"

3/8"

1/4"

GROOVE FOR
DISHES 1/4" x 1/4"

11-3/8"

UPPER
SECTION

3/4"
NOTCH

29-1/16"

42"

UPPER SECTION

32-1/16"

32-9/16"

27-1/16"

LOWER SECTION

2 INCH
SQUARES

RABBET
4 BACK
SECTIONS
1/4" x 3/8"

①

②

④ ③

13-3/4"

LOWER
SECTION

3/4"
NOTCH

Fig. 2-1. (left) The curved pediment adds to the appearance of the cabinet. Sand the edges before assembly.

Fig. 2-2. (right) Use a table saw to make the notches for the bottom pieces. Stop and cut as shown.

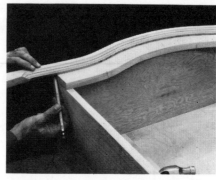

Fig. 2-3. (left) With a suitable cutter head, cut the molded edge on the shaper. Cut the top curve after shaping.

Fig. 2-4. (right) Before you make the miter cut, measure the shaped piece carefully for the best fit.

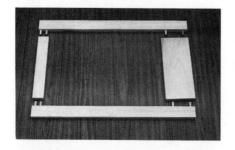

Fig. 2-5. (left) The door frame before assembly. Test the parts for an accurate fit before you begin gluing.

Fig. 2-6. (right) To make the raised panels for the front of the doors, shape the outline with a router.

Fig. 2-7. (left) Use 1-inch-wide strips of scrap wood to center the raised molded panel in the door.

Fig. 2-8. (right) Miter the shaped molding and attach to the edges. You can make the molding yourself.

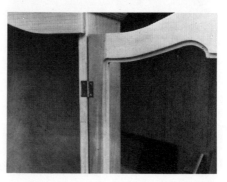

Fig. 2-9. (left) Rabbet the shelf supports ¼ inch wide × ⅛ inch deep to take the glass.

Fig. 2-10. (right) Hinges are fully mortised in the sides of cabinet. Brass butts will work well. The corner detail shows the construction of the door and the top piece.

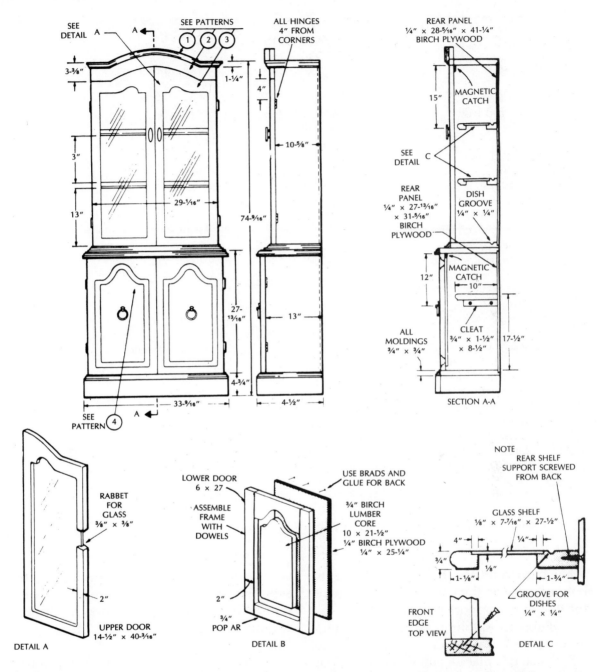

SEE
DETAIL   A   A

SEE PATTERNS
① ② ③

ALL HINGES
4" FROM
CORNERS

3-3/8"

1-1/4"

4"

3"

13"

29-1/16"

74-9/16"

10-5/8"

27-13/16"

13"

4-3/4"

33-9/16"

4-1/2"

SEE
PATTERN ④   A

REAR PANEL
1/4" × 28-5/16" × 41-1/4"
BIRCH PLYWOOD

MAGNETIC
CATCH

15"

SEE
DETAIL   C

REAR
PANEL
1/4" × 27-13/16"
× 31-5/16"
BIRCH
PLYWOOD

DISH
GROOVE
1/4" × 1/4"

MAGNETIC
CATCH

12"

10"

ALL
MOLDINGS
3/4" × 3/4"

CLEAT
3/4" × 1-1/2"
× 8-1/2"

17-1/2"

SECTION A-A

RABBET
FOR
GLASS
3/8" × 3/8"

2"

UPPER DOOR
14-1/2" × 40-3/16"

DETAIL A

LOWER DOOR
6 × 27

ASSEMBLE
FRAME
WITH
DOWELS

USE BRADS AND
GLUE FOR BACK

3/4" BIRCH
LUMBER
CORE
10 × 21-1/2"
1/4" BIRCH PLYWOOD
1/4" × 25-1/4"

2"

3/4"
POP AR

DETAIL B

NOTE
REAR SHELF
SUPPORT SCREWED
FROM BACK

GLASS SHELF
1/8" × 7-7/16" × 27-1/2"

4"

3/4"

1/8"

1-1/8"

1/4"

1-3/4"

GROOVE FOR
DISHES
1/4" × 1/4"

FRONT
EDGE
TOP VIEW

DETAIL C

of pliers to form grooves and so make for a tighter joint.

The upper section of the china cabinet differs from the lower in at least two respects. The top features a graceful curved pediment, and the base piece of the top is notched at the sides. Cut the sections to size, and then cut the curved pediment. Although we used a band saw, this task can be done with a saber saw. Use poplar or

MATERIALS LIST

Purpose	Size	Description	Quantity
Lower Section			
Top and base	¾" × 13¾" × 32¹⁄₁₆"	Birch	2
Sides	¾" × 13⅛" × 31⅞"	Birch	2
Rear	¼" × 27¹³⁄₁₆" × 31⁵⁄₁₆"	Birch	1
Shelf cleats	¾" × 1½" × 8½"	Poplar	2
Shelf	¾" × 10¼" × 30⁹⁄₁₆"	Birch	1
Base sides	¾" × 4" × 13¾"	Poplar	2
Base front	¾" × 4" × 33⁹⁄₁₆"	Poplar	1
Door sides	¾" × 2" × 27"	Poplar	4
Door top and bottom	¾" × 2" × 12"	Poplar	4
Raised panel	¾" × 10" × 21½"	Birch	2
Door back	¼" × 14" × 25¼"	Birch plywood	2
Upper Section			
Top	¾" × 10¹¹⁄₁₆" × 27⁹⁄₁₆"	Birch	1
Base	¾" × 11⅜" × 29¹⁄₁₆"	Birch	1
Sides	¾" × 10⅝" × 42"	Birch	2
Rear	¼" × 28⁵⁄₁₆" × 41¼"	Birch plywood	1
Rear shelf supports	¾" × 1¾" × 27⁹⁄₁₆"	Poplar	2
Front shelf supports	¾" × 1⅛" × 27⁹⁄₁₆"	Poplar	2
Pediment	¾" × 6" × 29¹⁄₁₆"	Poplar	1
Top molding	¾" × 1¼" × 25"	Poplar	1
Curved molding	¾" × 3¾" × 31"	Poplar	1
Outer door sides	¾" × 2" × 37¾"	Poplar	2
Inner door sides	¾" × 2" × 40³⁄₁₆"	Poplar	2
Door top	¾" × 4¾" × 10½"	Poplar	2
Door bottom	¾" × 2" × 10½"	Poplar	2
Molding for entire unit	¾" × 182"	Poplar	

Misc.: screws, glue, hinges, pulls, nails, brads, glass, dowels

other hardwood for this piece. Notch the bottom piece on the table saw using the miter gauge to support the work.

Before assembling, sand the pediment to remove all saw marks. Then join the sections. You can place a nail at the upper part of the pediment since the molding will conceal it. There is nothing wrong in using nails even where the heads will show, but it makes for a finer, better finished piece of furniture if they are hidden. Use clamps to hold the pieces while the glue sets. We have found that Weldwood white glue is fine for this type of work. It sets fast, is nonstaining, and has a very strong glue line.

The curved pediment molding looks tricky, but it is quite easy to make. Draw the outline of the molding onto a piece of poplar about 4 inches wide (see drawing). Then, using a router or shaper, cut the desired profile. The advantage of using the shaper is that a larger profile is possible than with the router. If you use the shaper, insert the starting pin to prevent kickback.

After the piece is shaped, cut the top line on the band saw, miter the corners, and mount it as shown. Using the same profile cutter, make the rest of the molding for the base and midsection.

The lower doors are made from poplar and consist of three sections: frame, raised panel, and backpiece. Cut the framing to size and assemble it with dowels. (A dowel drilling jig is handy because it ensures alignment of the pieces.) Do not cut the curved part of the upper rail until after the frame is glued. If you cut it before gluing, clamping pressure might split the narrow part. When the glue has set, cut the curve and then rout the edges to suit using a beading or ogee bit.

After routing the inside edge, cut the rear panel to size and mount it with glue and brads. Next, cut the panel inserts to size and use the router (with the same bit) to shape the edges. Center the panel in the door frame and again assemble with brads and glue. As an aid to centering the panel, cut three scraps of wood 1 inch wide, and use them as temporary spacers at the sides and bottom. This method will automatically center the panel.

Make the upper doors in a similar manner, but leave them open to accept the glass. After cutting the decorative bead on the inner edge, cut the rabbet on the underside for the glass. If desired, you may use a brass grille with the glass. The depth of the rabbet will be determined by the thickness of the glass and grille.

The lower shelf is supported by means of two cleats. Use screws to hold the wood strips that support the glass shelves, as indicated. The glass shelves should be of double-strength glass, which is a little thicker than window glass and is available at glazier shops. The door glass can be single strength. Use brass butt hinges for the doors. Cut full mortises in the side panels and mount the hinges carefully.

Sand the entire cabinet, then stain the desired shade. To complete the job, apply a suitable finish.

Cedar-lined Hope Chest

THIS ATTRACTIVE HOPE CHEST is lined inside with aromatic red cedar and is the perfect place for storing linens, blankets, curtains, and similar items. In addition, the chest lid is topped with a nice soft cushion, which adds to its appearance and function. This piece also can be used as a toy chest. The drawers and doors are dummies and serve only to enhance the appearance of this lovely piece.

Made mostly of 1-inch pine (¾ inch actual size) boards, the chest is rather easy to build. Some joints are doweled; others are dadoed and rabbeted. The table saw and router are the main tools needed for this project.

The inside of the cabinet has been lined with cedar, but you can eliminate this

step if you desire. The cushioned lid is fitted with four tension hinges. They permit the lid to be raised and lowered with ease. The hinges are fitted with springs, which can be tensioned to equalize the load.

The Materials List shows the sizes required for each piece; however, when gluing up boards for the front, rear, and end panels, you should make the pieces longer and wider than shown. You will trim these pieces to size after gluing. Because of the width required, you should make up these panels by gluing two or three narrow boards together.

The joints for the glued up boards can be tongued-and-grooved or butted with dowels. Of the two choices, the doweled

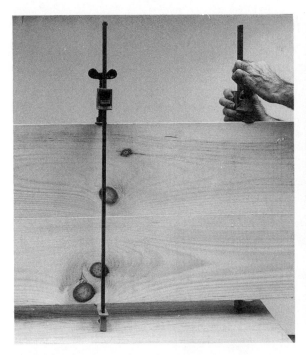

Fig. 3-1. Gluing up boards for the rear panel. If you can find large enough boards that are fairly flat, use two; otherwise use three or four.

Fig. 3-2. Grooves, dadoes, and rabbets can be made with a router or on a table saw, as shown. Make three passes.

Fig. 3-3. Fasten the router guide strip to a crosspiece to simplify mounting and clamping. The taped stick ensures a stopped cut.

Fig. 3-4. It's important that the corner posts be perfectly perpendicular to the base of the unit. Check accuracy with a square.

13

Fig. 3-5. A simple jig for gluing up the door frames consists of two 1 × 2s nailed to the board. You should space the two about 9½ inches apart. Next, apply glue to the joints and place the piece between the 1 × 2s. Tape a double wedge into place to tighten the assembly.

Fig. 3-6. Trim the corners of the raised panels, as shown. Check the cut on a scrap panel before cutting good work.

Fig. 3-7. Two brads placed in each cedar panel are sufficient because the interlocking tongues-and-grooves hold the pieces securely.

Fig. 3-8. Looking down into the chest, without cedar sides. Two cuts were made in the end panel to flatten it.

Fig. 3-9. Bottom view of the chest showing how the base pieces are fastened to the unit with screws.

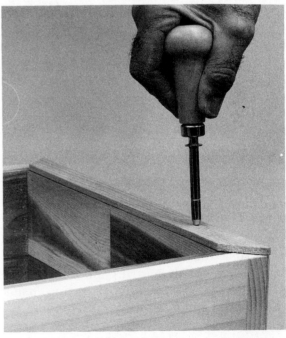

Fig. 3-10. The ¼-inch lattice is added to the top edge for a pleasing look. Note that all of the corners have been carefully mitered.

15

Fig. 3-11. With this particular hardware, the lid support hinges are adjustable. Here, the adjusting screw increases the tension.

Fig. 3-12. A peek into the completed chest, revealing the beautiful and aromatic red cedar lining. Stain the outside to your liking.

method is perhaps the easiest. The dowels should be $3/8 \times 2$ inches. Drill the holes for them $1 1/32$ inches deep in each board to ensure that the joints will close good and tight. To prevent the panels from cupping, reverse the annular rings in adjoining pieces as shown in the drawing.

Apply glue to the dowels and to all mating surfaces, then clamp securely. When applying clamping pressure, do not overdo. Excessive pressure can cause too much glue to squeeze out, resulting in a weak joint. After the glue has set remove the clamps then surface the boards to eliminate any irregularities at the joints. Use a plane followed with a good sanding. You may use the belt sander instead of the plane. Start with 80-grit paper then finish off with 120-grit. For final sanding, use a finishing sander with 220-grit paper.

Join the front, rear, and end pieces with tongue-and-groove joints. You can make these joints on any of the following machines: shaper, table saw, radial arm saw, or router. We used the table saw fitted with a Rockwell adjustable dado blade. If you lack the dado blade, you can get by just using the regular saw blade. Simply take several cuts, adjusting the fence after each pass. Make the groove near the bottom $1/2$ inch wide to take the $1/2$-inch plywood panel.

Assemble the front, rear, and end panels with the bottom panel in place. Before assembly, be sure to drill the screw holes along the lower part of each member.

To ensure a good strong joint, *glue-size* the end grain of the front and rear panels. Do this by thinning some glue and brushing it onto the ends of each board. When dry, in about 20 minutes time, sand lightly then apply glue full strength and join the pieces. Clamp and allow to set. Use cauls under the clamps to protect the wood. Since the bottom panel is already in place, the assembly should glue up square, but check it anyway.

Join the four base pieces with doweled

MATERIALS LIST

Purpose	Size	Description	Quantity
Chest			
Front	1″ × 16″ × 47″	Pine	1
Rear	1″ × 16″ × 47″	Pine	1
End	1″ × 16″ × 16″	Pine	2
Bottom	½″ × 15″ × 47″	Fir plywood	1
Filler	* 1″ × 2″ × 48″	Pine	1
Base front	1″ × 3½″ × 49½″	Pine	1
Base rear	1″ × 3½″ × 49½″	Pine	1
Base end	1″ × 3½″ × 16¾″	Pine	2
Corner post	1″ × 1½″ × 14″	Pine	2
Molding	⅝″ × ¾″	Nose and cove	12 ft.
Glue block	¾″ × ¾″ × 2″	Pine	4
Drawer front	1″ × 5¾″ × 12″	Pine	4
Door stile	1″ × 1½″ × 13″	Pine	4
Door rail	1″ × 1½″ × 5½″	Pine	4
Door panel	1″ × 4½″ × 8¾″	Pine	4
Lattice	¼″ × 1⅛″		12 ft.
Seat			
Frame front	1″ × 2″ × 48″	Pine	1
Frame rear	1″ × 2″ × 48″	Pine	1
Frame end	1″ × 2″ × 12¾″	Pine	2
Seat top	½″ × 14″ × 45¼″	Fir plywood	1
Seat plug	½″ × ⅝″ × 2″	Pine	4
Seat molding	⅝″ × ¾″	Nose and cove	8 ft.
Seat lattice	¹⁄₁₆″ × 1⅜″		8 ft.
Seat end	1″ × 4″ × 15½″	Pine	2
Seat rear	1″ × 4¹³⁄₁₆″ × 45½″	Pine	1
Aromatic red cedar	⅜″ × 3½″ (random lengths)		30 sq.ft.
Cushion base	¼″ × 14¾″ × 45¼″	Plywood	1
*Foam	2″ × 14¾″ × 45¼″		1
Miscellaneous			
*Drawer pull	2½″ centers (CH)		4
*Door pull	tear drop (TDP)		2
Screw	1¼″ 8 RH		16
Screw	1¼″ 8 FH		6
Staple	¼″		1 box
*Hinge	Adjustable tension (ATL)		4
Dowel	⅜″ × 2″		36

Items with asterisk are available from Armor Products. See text.

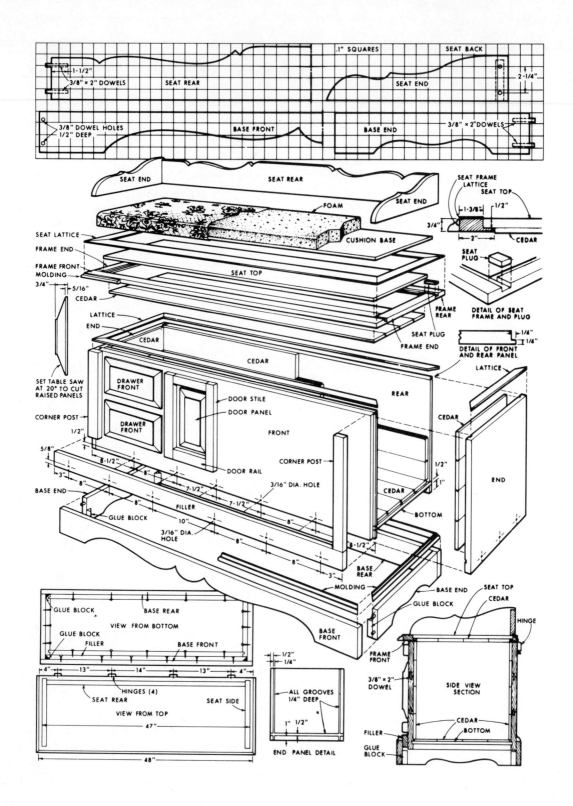

butt joints. Lay out the decorative shapes at the bottom of the front and end pieces, then drill the holes for the dowels. There are two dowels at each joint. Before gluing and assembling the base, glue-size the end grain of both end pieces. Glue, clamp, then set aside.

Prepare the filler strip next. It is used to fill the space between the front of the main assembly and the front base piece. The bottom view drawing shows how the filler strip is fastened to the front base piece with 1¼-inch flat-head screws.

With the filler strip in place, you can fasten the base assembly to the chest case. Drive screws through the previously drilled holes.

Make the dummy doors of pine strips ripped to 1½-inch widths. Cut the lengths for the rails and stiles, then assemble with butt joints. You can use dowels at the joints if desired, but they are not necessary because the doors are nonworking and they will be glued to the backboard (front panel).

Make the raised panels for doors and drawers on the table saw. Tilt the saw blade 20 degrees, then adjust the fence and blade height to produce the raised-panel effect. The blade should project 1¹⁄₁₆ inches above the table. The saw blade should be sharp for this operation. Hold the work firmly and feed it through the blade, using the fence as a guide.

After you cut the panels, you will need to run them through the saw to remove the slight angle left by the edge of the saw blade. Return the saw blade to 90 degrees and let it project about ³⁄₃₂ inch above the table. Make test cuts on the extra panel. When you are satisfied with the results, cut the panels. Drill the pull holes as indicated,

then mount the panels and door frames to the front panel. First, however, add the two corner posts.

The aromatic cedar is sold by the bundle in random lengths. Each piece is 3½ inches wide with tongue and groove. Start by applying the strips to the floor of the chest. Choose any length and place the first piece at the upper left corner as shown, but ¼ inch from the rear panel. Continue along the floor to the right end. Trim the piece to fit. Hold each piece in place with two ¾-inch brads.

Start the second row in the same manner, but stagger the joints by choosing a strip that is longer or shorter than the first piece in the first row. Continue the successive rows with staggered joints. The final row will fit back to front with a ¼-inch space.

Install the back vertical row of cedar next. Start at the lower left and work across to the right. Start the strips with the groove down. You will need to trim the top row flush with the panel sides and ends. Trim the top edge of the chest with ¼-inch lattice to conceal the two dissimilar woods (³⁄₈-inch cedar and ¾-inch pine). Miter the lattice at each corner. Fasten with glue and brads.

Next, add the nose and cove molding, but before doing so, you must round the corners of the base pieces. Use a router with ¼-inch rounding bit for this step. Then add the molding to the top of the base pieces. Milter all corners and fasten with glue and brads.

The top consists of a piece of plywood edged with a pine frame. The underside is lined with cedar and the top is covered with an upholstered cushion. Cut the front, rear, and end frame sections to length;

then, before assembly, rabbet the inner top edge to take the ½-inch plywood panel. When assembled, the frame will have gaps where the rabbets were cut. Fill them in with plugs. Glue the frame members without dowels—just plain butt joints. The plywood top will add sufficient strength to the assembly. When installing the top, use glue at the joint and reinforce with brads driven from the underside.

Add the cedar to the underside of the seat using the same procedure as for the chest. The only difference is that you first need to trim the leading edges to remove the grooves. You must also trim the last row to fit.

Now make the lattice from a piece of ¹⁄₁₆-inch-thick by 1⅜-inch-wide knot-free pine. Miter the corners then install with glue and brads. This lattice will conceal the butt joints as well as the plugs added previously.

Next, turn the seat upright and add the lattice. Cut the seat ends to shape and drill them to take the ⅜-inch dowels. Note that the holes in the end pieces are ½ inch deep.

Before assembly, round the top corners with a ¼-inch-rounding bit. Apply glue and clamp securely. Install the assembly with flat-head screws driven from the underside of the seat. Finally, add the nose and cove molding to the front and ends.

Fasten the seat to the chest with four lid hinges. Do not set the tension of the springs until you install the cushion because the weight will be increased slightly. Stain and finish as desired. Do not apply finish to the cedar. It should be left natural.

The cushion consists of a bottom board, urethane foam, and upholstery material. To make the cushion wrinkle-free, proceed as follows. Place the fabric on a flat surface, followed by the foam then the ¼-inch plywood panel. Cut a board slightly smaller than the plywood and place it on top of the pile. Now, using deep-throat clamps, squeeze the sandwich to about one-third its original thickness, then staple the fabric all around the perimeter into the ¼-inch plywood. When stapling is completed, cut away the excess material that has bunched up at the corners.

When you remove the clamps, the sandwich will expand to its original thickness and the edges will be neat and wrinkle-free. Simply place the cushion in its nook without fastening. If you like, you can hold it with several small pieces of Velcro glued to the underside of the cushion and the seat top.

Note: The items in the Materials List flagged by asterisks should be available locally. However if you cannot locate them in your area, write to Armor Products.

Cheese and Wine Cart

HOME CRAFTSMEN are often discouraged from making a rolling cart on wheels because they don't have a lathe for the spokes. This elegant cart was designed and built without a lathe. The turnings are ready-made and available at most lumberyards and home-improvement centers. Even the wheel hubs and rims are made with conventional tools: a router and saber saw.

The cart is made of ¾-, 1⅛-, and 1⅜-inch pine stock (nominal sizes 1, 1¼, and 1½ inches). It measures 18 × 29 × 29 inches and has a roomy drawer for storing odds and ends. Most rolling carts have a movable hand grip, which must be dropped out of the way to permit the drawer to open. We used a fixed hand grip and simply

made the drawer open from the front. It looks better and is more practical.

Make the top of the cart of 1⅜-inch pine. Glue up four boards, each 5 inches wide, to obtain the necessary width. Note that the Materials List shows the lengths to be 3 inches longer than the finished size. You will trim away the excess after gluing. Dowel pins are necessary to ensure a good, permanent glue line. To prevent warping, invert the first and third boards so the annular rings will alternate. Use four dowels in each section, locating them carefully. If you have a doweling jig, you will be able to center the dowel holes automatically. If you do not have a jig, drill the holes in the first board, then use dowel centers to transfer the location of the holes to the mating

Fig. 4-1. Top panel is made by doweling and gluing several boards together. When the glue dries, trim the excess at the ends of the panel.

Fig. 4-2. Make the decorative bead on the end panels with a router. Make a wooden template (see diagram) for the router base to follow.

board. Repeat for the four boards, then apply glue and clamp. After the glue sets, trim the ends to size.

If the surface joints are uneven, use a belt sander to even the surface. Belt sanders cut fast, especially on pine, so use care when sanding. Start with a medium-grit belt, followed by fine.

Make the upper rails of 1⅛-inch stock. After ripping the pieces to width, run a groove along the lower edge using the router fitted with a V-shaped cutter. Tack

a wood strip to the rail to guide the cutter. You will need two side rails and one rear rail. The front is left open for the drawer.

Make the lower side rails in a similar manner, but narrower. The front and rear rails are a bit more tricky to make.

The upper edge must be contoured. In addition, the upper edge is contour grooved. This process requires that you use a shaped wood template to guide the router. Trace the contour of the end panel onto a piece of scrap about 2 inches longer

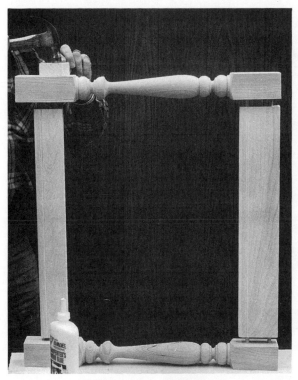

Fig. 4-3. Using ready-made legs saves a lot of work. Cut the legs to size and join to the apron with glue and dowels. Use the block to protect the legs.

Fig. 4-4. The rims for wheels are made in four sections. When cutting curved rims, leave end tabs for later assembly. Predrill for spokes.

than the panel. Use a narrow piece of wood for the template strip and nail it to the base piece. To contour-cut it parallel to the shape of the panel, you need to use a marking gauge to draw the shape of the template. (To set the gauge, measure the radius of the router base, then add ½ inch.) Trace the shape onto the guide strip and cut with a saber saw. Fasten the strip to the base with a couple of nails, then place the panel into the shaped base. Hold it securely with a stop on the table or with a clamp.

Cut the ⅜-inch deep groove in the rail pieces. They are for the top fasteners. Locate the groove ½ inch from the top edge. The width of the saw kerf is not important. Cut the lower shelf to size, but do not notch the corners yet.

The legs are standard 3- × -32-inch turnings available at your lumberyards. Since the finished length required is 24½ inches, you will need to trim the lengths to size. The square block at the top should measure 5 inches and the lower one 6 inches. (See drawing.) *Note:* If you have a lathe, simply make a template on kraft paper, then turn in the usual manner.

Use the doweling jig to locate and drill the ⅜-inch-diameter holes at the ends of

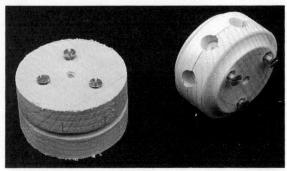

Fig. 4-5. Cut hubs from ¾-inch stock, then saw in half. Reassemble with wood screws and drill for spokes. Hubs are cross-grain for strength.

Fig. 4-6. Separate hub halves, insert spokes, glue, and re-join hubs with screws. Make the spokes from ready-made spindles cut in half.

Fig. 4-7. Attach the wheel shaft to the hub with three screws. The metal stem will snap into the socket that is placed in the leg.

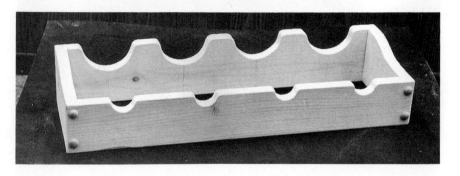

Fig. 4-8. The wine rack is removable. Cut the bottle rests so that bottles lie with necks down. Add wood buttons for looks.

24

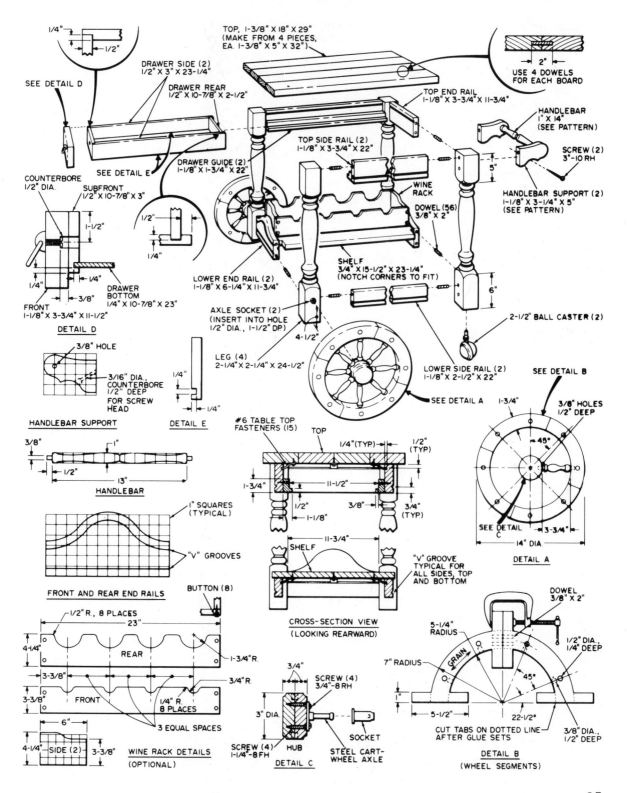

1/4" | 1/2"

SEE DETAIL D

TOP, 1-3/8" X 18" X 29"
(MAKE FROM 4 PIECES,
EA. 1-3/8" X 5" X 32")

DRAWER SIDE (2)
1/2" X 3" X 23-1/4"

DRAWER REAR
1/2" X 10-7/8" X 2-1/2"

2"

USE 4 DOWELS
FOR EACH BOARD

TOP END RAIL
1-1/8" X 3-3/4" X 11-3/4"

HANDLEBAR
1" X 14"
(SEE PATTERN)

DRAWER GUIDE (2)
1-1/8" X 1-3/4" X 22"

SEE DETAIL E

TOP SIDE RAIL (2)
1-1/8" X 3-3/4" X 22"

SCREW (2)
3"-10 RH

COUNTERBORE
1/2" DIA.

SUBFRONT
1/2" X 10-7/8" X 3"

1/2"

1/4"

WINE
RACK

HANDLEBAR SUPPORT (2)
1-1/8" X 3-1/4" X 5"
(SEE PATTERN)

5"

DOWEL (56)
3/8" X 2"

1-1/2"

1/4"

1/4"

3/8"

DRAWER
BOTTOM
1/4" X 10-7/8" X 23"

FRONT
1-1/8" X 3-3/4" X 11-1/2"

DETAIL D

LOWER END RAIL (2)
1-1/8" X 6-1/4" X 11-3/4"

SHELF
3/4" X 15-1/2" X 23-1/4"
(NOTCH CORNERS TO FIT)

6"

2-1/2" BALL CASTER (2)

3/8" HOLE

AXLE SOCKET (2)
(INSERT INTO HOLE
1/2" DIA., 1-1/2" DP)

4-1/2"

3/16" DIA.,
COUNTERBORE
1/2" DEEP
FOR SCREW
HEAD

1/4"

1/4"

LEG (4)
2-1/4" X 2-1/4" X 24-1/2"

LOWER SIDE RAIL (2)
1-1/8" X 2-1/2" X 22"

SEE DETAIL A

SEE DETAIL B

1-3/4"

HANDLEBAR SUPPORT

DETAIL E

3/8" HOLES
1/2" DEEP

#6 TABLE TOP
FASTENERS (15)

TOP

1/4"(TYP)

1/2"
(TYP)

45°

3/8"

1"

1/2"

13"

1-3/4"

11-1/2"

SEE DETAIL
C

3-3/4"

HANDLEBAR

1/2"

3/8"

3/4"
(TYP)

14" DIA.

DETAIL A

1" SQUARES
(TYPICAL)

"V" GROOVES

1-1/8"

1-1/4"(TYP)

11-3/4"

SHELF

"V" GROOVE
TYPICAL FOR
ALL SIDES, TOP
AND BOTTOM

DOWEL
3/8" X 2"

FRONT AND REAR END RAILS

CROSS-SECTION VIEW
(LOOKING REARWARD)

5-1/4"
RADIUS

1/2" DIA.,
1/4" DEEP

BUTTON (8)

1/2" R., 8 PLACES

23"

7" RADIUS

GRAIN

45°

4-1/4"

REAR

1-3/4" R.

3-3/8"

3/4" R.

1"

5-1/2"

22-1/2°

3/8" DIA.,
1/2" DEEP

3-3/8"

FRONT

1/4" R.
8 PLACES

3 EQUAL SPACES

3/4"

SCREW (4)
3/4"-8 RH

CUT TABS ON DOTTED LINE
AFTER GLUE SETS

6"

4-1/4"

SIDE (2)

3-3/8"

WINE RACK DETAILS
(OPTIONAL)

3" DIA.

SOCKET

SCREW (4)
1-1/4"-8 FH

HUB

STEEL CART-
WHEEL AXLE

DETAIL C

DETAIL B
(WHEEL SEGMENTS)

25

MATERIALS LIST

Purpose	Size	Description	Quantity
Top	1⅜″ × 18″ × 29″ (Make from 4 pieces, ea. 1⅜″ × 5″ × 32″)	Pine	1
Side rail (top)	1⅛″ × 3¾″ × 22″	Pine	2
End rail (top)	1⅛″ × 3¾″ × 11¾″	Pine	1
Handlebar support	1⅛″ × 3¼″ × 5″	Pine	2
Handlebar	1″ × 14″	Pine	1
Leg	2¼″ × 2¼″ × 24½″	Pine	4
Shelf	¾″ × 15½″ × 23¼″	Pine	1
Side rail (lower)	1⅛″ × 2½″ × 22″	Pine	2
End rail (lower)	1⅛″ × 6¼″ × 11¾″	Pine	2
Drawer front	1⅛″ × 3¾″ × 11½″	Pine	1
Drawer side	½″ × 3″ × 23¼	Pine	2
Drawer subfront	½″ × 10⅞″ × 3″	Pine	1
Drawer rear	½″ × 10⅞″ × 2½″	Pine	1
Drawer guide	1⅛″ × 1¾″ × 22″	Pine	2
Wheel segment	1⅛″ × 5″ × 12½″	Pine	8
Wheel hub	¾″ × 2¾″ dia.	Pine	4
Spoke	¾″ × 4¾″	Pine	16
Buttons	½″ × ⅝″	Pine	32
Wine rack front	3⅜″ × 23″	Pine	1
Wine rack rear	4¼″ × 23″	Pine	1
Wine rack side	4¼″ × 6″	Pine	2
		Ornament	3
	2½″	Ball casters	2
	#6	Table top fasteners	15
		Wheel axle assembly	2
	⅜″ × 2″	Dowels	56

Note: You should be able to purchase the necessary turnings and related parts at your local lumber dealer. Should you have difficulty in this respect, write to Armor Products, Box 290, Deer Park, N.Y. 11729. Ask for Cart Price List.

the rail pieces. The holes should be 1 inch deep. You can also drill the holes for the caster and wheel sockets into the legs at this time.

Use dowel centers to transfer the dowel holes from the rail ends to the legs. Drill the holes carefully to ensure that they are straight.

Fasten the legs to the side (long) rails with dowels as shown. Use care when ap-plying glue to the rail ends and use it sparingly. Clamp the sections. When the glue has set, remove the clamps and fasten these sections to the end (short) rails. To keep the unit square while clamping, nail a temporary cleat across the upper front.

Next, install the top and lower shelf. Use tabletop brackets to fasten them. You must notch the lower shelf at the corners before installation. Place the shelf in position and, with a pencil, mark exactly where the cuts are to be made. Cut and fit the shelf into place, then fasten with the brackets. Next cut and install the drawer runners, then make the drawer as shown.

To make the wheels, cut eight curved pieces with tabs as indicated. You will use the tabs as an aid to gluing and remove them when the glue has set. Drill the dowel holes in each section. Also drill the spoke holes by supporting the segments in a scrap of wood cut to the same contour as the segment. Drill the ⅜-inch-diameter holes ½ inch deep.

After the holes are drilled, glue up pairs of segments to make half rims. Insert the dowels, glue, and then clamp. When the glue has set, glue up the half sections to complete the rims. Use a saber saw or table jigsaw to cut away the tabs. You will now have a rim with 8 spoke holes on the inside diameter.

Make a curved sanding block and smoothen the rim until all saw marks are removed. Drill the eight ½-inch-diameter button holes around the face of each rim and drill four holes on the back side.

Cut the spokes from 11-inch spindles. Each spindle will yield two spokes. Cut the spindles in half and then with a sharp knife shape the ends to form the ⅜-inch tenon. Fit these into the rim without glue.

Now make the hub. Screw two 4-inch-square pieces of ¾-inch pine together and be sure to cross the grain of each at right angles to each other. Do not glue at this time. Lay out a 13¾-inch circle on the lay-up and cut with a saber saw. Sand the disc until it is perfectly smooth, then shape the outer edge with a router. Next, drill eight ⅜-inch-diameter, equally spaced holes around the circumference of the disc. The holes must be centered on the parting line.

Remove the screws from the hub to disassemble it. Place the spokes into the sockets formed by drilling, then apply glue to the inner hub surface. Add the second half of the hub and rescrew. Add buttons to complete the wheel.

A special wheel shaft with socket is available. (See Materials List.) Fasten it to the wheel with three round-head screws. Simply force the socket part into the holes previously drilled into the legs. Insert the ball casters into the holes made at the bottom of the rear legs in the same manner.

Add the ornaments to complete the piece. The wine rack is optional. Finish as desired. We used Sapolin stain and three coats of clear gloss lacquer.

Classic China Cabinet

THIS HANDSOME CHINA CABINET is made of common pine. You may substitute hardwood, but if the hardwood is thicker than the ¾-inch thickness of the pine, be sure to revise the dimensions accordingly. We used pine in the original design to keep down the cost.

The basic tools needed are a table saw, router, and saber saw. A band saw and shaper are helpful, but not essential.

The cabinet is made in two sections—upper and lower. These sections are built as separate units then assembled with four screws after they have been completed and moved to where the cabinet will be used.

The arched door and frieze above it are glued up from four pieces of stock, with the grain in each piece running the length of the piece. The author has devised a unique method of gluing the pieces so that the joints are pulled tightly for a perfect glue line.

Other features are fluted pilasters, raised panels, and a plywood grille—all add to the professional appearance of this fine piece.

Cut all parts to size as shown in the Materials List. If you have a jointer, make all pieces a trifle wider, then dress down to the size given. To prevent cupping, make the top, bottom, and side members by gluing narrow boards. Be sure to reverse the annular rings in alternate pieces.

Starting with the lower section, rabbet the ends of the side pieces to take the top and bottom panels. Make this rabbet ⅜ × ¾ inch. Rabbet the front edges of the side panels to a depth of ¼ inch and a width of ½ inch. Also make the ¼- × -⅜-inch rabbets for the rear panel at this time.

After the rabbets are cut, drill the two rows of holes to take the adjustable shelf brackets. These holes should be ¼ inch in diameter and ⅜ inch in depth. Lay out the spacing as shown for the upper cabinet.

Set aside the pieces just cut and make up the front frame. Drill the holes in the upper rail to take the dummy drawer front screws. The ½-inch-diameter holes are to allow clearance for the drawer-pull screw heads. Also drill the dowel holes at this time. A doweling jig is useful for this operation because it will ensure perfectly aligned holes for the dowel pins. Use two dowels at each joint, except for the center divider where only one hole is required.

Before gluing these pieces, cut the groove at the back of the stiles. Make the groove ¼ inch wide × ¼ inch deep. Check the fit with the side member.

Next, glue up the front frame. Glue upper and lower rails to the divider first, then add the stiles. Use cauls under the clamp jaws to protect the edges of the stiles. Next assemble the sides, top, and bottom using glue and screws. Be sure the assembly is square then set it aside until the glue sets. Then fasten the front frame to the case. Use glue at all joints and clamp securely.

Cut the pilasters from ½-inch stock. Make the grooves with a router or shaper. The shaper is the easier to use because the piece is made to ride against the fence. Use start and stop blocks to locate the grooves on the stock. If you use a router, mount it on a board large enough so you can use similar stops as with the shaper. Mount the router so that the round end bit protrudes ¼ inch. Use a movable side guide so the five grooves are cut as shown in the detail.

When the pilasters are finished, sand them smooth, breaking all sharp edges, then fasten to the stiles as indicated. Place the nails so they will be hidden under the rosettes. Be careful with the glue. Keep it

Fig. 5-1. Assemble the front frame with dowels. The center divider has already been glued. Use spiraled dowels in all cases because they allow air to escape from the hole.

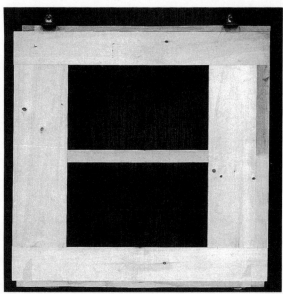

Fig. 5-2. Use cauls under the clamps to protect the edge of the frame. Be sure the assembly is square, then set the piece aside until the glue sets. Then fasten to the case.

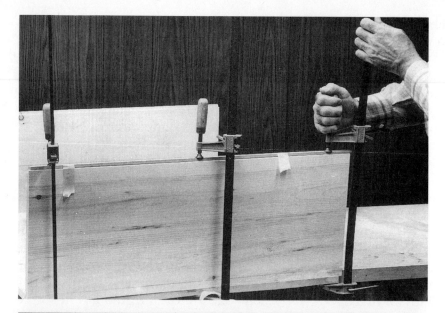

Fig. 5-3. The cabinet sides are being glued to the front frame. The cauls have been taped to the sides to prevent any shifting. Be sure to clean away any excess glue from the wood.

Fig. 5-4. Fasten the top panel for the bottom section with glue and nails. You can use nails here because they will be hidden by the top section of the cabinet.

Fig. 5-5. Use start and stop guides on the shaper fence to control the position of the flutes on the pilasters. This is very important for uniform flutes.

away from the edges because you do not want any to squeeze out and get onto the face of the stiles.

Make the lower doors with doweled joints (two dowels per joint). Drill the rails and stiles for the dowels, then assemble them with glue and clamps. When the glue has set, cut the 3/8- x -3/8-inch rabbets on the inner and outer edges, as shown in the sectional drawing.

Cut the door panels from a piece of 3/4- x -7- x -14-inch stock. Use the table saw to raise the panel. Elevate the blade 1 1/4 inches and tilt it 15 degrees. Adjust the fence so that it is 1/4 inch from the blade at the table surface. Holding the panel vertically, rest it against the fence and feed it slowly through the blade. Repeat for all four sides. When done, the waste will hang on lightly. Return the blade to the vertical position, lowering it so only 1/8 inch projects from the table top. Set the fence 1 1/4 inches away from the blade and recut each edge to remove the waste and to square off the angular cut left by the previous operation.

The inside corners of the rabbeted door frame will have a radius left by the router bit. Use a chisel to square off the corners. The door panels should fit easily into the rabbeted area. If necessary, trim the panels slightly, especially at the sides, because the wood will expand and contract during weather changes. If left too tight, some damage is bound to result. Use panel retainers to hold the panels—six per door as shown.

Now add the base ends, front, and front blocks. Assemble with glue and fasten with 1-inch wire brads. The front blocks must be centered over the pilasters. Center the rosettes in the space provided and fasten with glue and one brad.

Next add the moldings to complete the base section. The stock is 5/8- x -3/4-inch nose and cove molding. Cut each piece and miter to fit by taking measurements directly from the cabinet. Thus, each piece is custom-fit to allow for any discrepancies. The returns at the sides of the pilasters will require an inside and outside miter. These pieces are very short (about 1 1/8 inches), so you must use care in making them. You can make them with a miter box, table saw, radial arm saw, or cutoff saw. Use glue to hold these pieces, but fasten the longer moldings with glue and brads. Use glue sparingly. If it squeezes out, it will cause finishing problems.

Make the upper section case with the same type of joints you used for the lower case. The front frame is different, however.

Fig. 5-6. Use a marking gauge to position the pilaster on the stile. Cut the pilasters from 1/2-inch stock and make the flutes or grooves with a router or shaper.

Fig. 5-7. This rear view of the lower door shows how the panels are held in position by retainers. Use nonmortise hinges.

Fig. 5-8. After shaping the molding, trim it to size on a band saw. It should match the top edge of crown.

In order to save lumber, make the crown section of the front frame as a separate unit. Fasten it to the stiles later.

To make the crown piece, glue up four 24-inch lengths of stock, each measuring $5^{17}/_{32}$ inches wide. Use two dowels in each piece and locate them so they will not be cut away later when the arch and crown are cut. Determine their location by lightly penciling the outline of the arch and crown from the pattern and measurements shown.

When glued up, the four pieces should total $22^1/_8$ inches in width. Using dowels, but no glue, fasten this center section to the two stiles. Then proceed to lay out the arch and crown cutting lines. Use a paper pattern made by enlarging the squared drawing. True up the curved arch by using a beam compass made from a strip of wood about ⅛ inch thick and ½ inch wide. Place a pin through the strip near one end and drill a ¹/₁₆-inch diameter hole $11^1/_{16}$ inches from the pin. This will give you the radius for the arch. Locate the center on some scrap wood placed on the table then scribe the arc. You can use the compass later for the other arcs needed for the door and frieze.

After you lay out the cutting lines on the front frame, remove the stiles and cut the lines using a saber saw, jigsaw, or band saw. Set these pieces aside now and prepare to make the crown moldings.

Lay out the crown moldings on a piece of wood about 5 inches wide. Cut the lower edge only and be sure to extend the ends about 3 or 4 inches in a horizontal plane perpendicular to the imaginary vertical centerline of the crown. This step is very important because the ends will provide a support for cutting the crown miter later. After you have cut the lower (or bottom)

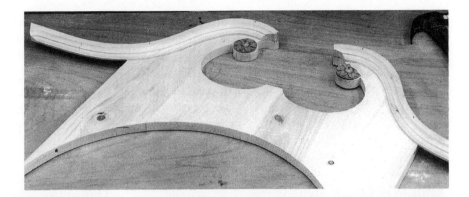

Fig. 5-9. Temporarily tack the molding to the crown with 1-inch brads. Trim the ends and remove the molding.

Fig. 5-10. Make the arched part of the door and frieze from small sections of glued-up stock with tabs at the ends to permit clamping.

Fig. 5-11. The final assembly of the glued segments form the arch. Make sure you cut each segment at a precise 45-degree angle.

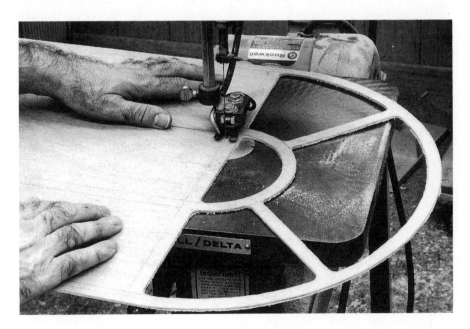

Fig. 5-12. Cut the grille very carefully with a jigsaw. Use a fine blade to produce the desired smooth edge.

edge of the moldings, you must shape the edge with a router or on the shaper using a suitable cutter. Note: You should also make two straight pieces for the returns, about 15 inches long, at this time. After shaping, cut the upper edge of the molding. It should match the top edge of the crown, which was previously cut. Using 1-inch brads, temporarily fasten the moldings to the crown, then proceed to trim the ends to the shape shown. Then remove the moldings.

Now you can glue the crown section to the stiles. Be sure to install the lower rail piece at the same time. Next you can glue the front frame to the case, which was prepared earlier. Again, tack on the crown moldings, then mark the mitering line on the left and right pieces. Support the moldings on the extended ends and miter carefully. Miter the returns in the normal manner. You can now fasten them permanently. Apply glue sparingly, then join securely with brads. You will need to rest the overhanging crown on a solid support when bradding because you will have trou-ble with the wood bouncing, which will make nailing almost impossible. Have an assistant hold the case steady with just the crown resting on the workbench.

Make the arched parts of the door and frieze from small sections of glued-up stock. This method will save stock, but more important, the grain will be running in the proper direction around the curve. Cut each segment with tabs at the ends. They permit proper clamping of the joints. The tabs are cut away afterwards. Note that you should make the segments oversize to permit accurate trimming to a compass-drawn line, which you will lay out after you glue up the segments.

The frieze will not require doweling, but the door must have dowels for strength—two dowels per joint. Cut the ends of each segment at 45-degree angles so that when joined, all four will make up a semicircle. Note: When cutting the stiles for the doors, leave tabs at the top so that the stile can be clamped to the semicircle easily. Glue the stiles to the lower rail then proceed to glue the segments as shown. Af-

Fig. 5-13. Add rosettes to the pilaster as an elegant decoration. Apply them with glue and a countersunk brad.

34

MATERIALS LIST

Purpose	Size	Description	Quantity
Base Section			
Top and bottom	¾″ × 10⅞″ × 29″	Pine	2
Side	¾″ × 11⅜″ × 31¾″	Pine	2
Lower rail	¾″ × 6½″ × 22″	Pine	1
Upper rail	⅜″ × 3⅛″ × 22″	Pine	1
Stile	¾″ × 4″ × 31¾″	Pine	2
Divider	¾″ × 1½″ × 17⅛″	Pine	1
Rear panel	¼″ × 29¼″ × 31¾″	Plywood	1
Base end	½″ × 4¾″ × 11⅞″	Pine	2
Base front	½″ × 4¾″ × 31″	Pine	1
Base block	½″ × 3¼″ × 4¾″	Pine	2
Pilaster	½″ × 2½″ × 27″	Pine	2
Dummy drawer	½″ × 4½″ × 22½″	Pine	1
Door stile	¾″ × 2⅛″ × 17⅝″	Pine	4
Door rail	¾″ × 2⅛″ × 6½″	Pine	4
Door panel	¾″ × 7″ × 14″	Pine	2
Upper Section			
Top and bottom	¾″ × 10⅛″ × 29″	Pine	2
Side	¾″ × 11⅜″ × 38¾″	Pine	2
Lower rail	¾″ × 1″ × 22⅛″	Pine	1
Stile	¾″ × 3¹⁵⁄₁₆″ × 38¾″	Pine	2
Upperframe	¾″ × 5¹⁷⁄₃₂″ × 24″	Pine	4
Pilaster	½″ × 2½″ × 24″	Pine	2
Frieze	½″ × 7″ × 13″	Pine	4
Molding	⅝″ × ¾″ × 2½″	Pine	2
Crown molding	¾″ × 5″ × 18″	Pine	2
Crown return molding	¾″ × 1″ × 13″	Pine	2
Final	1¾″ × 7½″	Pine	1
Final base	¼″ × 1⅞″ × 2⅛″	Pine	1
Door stile	¾″ × 2⅛″ × 23⅜″	Pine	2
Door rail	¾″ × 2⅛″ × 18½″	Pine	1
Door arch	¾″ × 6½″ × 10″	Pine	4
Grille	⅛″ × 19″ × 31¼″	Plywood	1
Rear	¼″ × 29½″ × 37¾″	Plywood	1
Latch support	¾″ × 1⅜″ × 2″	Pine	1
Shelf	¾″ × 9¾″ × 28⅜″	Pine	4
Rosette	1¾″ dia. (ROS)		10
Pull	(TDP)	Tear Drop	3
Pull	(CH)	Chippendale	2
Magnetic catch	(MC)		2
Touch latch	(TVC)		1
Panel retainer	(PRB)		12
Glass holder	(GH)		8
Molding	⅝″ × ¾″ (NC)		18 ft.
Shelf support	(SHS)		16
Hinge, nonmortise	(FH)		6
Screw	1″ 8 RH		6
Screw	⅝″ 4 RH		24
Screw	4⅝″		20
Nail	2″	finishing	24
Brad	1″	#18	36
Dowel	⅜″ × 2″ (SD)		59

Note: The items in parentheses were obtained from Armor Products.

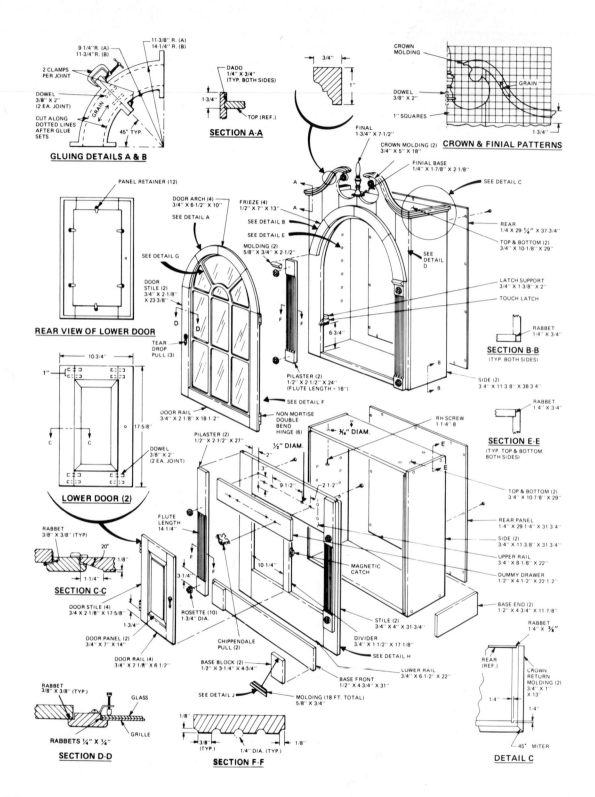

GLUING DETAILS A & B

2 CLAMPS PER JOINT

9-1/4"R. (A)
11-3/4"R. (B)

11-3/8" R. (A)
14-1/4" R. (B)

DOWEL
3/8" X 2"
(2 EA. JOINT)

GRAIN

CUT ALONG
DOTTED LINES
AFTER GLUE
SETS

45° TYP.

SECTION A-A

DADO
1/4" X 3/4"
(TYP. BOTH SIDES)

1-3/4"

TOP (REF.)

3/4"

1"

CROWN & FINIAL PATTERNS

CROWN MOLDING

GRAIN

DOWEL
3/8" X 2"

1" SQUARES

1-3/4"

REAR VIEW OF LOWER DOOR

PANEL RETAINER (12)

DOOR ARCH (4)
3/4" X 6-1/2" X 10"

SEE DETAIL A

FRIEZE (4)
1/2" X 7" X 13"

SEE DETAIL B

SEE DETAIL E

MOLDING (2)
5/8" X 3/4" X 2-1/2"

SEE DETAIL G

DOOR
STILE (2)
3/4" X 2-1/8"
X 23-3/8"

FINAL
1-3/4" X 7-1/2"

CROWN MOLDING (2)
3/4" X 5" X 18"

FINIAL BASE
1/4" X 1-7/8" X 2-1/8"

SEE DETAIL C

REAR
1/4 X 29-1/4" X 37-3/4"

TOP & BOTTOM (2)
3/4" X 10-1/8" X 29"

SEE DETAIL D

LATCH SUPPORT
3/4" X 1-3/8" X 2"

TOUCH LATCH

RABBET
1/4" X 3/4"

SECTION B-B
(TYP. BOTH SIDES)

SIDE (2)
3/4" X 11 3/8" X 38 3/4"

6-3/4"

TEAR DROP PULL (3)

DOOR RAIL (2)
3/4" X 2-1/8" X 18-1/2"

PILASTER (2)
1/2" X 2 1/2" X 24"
(FLUTE LENGTH = 18")

SEE DETAIL F

NON-MORTISE
DOUBLE-
BEND
HINGE (6)

10-3/4"

1"

17-5/8"

DOWEL
3/8" X 2"
(2 EA. JOINT)

LOWER DOOR (2)

PILASTER (2)
1/2" X 2-1/2" X 27"

1/2" DIAM.

3"

9-1/2"

2-1/2"

RH SCREW
1-1/4" 8

3/8" DIAM.

RABBET
1/4" X 3/4"

SECTION E-E
(TYP. TOP & BOTTOM,
BOTH SIDES)

TOP & BOTTOM (2)
3/4" X 10-7/8" X 29"

REAR PANEL
1/4" X 29-1/4" X 31-3/4"

SIDE (2)
3/4" X 11-3/8" X 31-3/4"

UPPER RAIL
3/4" X 8-1/8" X 22"

DUMMY DRAWER
1/2" X 4-1/2" X 22-1/2"

RABBET
3/8" X 3/8" (TYP)

20°

1/8"

1-1/4"

SECTION C-C

FLUTE
LENGTH
14-1/4"

10-1/4"

3-1/4"

MAGNETIC
CATCH

BASE END (2)
1/2" X 4 3/4" X 11-7/8"

RABBET
1/4" X 3/8"

DOOR STILE (4)
3/4 X 2-1/8" X 17-5/8"

1-3/4"

ROSETTE (10)
1-3/4" DIA.

STILE
3/4" X 4" X 31-3/4"

DIVIDER
3/4" X 1-1/2" X 17-1/8"

SEE DETAIL H

REAR
(REF.)

CROWN
RETURN
MOLDING (2)
3/4" X 1"
X 13"

DOOR PANEL (2)
3/4" X 7" X 14"

CHIPPENDALE
PULL (2)

LOWER RAIL
3/4" X 6-1/2" X 22"

1/4"

1/4"

DOOR RAIL (4)
3/4" X 2-1/8" X 6-1/2"

RABBET
3/8" X 3/8" (TYP.)

GLASS

GRILLE

RABBETS 1/4" X 1/4"

SECTION D-D

BASE BLOCK (2)
1/2" X 3-1/4" X 4-3/4"

SEE DETAIL J

MOLDING (18 FT. TOTAL)
5/8" X 3/4"

BASE FRONT
1/2" X 4-3/4" X 31"

1/8"

3/8"
(TYP.)

1/4" DIA. (TYP.)

1/8"

SECTION F-F

45° MITER

DETAIL C

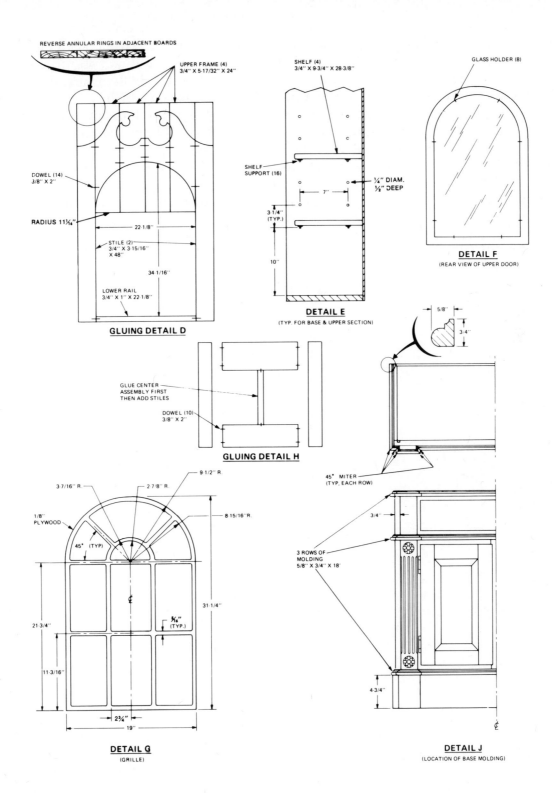

REVERSE ANNULAR RINGS IN ADJACENT BOARDS

UPPER FRAME (4)
3/4" X 5-17/32" X 24"

DOWEL (14)
3/8" X 2"

RADIUS 11¼"

22-1/8"

STILE (2)
3/4" X 3-15/16"
X 48"

34-1/16"

LOWER RAIL
3/4" X 1" X 22-1/8"

GLUING DETAIL D

SHELF (4)
3/4" X 9-3/4" X 28-3/8"

SHELF
SUPPORT (16)

¼" DIAM.
½" DEEP

7"

3-1/4"
(TYP.)

10"

DETAIL E
(TYP. FOR BASE & UPPER SECTION)

GLASS HOLDER (8)

DETAIL F
(REAR VIEW OF UPPER DOOR)

GLUE CENTER
ASSEMBLY FIRST
THEN ADD STILES

DOWEL (10)
3/8" X 2"

GLUING DETAIL H

5/8"

3/4"

45° MITER
(TYP. EACH ROW)

9-1/2" R.

3-7/16" R.   2-7/8" R.

1/8"
PLYWOOD

8-15/16" R.

45° (TYP)

31-1/4"

21-3/4"

¾"
(TYP.)

11-3/16"

2¾"

19"

DETAIL G
(GRILLE)

3/4"

3 ROWS OF
MOLDING
5/8" X 3/4" X 18'

4-3/4"

DETAIL J
(LOCATION OF BASE MOLDING)

37

ter the glue sets, lay out the cutting lines using the beam compass, then trim with a saber saw or jigsaw.

Rabbet the back of the door at the inner and outer edges. Use a chisel to square up the radius left by the router.

Cut the grille from a piece of ⅛-inch door skin, which is available at most lumberyards. This is the same material used for facing hollow doors.

Fasten the frieze, pilasters, and rosettes with glue and brads. Cut the short lengths of molding atop the pilasters square at the edges.

Cut the shelves, and add the rear panels. Install the finial at the top of the crown by gluing it and slipping it over a ⅜-inch dowel. Add hardware, then remove before applying finish.

If you used pine, you need not fill it, but you should give the grille door skin a treatment of paste wood filler—the rear panels, too, if they are of open grain stock.

Give the entire cabinet a thinned application of sealer so that staining will take evenly. (Do not use sealer straight because this method will prevent stain from taking at all). Make tests on scrap wood beforehand to make sure that it will take stain to your liking.

Classic Colonial Desk

THIS SLANT-TOP DESK has a large writing surface, ample storage under the lid, and plenty of shelf space. The lower shelf is contoured to allow comfortable leg space. Its well-proportioned and uncluttered lines make it an ideal functional piece of furniture. To top it all, it is not difficult to make.

Made of 1-inch pine (¾ inch actual size), the piece can easily be made with ordinary home-shop tools. You can glue up the wide boards from narrow stock using doweled joints. If you have a shaper, you might want to use a glue joint instead of dowels. If the lumber has knots, be sure they are good and tight. The Materials List indicates the final size of the various parts. For glued-up stock, cut the wood slightly larger to allow for trimming after gluing.

Start construction with the base. Glue up three boards for the side panels, assembling them with dowels as indicated. Before drilling the dowel holes, roughly sketch the outline of the panel on the board, then locate the dowels so they won't fall on one of the cutting lines. Do the same for the lower shelf.

In addition to the lower shelf and sides, you will need to glue up boards for the desk bottom and desk lid. The lid must be glued in two stages. The first step is to glue up three or four narrow boards to make the required width. Follow by adding the end pieces. When laying out the pieces

Fig. 6-1. (left) To cut the contoured shape of the desk's side panel, use a band saw, as shown. You can also use a saber saw.

Fig. 6-2. (right) Cut dadoes with the aid of a dadoing square. Clamp the square securely to the work and tabletop, as shown.

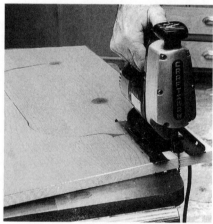

Fig. 6-3. (left) The rabbet to accept the top board is cut last. The notched piece shown is being used as straightedge.

Fig. 6-4. (right) The contour of the desk's side is being cut here with a saber saw. As is evident, the piece is too large for the use of a band saw.

Fig. 6-5. (left) Clamp a straight board to the work, as shown, to true up the line cut by the saber saw for the side contour. Here a straight board is being set to guide the router in making a rabbet cut at the rear edge of the desk's side panel.

Fig. 6-6. (right) The completed rabbet cut in a side panel is shown.

Fig. 6-7. (left) The desk's side panels after dadoing for the shelves. Still to be added is the short dado for the desk front.

Fig. 6-8. (right) For dadoing the desk front, clamp a guide at both ends. Here, a stop is nailed to the router guide to control the length of the dado.

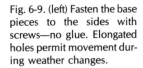

Fig. 6-9. (left) Fasten the base pieces to the sides with screws—no glue. Elongated holes permit movement during weather changes.

Fig. 6-10. (right) Use a table saw to bevel the desk lid, as shown. When you bevel the opposite edge, merely flop the board upside down.

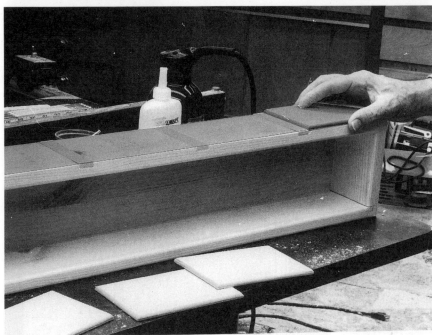

Fig. 6-11. Here drawer fronts are being glued to the subfront. Note the inserted strips, which will give the appearance of partitions.

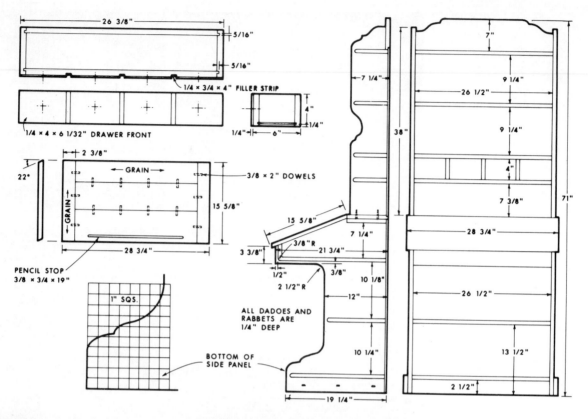

26 3/8"
5/16"
5/16"
1/4 × 3/4 × 4" FILLER STRIP
1/4 × 4 × 6 1/32" DRAWER FRONT
4"
1/4"
1/4"   6"
2 3/8"
22°
GRAIN
GRAIN
3/8 × 2" DOWELS
15 5/8"
28 3/4"
PENCIL STOP
3/8 × 3/4 × 19"
1" SQS.
ALL DADOES AND
RABBETS ARE
1/4" DEEP
BOTTOM OF
SIDE PANEL

7 1/4"
38"
15 5/8"
7 1/4"
3/8" R
3 3/8"
21 3/4"
1/2"   3/8"
2 1/2" R
10 1/8"
12"
10 1/4"
19 1/4"

7"
9 1/4"
26 1/2"
9 1/4"
4"
7 3/8"
28 3/4"
71"
26 1/2"
13 1/2"
2 1/2"

Fig. 6-12. Use flat-head screws when installing lid-support hardware. Locate holes for the screws as indicated in the drawing.

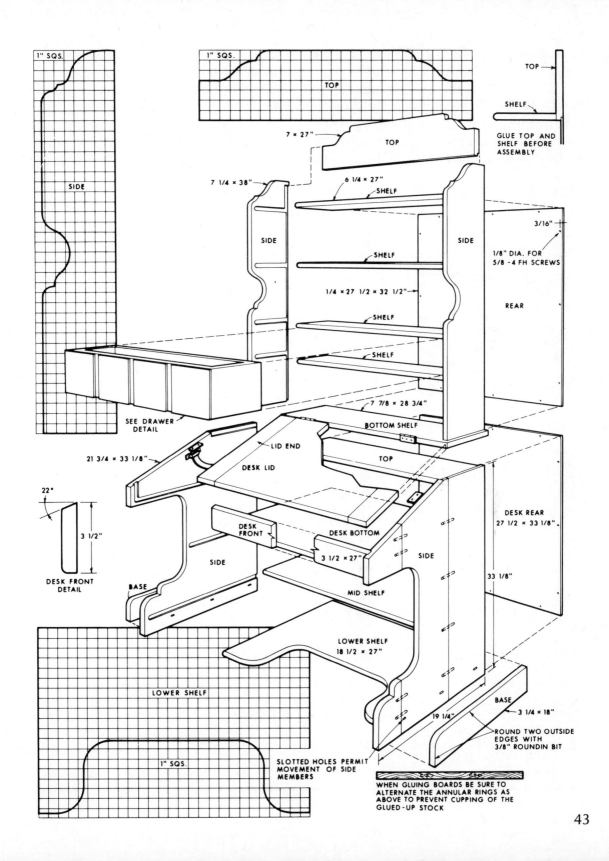

1" SQS.

SIDE

1" SQS.

TOP

7 × 27"

TOP

7 1/4 × 38"

6 1/4 × 27"

SHELF

SIDE

SHELF

SIDE

1/4 × 27 1/2 × 32 1/2"

SHELF

SHELF

7 7/8 × 28 3/4"

BOTTOM SHELF

TOP

TOP

SHELF

GLUE TOP AND
SHELF BEFORE
ASSEMBLY

3/16"

1/8" DIA. FOR
5/8 - 4 FH SCREWS

REAR

SEE DRAWER
DETAIL

21 3/4 × 33 1/8"

LID END

DESK LID

22°

3 1/2"

DESK FRONT
DETAIL

DESK
FRONT

BASE

SIDE

DESK BOTTOM

3 1/2 × 27"

MID SHELF

SIDE

DESK REAR
27 1/2 × 33 1/8"

33 1/8"

LOWER SHELF
18 1/2 × 27"

LOWER SHELF

1" SQS.

SLOTTED HOLES PERMIT
MOVEMENT OF SIDE
MEMBERS

19 1/4"

BASE

3 1/4 × 18"

ROUND TWO OUTSIDE
EDGES WITH
3/8" ROUNDIN BIT

WHEN GLUING BOARDS BE SURE TO
ALTERNATE THE ANNULAR RINGS AS
ABOVE TO PREVENT CUPPING OF THE
GLUED-UP STOCK

43

to be glued, be sure to alternate the annular rings. (See detail.)

The holes for the dowels must be accurate. We highly recommend that you use a doweling jig, which will assure you of perfectly centered perpendicular holes. After you have drilled a row of holes into one edge, use dowel centers to transfer the hole positions to the mating edge. Drill ⅜-inch-diameter holes 1¹⁄₁₆ inches deep into each piece.

Before applying glue, be sure to have your clamps on hand and opened to the proper size. Also, you should have pre-

MATERIALS LIST

Purpose	Size	Description	Quantity
Upper Section			
Side	¾" × 7¼" × 38"	Pine	2
Shelf	¾" × 6¼" × 27"	Pine	4
Bottom Shelf	¾" × 7⅞" × 28¾"	Pine	1
Top	¾" × 7" × 27"	Pine	1
Rear	¼" × 27½" × 32½"	Plywood	1
Drawer subfront	¾" × 4" × 25½"	Pine	1
Drawer rear	¾" × 4" × 25½"	Pine	1
Drawer side	¾" × 4" × 6"	Pine	2
Drawer bottom	¼" × 5" × 25¼"	Plywood	1
Drawer front	¼" × 4" × 6¹⁄₃₂"	Plywood	4
Drawer filler	¼" × ¾" × 4"	Plywood	3
Lower Section			
Side	¾" × 21¾" × 33⅛"	Pine	2
Top	¾" × 7⅝" × 27"	Pine	1
Desk bottom	¾" × 20¼" × 27"	Pine	1
Mid shelf	¾" × 11¼" × 27"	Pine	1
Lower shelf	¾" × 18½" × 27"	Pine	1
Desk lid	¾" × 15⅝" × 24"	Pine	1
Lid end	¾" × 2⅜" × 15⅝"	Pine	2
Desk front	¾" × 3½" × 27"	Pine	1
Desk rear	¼" × 27½" × 33⅛"	Plywood	1
Base	¾" × 3¼" × 18"	Pine	2
Lag screw	⁵⁄₁₆" × 1½"		4
Flat washer	⁵⁄₁₆" ID		4
Screw	2½" 10 FH		4
Screw	⅝" 4 FH		24
Screw	1½" 8 RH		6
Screw	⅝" 6 FH		4
Flat washer	⅛" ID		6
Knob		Screw-type	4
Hinge (NMH)	2"	nonmortise	2
Lid stay (LLS)			1

pared cauls (sticks) to protect the work edges from the clamp jaws. Apply glue with a brush to both surfaces and to the dowels. Join the pieces and clamp securely.

When the glue has set, remove the clamps and trim the boards to the exact size. Follow by laying the contours shown and cut with a saber saw or band saw.

The sides are now ready to be rabbeted and dadoed. Make the ¾-inch dadoes first. Mark the position of each dado at the edge of the board, then clamp a board to the work to guide the router. The location of the guide board is determined by the size of the router base and cutter. Take one-half the diameter of the base (radius) and subtract one-half the diameter of the cutter. This measurement will indicate the distance from the edge of the dado to the edge of the guide. Another method is to locate the center of the dado on the work, then simply take one-half the diameter (radius) of the base and locate the guide at this distance. The method you choose to locate the guide is a matter of preference.

You will note that all of the dadoes are stopped; that is, they do not extend to the edge of the board at the front edge. To make stopped dadoes, clamp or nail a stop to the guide to limit the travel of the router. For the base piece and upper sections, place the stops so they will stop the cutter ½ inch from the leading edge. The only exception is the short vertical dado that accepts the desk front. This dado comes to within ⅜ inch of the edge. Bear in mind that the inside surfaces are to be dadoed. Thus, one piece is dadoed face-up and one face-down.

Leave the ends of the dadoes half-round except for the uppermost one on the base side pieces. Square this one off at the front end using a chisel. After cutting the dadoes, make the ¼-inch rabbet cuts to accept the rear panel.

Cut the shelf members to size and then round the front edges using a router fitted with a ⅜-inch rounding overbit. The resulting round edge will match the half-round of the dadoed groove in the side members.

You can now make the lag-screw clearance holes in the top piece of the lower section. Space them 4 inches apart and 3½ inches from each end. Drill the bottom shelf of the upper section to accept the 2½-inch screws. Space the holes as shown in the detail.

Next, sand the members smooth then dry-assemble them to make sure they fit properly. Although the rear panels are not installed yet, you should cut them because you will use them temporarily in the gluing and clamping operation. Apply a thinned coat of glue to the ends of all shelf members. This is called *sizing* and will prevent the end grain from absorbing too much glue. Allow the sized pieces to air-dry then sand lightly to remove the roughness, which will be apparent.

Next, apply the glue full strength and assemble and clamp the parts securely. Be sure to have an assistant on hand to help with assembling and clamping. Use cauls under the clamp jaws to protect the work surfaces.

After you have assembled the parts and before you have installed the clamps, place the rear panel in place to ensure that the assembly remains square while you install and tighten the clamps. After you glue both sections, final assembly can take place. Apply glue to the joint, then fasten the bottom shelf to the sides using 2½-inch flat-head screws. Join the two sections using the 1½-inch lag screws. Be sure to use flat washers under the screw heads. They serve two purposes: they prevent the heads from crushing the wood surface, and they tend to shorten the screw slightly so the points do not penetrate the surface of the adjoining shelf.

Bevel the desk lid 22 degrees at the front and rear edges as indicated. Then round the ends with a 3/16-inch rounding bit (not 3/8-inch as was used on the shelves). Do not use a router on the beveled edges. You must round them by hand using a plane or sandpaper. Next, fasten the lid to the lower shelf using 2-inch nonmortise hinges. Install them with the larger leaf on the lid. Fasten the lid support using flat-head screws. Locate the screw holes as indicated on the drawing.

Make the drawer next. Cut the pieces to the sizes shown in the Materials List, then cut the rabbets and grooves on the table saw. Make the three dadoes in the drawer subfront to take the filler strips, which are used to give the appearance of four separate drawers. Glue the strips into the grooves, then sand the surface smooth before you attach the four 1/4-inch plywood fronts. Fasten the fronts with glue and hold in place with spring clamps. Assemble the drawer by inserting the plywood bottom into the grooves as you assemble the subfront, rear, and ends.

Now add the two base pieces to complete the assembly. Because the grain direction in these pieces runs at right angles to the sides, install them without glue. Use screws and flat washers as shown to assemble them.

To simplify staining and finishing, do not install the rear panels yet. You will find it easier to get into the corners without the panels in place. Stain as desired. We used Carters Spanish Oak Stain and two coats of sanding sealer, followed by two coats of gloss lacquer. After the lacquer dried thoroughly—about three days—we rubbed the surface with rubbing compound.

Classic Hall Tree with Mirror

THIS CHARMING HALL TREE will make a practical addition to your home. It is constructed of solid oak, is easy to build, and will give years of attractive, trouble-free service.

The hall tree was so named because the hooks used on it resemble the branches of a tree. Our version uses brass hooks with ceramic knobs, but early models of this piece were made with stag horns. This piece has been made in many different forms, but the basic design is always the same: a large mirror, several hat hooks, a small table or tray, and a storage area for umbrellas.

We selected oak for our tree, but you may substitute any wood species. The piece is 24 inches wide and 78 inches tall. It is only 14 inches deep, so it will easily fit into a small hallway or foyer.

The turned legs are store-bought, making it possible for those without a lathe to produce the piece. Of course, lathe owners will have no difficulty in turning the legs.

Construction consists of doweled and screwed joints. You can eliminate the screws, however, and use the dowels throughout. We found that using both screws and dowels in assembly greatly simplified the procedure.

Use flat boards with a pleasant grain pattern, then rip the two stiles to size. Trim the ends so both pieces will be exactly 78 inches long. Next cut the three rail members to size, then shape the top piece so it

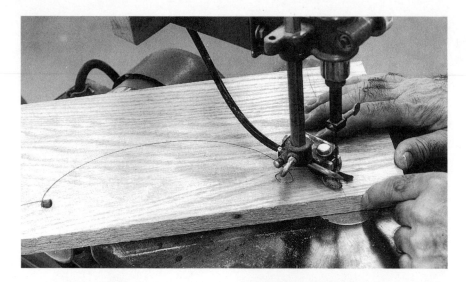

Fig. 7-1. Use a jigsaw to cut the scalloped section of the top rail. A saber saw or band saw can be substituted. The drawings show the correct pattern.

Fig. 7-2. (left) To prevent errors during assembly, identify all pieces with markings. The doweling jig ensures perfectly centered holes for the dowels.

Fig. 7-3. (right) Transfer hole locations in the rail to the stile using the dowel centers. The strip of wood at the bottom ensures you will be able to line them up perfectly before gluing them together.

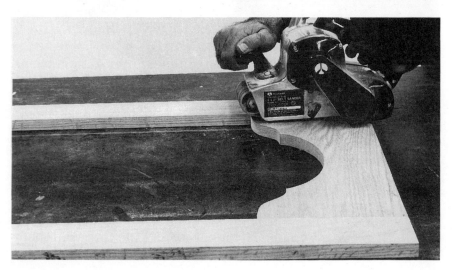

Fig. 7-4. Clamp and set aside the glued-up frame until the glue sets. Later, use a belt sander to level the discrepancies between pieces.

Fig. 7-5. Use a router to cut the rabbet for the mirror of the hall tree. The depth of the rabbet cut must match the thickness of the mirror you buy.

Fig. 7-6. The setup for grooving the frame to take the plywood shelf. Again, you will use a router for this procedure. The clamped straightedge guides the router.

Fig. 7-7. Trim ready-made legs to size on a radial arm saw. Then round the ends of the legs, using sandpaper on a stick.

Fig. 7-8. To make the top of the leg, use a ball and wheel. They are available ready made.

conforms to the drawing.

Locate the dowel positions, then drill the ⅜-inch-diameter holes 1¹⁄₁₆ inches deep into the ends of the rails. A doweling jig will help a great deal in drilling these holes because it will ensure that the holes are perfectly centered.

After the holes have been drilled in all three rail pieces, lay the parts on the table in the manner in which you will assemble

them. If you haven't yet made the identification marks for each piece, do so now to prevent mixing up the pieces.

Transfer the dowel holes that you drilled into the rails to the stiles. The best way is to use *dowel centers*, which are short steel dowels with a sharp point centered at one end. Insert them into the previously drilled holes, then align the mating parts and bring them together. The sharp point automatically transfers the exact location of the drilled hole to the stile.

To ensure that the stiles and rails are aligned at the top and bottom edges, use a piece of wood at the top edge, as shown in the illustration. Slide the pieces together, then use a square to draw a pencil line through the center mark left by the dowel center. Slide the doweling jig until the reference mark for the ⅜-inch bushing aligns with the pencil mark. Drill the holes to a depth of 1¹⁄₁₆ inches.

Before gluing the parts, glue-size the end grain of the rails to ensure a good, tight glue joint. If the end grain is left unsized, it will absorb too much glue, resulting in a glue-starved, and thus a poor, joint. To make sizing glue, thin the regular glue by

Fig. 7-9. When both legs are assembled, fasten them to the front members. Always use pads under the jaws of the clamps to prevent damage to wood. Allow the glue to dry.

Fig. 7-10. Here the crown molding is being fitted into place. Note the perfect miter joint. It was accomplished with a fine-toothed back saw in a miter box. Do it carefully.

Fig. 7-11. Hold both the rear panel and the mirror in place with plastic panel retainers. They make for easy removal when you want to clean or polish the tree's mirror.

Fig. 7-12. To remove paste wood filler/stain, wipe across the grain. Note that small sections are done at one time. Don't worry, stain will blend without streaks.

adding a little water to it. Brush it on and let it dry for about 15 minutes. Then apply full-strength glue to the joints and dowels, assemble the parts, and clamp securely.

A word of advice about the dowels. When using them on hardwood, you might find they are too snug. If so, sand them down until they fit without being forced. After all, the dowels in this application are mostly used for alignment, not for strength.

To save time when gluing up the frame, tape strips of wood to the outer part of the stiles. The strips will prevent the clamp jaws from marring the work. Apply glue to all members, then clamp securely. The members should square up automatically but it is a good idea to check the assembly with a square to make sure everything is in order.

After the glue has set, sand the frame, preferably with a belt sander, until all joints are perfectly level. Then use a vac or brush and remove all traces of sanding grit before the next operation, which requires the use of the router. If any traces of abrasive particles are left on the work, the router bit will quickly dull, so be sure to dust off carefully.

Use the router to rabbet the rear edges

MATERIALS LIST

Purpose	Size	Description	Quantity
Stile	$^{13}/_{16}$″ × $^{3}/_{4}$″ × 78″	Oak	2
Upper rail	$^{13}/_{16}$″ × 8½″ × 17½″	Oak	1
Center rail	$^{13}/_{16}$″ × $7^{7}/_{8}$″ × 17½″	Oak	1
Lower rail	$^{13}/_{16}$″ × 5″ × 17½″	Oak	1
Crown molding	½″ × 2½″	#52501	42″
Upper front	$^{13}/_{16}$″ × $5^{3}/_{4}$″ × $19^{5}/_{16}$″	Oak	1
Lower front	$^{13}/_{16}$″ × $3^{5}/_{8}$″ × $19^{5}/_{16}$″	Oak	1
Upper side	$^{13}/_{16}$″ × $8^{7}/_{8}$″ × $10^{3}/_{4}$″	Oak	2
Tray side	$^{13}/_{16}$″ × 5″ × $11^{5}/_{8}$″	Oak	2
Tray	¼″ × $11^{3}/_{4}$″ × 12½″	Plywood	1
Lower side	$^{13}/_{16}$″ × $3^{5}/_{8}$″ × $10^{3}/_{4}$″	Oak	2
Bottom panel	$^{13}/_{16}$″ × $11^{3}/_{16}$″ × $21^{1}/_{8}$″	Oak	1
Bottom divider	$^{13}/_{16}$″ × 1¼″	Oak	2
Rear panel	¼″ × $18^{1}/_{8}$″ × 22″	Plywood	1
Leg	$2^{3}/_{8}$″ × $2^{3}/_{8}$″ × 30″	#51001	2
Disc	$^{13}/_{16}$″ × $^{3}/_{4}$″ × 2¼″	Oak wheel	4
Ball	1½″ dia.		2
Dowel	$^{3}/_{8}$″ × 2″	#51017	24
Screw	2″ 14 FH		12
Screw	½″ 4 FH		20
Glue Block	$^{13}/_{16}$″ × 1″ × $^{3}/_{4}$″	Oak	6
Mirror	$^{1}/_{8}$″ × 18″ × $40^{7}/_{8}$″		1
Retainer		#77527	20
Hook		#64000	4

Note: The hooks, legs, and other accessories are available from Armor Products. The numbers shown are from the Armor catalog.

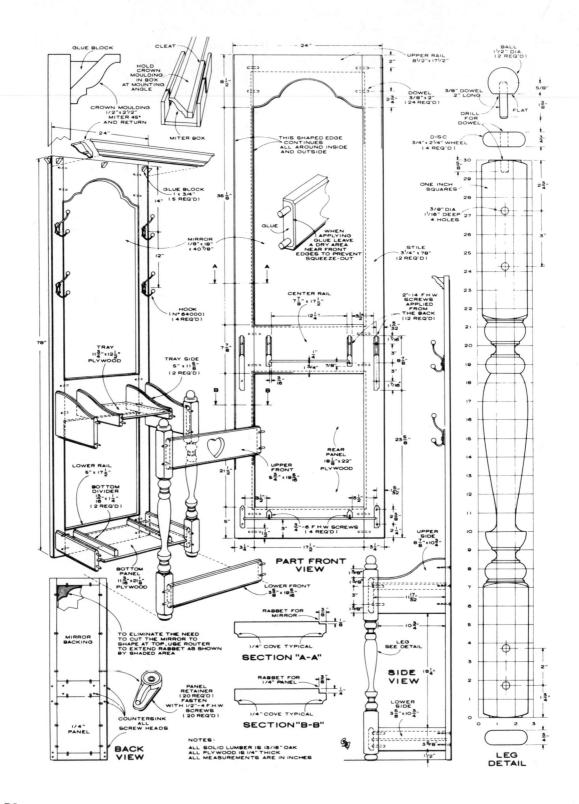

GLUE BLOCK

CLEAT

BALL
1½" DIA
(2 REQ'D)

HOLD CROWN MOULDING IN BOX AT MOUNTING ANGLE

UPPER RAIL
8½" x 17½"

24"

2"

CROWN MOULDING
1½" x 2½"
MITER 45°
AND RETURN

8½"

DOWEL
3/8" x 2"
(24 REQ'D)

3/8" DOWEL
2" LONG

FLAT

2¾"

8½"

DRILL
FOR
DOWEL

5/8"

DISC
3/4" x 2¼" WHEEL
(4 REQ'D)

24"

MITER BOX

THIS SHAPED EDGE CONTINUES ALL AROUND INSIDE AND OUTSIDE

¾"

30

GLUE BLOCK
1 x 1¾"
14" (5 REQ'D)

36¾"

29

2¾"

ONE INCH SQUARES

28

14"

27

3/8" DIA
1 1/16" DEEP
4 HOLES

3"

MIRROR
1/8" x 18"
x 40⅞"

GLUE

12"

WHEN APPLYING GLUE LEAVE A DRY AREA NEAR FRONT EDGES TO PREVENT SQUEEZE-OUT

STILE
3¼" x 78"
(2 REQ'D)

26

25

24

CENTER RAIL
7⅞" x 17½"

2"-14 FHW SCREWS APPLIED FROM THE BACK (12 REQ'D)

23

HOOK
(N° 64000)
(4 REQ'D)

12¼"

5/32"

22

21

1 7/16"

TRAY
11¾" x 12½"
PLYWOOD

7⅞"

1"

7/8"

3"

8⅞"

20

19

TRAY SIDE
5" x 11⅝"
(2 REQ'D)

1¾"

7/8"

3"

18

3/16"

1 7/16"

79"

REAR PANEL
18⅝" x 22"
PLYWOOD

23⅝"

LOWER RAIL
5" x 17½"

UPPER FRONT
5¾" x 19 15/16"

21½"

BOTTOM DIVIDER
13/16" x 1¼"
(2 REQ'D)

½"

5/32"

½"

3"

2¾"

2¼"

5"

3-6 FHW SCREWS
(4 REQ'D)

UPPER SIDE
8⅞" x 10¾"

BOTTOM PANEL
11½" x 12½"
PLYWOOD

1½"

3"

1½"

3¼"

17½"

3¼"

PART FRONT VIEW

LOWER FRONT
3⅝" x 19⅝"

LEG
SEE DETAIL

SIDE VIEW

RABBET FOR MIRROR

3/8"

1½"

¼" COVE TYPICAL

11 17/32"

10¾"

SECTION "A-A"

MIRROR BACKING

RABBET FOR ¼" PANEL

3/8"

1½"

TO ELIMINATE THE NEED TO CUT THE MIRROR TO SHAPE AT TOP, USE ROUTER TO EXTEND RABBET AS SHOWN BY SHADED AREA

LOWER SIDE
3⅝" x 10¾"

¼" PANEL

PANEL RETAINER
(20 REQ'D) FASTEN WITH ½"-4 F.H.W. SCREWS
(20 REQ'D)

¼" COVE TYPICAL

SECTION "B-B"

3⅝"

COUNTERSINK ALL SCREW HEADS

NOTES:
ALL SOLID LUMBER IS 13/16" OAK
ALL PLYWOOD IS ¼" THICK
ALL MEASUREMENTS ARE IN INCHES

½"

¾"

BACK VIEW

LEG DETAIL

52

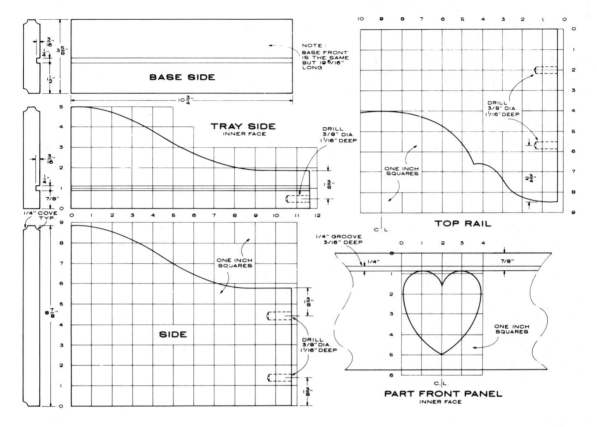

BASE SIDE

NOTE: BASE FRONT IS THE SAME BUT 19 5/16" LONG

TRAY SIDE
INNER FACE

DRILL 3/8" DIA. 1 1/16" DEEP

ONE INCH SQUARES

TOP RAIL

DRILL 3/8" DIA 1/16" DEEP

SIDE

DRILL 3/8" DIA. 1 1/16" DEEP

ONE INCH SQUARES

1/4" GROOVE 3/16" DEEP

ONE INCH SQUARES

PART FRONT PANEL
INNER FACE

of the frame for the mirror and plywood panel, as well as to shape the front of the frame.

A ball bearing rabbeting bit is recommended because it will not leave burn marks on the workpiece. Set the cutter to produce a 3/8- × -1/8-inch rabbet for the mirror and then reset it to produce a 3/8- × -1/4-inch rabbet for the plywood.

The mirror can be cut to the contoured shape at the top of the frame, but this is not easily done, so we decided to cut the mirror square and extend the rabbet into a rectangular shape as shown in the drawing. To rout this area use a straight bit and set the depth so it matches the depth of the rabbet, which is 1/8 inch.

After the rabbeting is completed, turn the frame upside down (face up) and cut

the cove bead. You can use just a portion of a Roman ogee cutter to make the cut, or substitute other shapes.

After the beading is completed, locate and drill the screw clearance holes as indicated. You also can cut the two grooves now. Clamp a straight piece of wood to guide the router. Fit the router with a 1/4-inch straight bit, then cut the groove 3/16 inch deep.

The legs are ready-made turnings which are modified slightly. They are available in various lengths. We used the 32-inch size and trimmed 1 inch off the top and bottom. After trimming, locate the center of the square section at the top and bottom, and drill the 5/8-inch-deep, 3/8-inch-diameter holes for the dowels.

The top and bottom of the legs looked

too plain with just the square cut so we decided to add the ball and disc to the top and a disc to the bottom. This task can be easily done with a lathe, but poses a problem for those without a lathe. You can improvise by using a ball and wheel, which are readily available. Flatten the ball at the bottom, the dowel it and the wheel to the leg. At the bottom of the leg, use a wheel without a ball. Flatten the ball on the sander, or use a hand saw.

Before mounting the ball and disc, break the sharp corners at the top and bottom of the legs with sandpaper. Wrap the sandpaper on a flat stick and use it as you would a rasp or file. Follow by drilling the holes for the dowels.

Cut the side and front members to size then sand and shape them with the router, as you did for the frame. Groove the rear of the upper front panel after you cut out and bead the heart shape because the groove runs very close to the top of the cutout.

Drill the dowel and screw holes as indicated, then glue-size the end grains as you did for the rails previously.

Assembly can now begin. The first step is to fasten the legs to the front members. Use care when applying glue because any squeezing-out will cause problems when staining later. Apply the glue sparingly with a small brush. (See drawing.) When clamping, be sure to use wood pads under the clamp jaws.

Next, glue the side members to the legs. You can simplify the clamping operation by using the method shown. Place the glued-up assembly on a flat surface with 2 × 4s stretched across both legs. Apply clamps, but before tightening securely, check to make sure the side members are square and perpendicular. Make adjust-

ments as necessary.

Now add the two inner side members.

Fasten the leg assembly to the rear frame with screws. Place the bottom plywood panel and upper tray into the grooves, then fasten securely with screws driven from the rear. If desired, you can use glue at the rear of each side member.

Finally, miter and install the crown molding at the top. When mitering, be sure to hold the molding at the mounting angle. (See detail.) Glue the molding to the top of the frame then add glue blocks behind to reinforce it.

Oak is an open-grain wood so you should give it an application of paste wood filler before you apply topcoats. This will result in a smooth professional finish. The filler is available mixed with stain so one application will do both operations—staining and filling.

Apply the filler with a brush, as if you were painting the surface. Before using the filler, you must thin it to the consistency of enamel. After applying the filler with the brush, allow it to set—usually about 15 minutes—then wipe off across the grain using burlap or other rough cloth. A terry cloth towel is a good substitute. Wipe across the grain so that the pores of the wood will be packed with filler.

Allow the filler to dry overnight, then apply a coat of sanding sealer. After the sealer has dried, follow with several coats of clear lacquer. Sand lightly between coats using 600- or 800-grit paper. Rub down the final coat with rubbing compound for a professional finish.

To attach the mirror and rear panel, use panel retainers screwed from the rear. Add the brass hooks to complete the project. Now your hall tree is ready for hats, coats, umbrellas, and whatall. Enjoy it.

Classic Mantel Clock

THIS ELEGANT CLOCK was made popular in the 1800s by the famous Connecticut clockmaker Eli Terry. Made of oak, the pendulum clock features a Westminster movement, which strikes every quarter hour. The solid brass tubing and finials add an elegant decorative touch to this fine timepiece. Although we used oak for the case, you can substitute other wood species. The lumber used was ½ inch thick, except for the bottom panel and posts which were cut from ¹³⁄₁₆-inch stock.

Choose good, flat stock for this project, then cut the pieces to size as per the Materials List. Before cutting apart the board into the individual pieces, you might want to sand the long board. You will find it easier and faster to sand the board beforehand so you won't have to sand a bunch of small parts, which at best are difficult to hold. A belt sander is great for this task. Start with an 80-grit belt, then finish with 120-grit. You can do further fine sanding just before final assembly.

Rabbet the sides, top, and bottom panels at the rear edge to accept the rear panel. You can make the rabbet on the table saw, but since the top and bottom panels require stopped rabbets, you might find it easier to make the rabbets with a router. We used a router fastened to the underside of a table. A straight board with a blade clearance notch converted the setup to a mini shaper.

Set and adjust the cut, making trial runs on scrap wood. The rabbets on the two side members run the full length of the piece. The top and bottom require blind rabbets, which are 9¼ inches long. Mark pencil lines on the edge of the boards where the rabbets are to start and stop. Pivot one end of the stock against the fence then angle the work into the cut, feeding the work from right to left.

The screw and tubing holes in the top and bottom panels must be laid out carefully. In order to avoid errors and to make for a more accurate job, we suggest that you drill the top and bottom panels together.

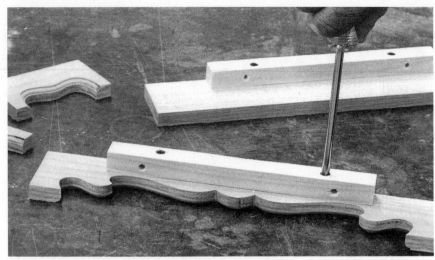

Fig. 8-1. The jigsaw is ideal for cutting the scalloped base. Add cleats to the base before assembly. Countersink screws.

Fig. 8-2. Before gluing rosettes, rub the back surface on sandpaper to flatten. Double-pointed brads prevent parts from sliding.

Fig. 8-3. Use a jig to clamp the door after gluing. A spacer locates the intermediate rail. After gluing, assemble the parts and clamp tightly.

Fig. 8-4. Install the pivot hinge by dropping it into the socket then screwing it to the back of the door. Insert the brass tubing before the top.

Fig. 8-5. Center the crown assembly over the top panel and fasten with screws. This is a view of the speaker and hinge socket on the underside of the top.

Center the top over the wider and longer bottom panel, then tape together and drill ⅛-inch pilot holes through both pieces at the ends only. Make the two holes at the front edge only in the top panel. Redrill the holes to the proper sizes and countersink as shown.

Cut the base and crown pieces on a jigsaw, band saw, or coping saw. If you use a band saw, a ⅛-inch-wide blade is recommended.

After the wood parts are cut, sand the edges to remove the kerf marks. Then dust carefully and shape the edges using a router fitted with a beading cutter. Use a ⅛-inch bead on the front and side base pieces and the top panel. Use a ⅜-inch beading cutter for the thicker bottom panel. Cut beads only at the ends and front of the top and bottom panels.

Before assembling the bottom base pieces, install the cleats to the front and rear pieces. We used drywall screws because they have sharp points and sharp threads.

Since we used butt-joint construction throughout, the gluing was done with great care. End grain is very absorbent, so we suggest that you glue-size all end grain. Allow to dry then sand lightly and apply the glue full strength.

To prevent the pieces from sliding when clamping, insert double-pointed brads into the mating parts. You can make the pins by snipping brads at an angle. Then press them into one member of the joint, using a pair of pliers. A better method uses special brads and a low-cost application tool. Be sure to use cauls under the clamp jaws to prevent damage to the work surface.

Round the crown panel with a ⅛-inch rounding over bit. Do not round the area to be covered by the rosette.

After the rosettes have been glued, add the corner posts and end pieces, again using the double-pointed brads.

Make the door of ½-inch stock. Rip the pieces ¹⁵⁄₁₆ inch wide, then cut the lengths as shown. You will need two stiles and three rail pieces. Top, bottom, and intermediate rails are 7 inches long. Glue-size

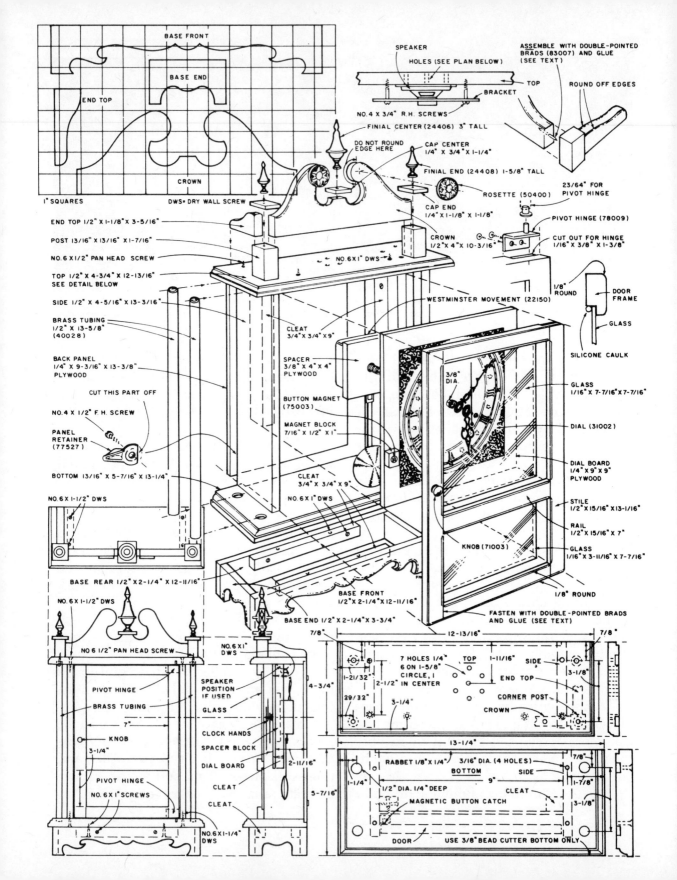

MATERIALS LIST

Purpose	Size	Description	Quantity
Bottom	$^{13}/_{16}$" × 5$^7/_{16}$" × 13¼"	Oak	1
Top	½" × 4¾" × 12$^{13}/_{16}$"	Oak	1
Side	½" × 4$^5/_{16}$" × 13$^3/_{16}$	Oak	2
Base front/rear	½" × 2¼" × 12$^{11}/_{16}$"	Oak	2
Base end	½" × 2¼" × 3¾"	Oak	2
End, top	½" × 1⅛" × 3$^5/_{16}$"	Oak	2
Post	$^{13}/_{16}$" × $^{13}/_{16}$" × 1$^7/_{16}$"	Oak	2
Cap, end	¼" × 1⅛" × 1⅛"	Oak	2
Cap, center	¼" × ¾" × 1¼"	Oak	1
Crown	½" × 4" × 10$^3/_{16}$"	Oak	1
Rosette	1¼" Dia.	50400	2
Back panel	¼" × 9$^3/_{16}$" × 13⅜"	Plywood	1
Rail	½" × $^{15}/_{16}$" × 7"	Oak	3
Stile	½" × $^{15}/_{16}$" × 13$^1/_{16}$"	Oak	2
Cleat	¾" × ¾" × 9"		4
Brass tubing	½" × 13⅝"	40028	4
Dial board	¼" × 9" × 9"	Plywood	1
Spacer	⅜" × 4" × 4"	Plywood	1
Magnet block	$^7/_{16}$" × ½" × 1"		1
Button magnet		75003	1
Glass	$^1/_{16}$" × 7$^7/_{16}$" × 7$^7/_{16}$"		1
Glass	$^1/_{16}$" × 3$^{11}/_{16}$" × 7$^7/_{16}$"		1
Pivot hinge		78009	1 pr.
Final, end		24408	2
Final, center		24406	1
Retainer		77527	4
Screw	#6x½ pan head		4
Screw	#6x1" dry wall		18
Screw	#6x1¼ dry wall		4
Screw	#4x½ FH		4
Screw	#4x¾ RH		4
Brad, double-pointed		83007	24
Brad tool		84037	1
Silicone Caulk		GE Clear	1 tube
Knob		71003	1
Dial		31002	1
Westminster movement		22150	1

the ends of the rails, then set aside to dry.

Make a simple door-gluing jig by nailing four cleats to a plywood board. Place the cleats to surround the outside of the door, except for one long cleat, which you should place farther away, as shown. To prevent the door from being accidentally glued to the board of the jig, protect the area of the door by placing a piece of wax paper (or melted paraffin) onto the board of the jig to cover that area.

Now use the jig as follows. Insert one

stile in place then add glue to both ends of the top rail. Install a 7- x -7-inch filler block, then glue and add the second and bottom rail. Add the second stile, then install the wedges and tap into place.

When the glue has set, sand the door frame then rabbet the back to take the glass. Use a sharp chisel to square the rounded corners of the rabbet left by the router.

The right top and bottom sections of the door must be mortised to accept the pivot hinge. Use a table-mounted router for this task. Set the fence to produce a $\frac{1}{16}$- x -$\frac{3}{8}$ inch rabbet. Be sure to make a test cut on scrap wood first.

The brass tubing and top panel must be installed together. Do not use glue at this time. Screw the base piece to the bottom panel, then the bottom to the side panels. Insert the tubes, align the holes, then add the top panel. The door hinges consist of a pin and socket. Install the sockets into the top and bottom pieces. Fasten the hinges with pan-head screws. The hinge holes are elongated to permit adjustment from side to side.

To fasten the glued-up crown section to the top panel, use the two screws at the front and those at the rear sides.

Assemble the entire clock without glue so that the brass parts can be removed when stain and finishing materials are applied. Fasten the cleats for the dial board to the side panels. Then fasten the dial board with 1-inch screws driven from the rear of the cleats.

The electronic clock movement used here has a separate loudspeaker. Mount the loudspeaker to the underside of the top panel and center it over the acoustical holes in the panel. A special bracket holds the speaker in place. Fasten it with two round-head screws. Fasten the movement to the

dial board with the hardware provided. A spacer block and rubber washer will place the movement in the proper place relative to the door glass. Fasten the dial with small round-head screws.

Drill the magnetic catch block $\frac{5}{16}$ inch to take the catch and two mounting screws. Insert the magnet into the block, then mount the strike plate on the door. Let the catch adhere to the strike plate, then close the door so it sets into the frame equally at the left and right sides. Mark the position of the block, then screw it into place.

Remove the movement, tubing, and finials, then prepare to finish the clock case. Sand all surfaces with 220-grit paper, then apply a coat of paste wood filler. You might find it easier to apply the filler with the parts disassembled so you won't need to work in tight corners. Be sure to tape over the areas where glue is to be applied because glue will not take over stain and filler.

The filler used here is dark walnut, which means that it stains and fills in one operation. Apply it with a brush and let it set for about 10 minutes. then rub it off with a rough cloth or burlap, rubbing across the grain.

Note: Do not coat the entire clock at one time. Work in sections. Use a stiff brush to remove the filler from the rosettes.

When the filler is completely dry, apply a sealer coat and follow with several coats of clear lacquer. Follow the manufacturer's instructions when applying these materials. Install the glass by applying a bead of silicone caulk around the edge of the glass and rabbet.

The items in the Materials List described by numbers are available from Armor Products.

Classic Rolltop Desk

THIS ELEGANT ROLLTOP DESK is designed along the lines of those that were popular in the nineteenth century. Constructed of solid and veneer oak, this functional masterpiece will make a fine addition to any home. The all-wood tambour operates with ease in a graceful curve, and when retracted it disappears behind the pigeonhole shelves. Two manuscript boards are also included, one located at the top of each pedestal.

The desk has seven drawers, two which are made to hold letter-size folders. Additionally, the drawers have aluminum rails to support hanging files. Center guides allow the drawers to operate without binding. Dust panels between each drawer are included.

Happily, the value is tremendous. Material will cost you just a few hundred dol-lars. Store-bought, the unit would cost thousands.

To simplify construction, the top is made as a separate unit and is fastened to the pedestal base with lag screws. All frame members are doweled for added strength.

Begin construction by cutting all parts to size as shown in the Materials List. The 1-inch oak stock is $13/16$ inch thick, and all measurements are based on this thickness. If you decide to use pine for construction, be sure to allow for the difference in thickness of the pine, which is ¾ inch.

Work on the base section first. Rip the stiles and rails for the end-frame section to size, then trim them to length. Locate the ⅜-inch dowel holes as indicated then drill to a depth of 1 1/16 inch. The use of a dowel jig is recommended for this operation because accuracy is most important. After

Fig. 9-1. (left) The end frame after the dadoes have been cut. You can use various tools, such as a dado head.

Fig. 9-2. (right) When you assemble the pedestal sections, bar clamps are indispensable because the proper pressure must be applied.

Fig. 9-3. (left) The rolltop frame being squared. Use waste pieces so that pressure is applied evenly to all frame members.

Fig. 9-4. (right) The template guide has been inserted into the router base. The cutter projects the distance of the groove depth and template thickness.

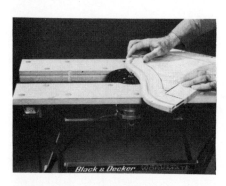

Fig. 9-5. (left) After the groove has been cut, round or bead the corners of the frame. A router makes an excellent tool for this job.

Fig. 9-6. (right) Crosspieces with end frames attached are being fastened to the top of the desk with lag screws for strength.

Fig. 9-7. (left) Tambour, drawers and other components can be fitted into the partially built unit.

Fig. 9-8. (right) The completed tambour. Remove the tape so the tambour can be lifted from the supporting backboard.

Fig. 9-9. (left) Assemble pigeonhole compartments in sections. The top and the bottom boards of each will be added later.

Fig. 9-10. (right) For good looks, miter the nose and cove moldings. Here, they are being secured to the drawer front. Use glue and brads for the job.

you have drilled the holes in one member, use dowel centers to transfer the hole locations to the mating parts.

When setting up the pieces for the frames, note that the stiles at the rear are wider than those at the front. To avoid errors, identify each joint by matching numbers or letters, such as A-A and B-B.

After you have drilled the frame members for the dowels, groove them to take the ¼-inch plywood panels. Note that the grooves are not centered; they are closer to the outside.

The ¼- × -¼-inch grooves run through from end to end on the short rail pieces, but not on the stiles. Instead, they stop ¼-inch before the dowel holes. You can make the grooves with a router, shaper, or table saw fitted with a dado blade.

After the pieces are grooved, assemble the frames temporarily with loose-fitting dowels. To make the dowels loose fitting, sand them down slightly.

With the frames temporarily assembled, bead the edges using a router, or use a shaper if available. Bead (or round) only the exposed edges adjacent to the grooves. (See detail drawing.) When making the bead or round, be sure the pilot of the router cutter is riding on a solid surface. If necessary, place a filler strip into the groove while you are making the cut.

Disassemble the members, then proceed to drill the holes for the front frame assembly. These holes are made in the edge of the forward stiles and will take dowels from the front frame. Also make the dowel holes for the rear apron and center frame at this time. You should drill the holes before you assemble the frame because it is easier to handle the separate pieces than the assembled frame.

After the necessary holes have been drilled, cut the rabbets into the rear stiles for the rear panel. Carefully note into which pieces the rabbet is to be made.

Drill the rear crosspieces, upper and lower, for dowels. Drill two holes in each 1 ½ inches deep. This depth will allow the dowel to protrude ½ inch, and you will later insert this part into the rear stiles. After the holes are made, use dowel centers to transfer the dowel hole centers to the stiles. Be sure that the rear edge of the crosspiece is flush with the rabbeted edge of the stile.

After the pedestals are completely assembled, fasten them to the top with flathead screws.

Cut the four end panels from ¼-inch oak plywood. Each piece is 5 ½ × 21 ⁷⁄₁₆ inches, but check these dimensions out carefully with the actual opening because these pieces will be inserted into the

MATERIALS LIST

Purpose	Size	Description	Quantity
Roll Top Unit			
Top	$\frac{3}{4}" \times 8\frac{1}{4}" \times 54"$	Plywood	1
Upper crosspiece	$\frac{13}{16}" \times 1\frac{1}{2}" \times 51\frac{7}{16}"$	Poplar	1
Lower crosspiece	$\frac{13}{16}" \times 2\frac{1}{2}" \times 51\frac{7}{16}"$	Poplar	1
Rear panel	$\frac{1}{4}" \times 13" \times 52\frac{7}{16}"$	Plywood	1
End frame rear	$\frac{13}{16}" \times 2\frac{1}{2}" \times 13"$	Oak	2
End frame top	$\frac{13}{16}" \times 2\frac{1}{2}" \times 5\frac{3}{4}"$	Oak	2
End frame front	$\frac{13}{16}" \times 5" \times 17\frac{1}{2}"$	Oak	2
End frame bottom	$\frac{13}{16}" \times 2\frac{1}{2}" \times 14\frac{1}{2}"$	Oak	2
End panel	$\frac{1}{4}" \times 8\frac{1}{2}" \times 14"$	Plywood	2
Tambour slat	$\frac{1}{2}" \times \frac{3}{4}" \times 52"$	Oak	21
Tambour lead slat	$\frac{1}{2}" \times 1\frac{3}{4}" \times 52"$	Oak	1
Pigeonhole Unit			
Top	$\frac{1}{2}" \times 6\frac{5}{8}" \times 51\frac{3}{8}"$	Oak	1
Bottom	$\frac{1}{2}" \times 6\frac{5}{8}" \times 51\frac{3}{8}"$	Oak	1
Shelf	$\frac{1}{2}" \times 6\frac{5}{8}" \times 18"$	Oak	1
Shelf	$\frac{1}{2}" \times 6\frac{5}{8}" \times 9\frac{7}{16}"$	Oak	4
Panel	$\frac{1}{2}" \times 6\frac{5}{8}" \times 10"$	Oak	8
Rear	$\frac{1}{4}" \times 10\frac{1}{2}" \times 51\frac{3}{8}"$	Plywood	1
Desk Unit			
Top	$\frac{3}{4}" \times 20\frac{1}{2}" \times 54"$	Oak plywood	1
End frame stile rear	$\frac{13}{16}" \times 2\frac{1}{2}" \times 29\frac{3}{8}"$	Oak	4
End frame stile front	$\frac{13}{16}" \times 1\frac{11}{16}" \times 29\frac{3}{8}"$	Oak	4
End frame rail upper	$\frac{13}{16}" \times 2\frac{1}{2}" \times 15"$	Oak	4
End frame rail lower	$\frac{13}{16}" \times 6" \times 15"$	Oak	4
End frame panel, rear	$\frac{1}{4}" \times 15\frac{1}{8}" \times 29\frac{3}{8}"$	Plywood	2
End frame apron, upper	$\frac{13}{16}" \times 2\frac{1}{4}" \times 14\frac{1}{2}"$	Oak	2
End frame apron, lower	$\frac{13}{16}" \times 3\frac{1}{4}" \times 14\frac{1}{2}"$	Oak	2
End frame panel	$\frac{1}{4}" \times 15\frac{3}{8}" \times 21\frac{3}{8}"$	Plywood	4
Dust frame side	$\frac{3}{4}" \times 2" \times 18\frac{7}{8}"$	Pine	16
Dust frame front	$\frac{3}{4}" \times 2" \times 10\frac{7}{8}"$	Pine	8
Dust frame rear	$\frac{3}{4}" \times 2" \times 10\frac{7}{8}"$	Pine	8
Dust frame panel	$\frac{1}{4}" \times 11\frac{1}{4}" \times 15\frac{3}{8}"$	Plywood	8
Spline	$\frac{1}{4}" \times \frac{1}{2}" \times 1\frac{3}{4}"$	Plywood	36
Front frame stile	$\frac{13}{16}" \times 1\frac{1}{4}" \times 29\frac{3}{8}"$	Oak	4
Front frame rail	$\frac{3}{4}" \times \frac{13}{16}" \times 13\frac{7}{8}"$	Oak	6
Front frame rail, lower	$\frac{13}{16}" \times 4" \times 13\frac{7}{8}"$	Oak	2
Multiscript board	$\frac{3}{4}" \times 14\frac{3}{8}" \times 19\frac{1}{8}"$	Plywood	2
Manuscript trim	$\frac{1}{16}" \times \frac{3}{4}" \times 13\frac{1}{4}"$	Oak	4
Manuscript front edge	$\frac{3}{4}" \times \frac{13}{16}" \times 13\frac{3}{8}"$	Oak	2
Desk Unit Center			
Rear apron	$\frac{13}{16}" \times 4\frac{1}{4}" \times 20\frac{7}{8}"$	Oak	1

Part	Dimensions	Material	Qty
Rear frame, upper rail	$^{13}/_{16}" \times 2^{1}/_{2}" \times 16$	Oak	1
Rear frame, lower rail	$^{13}/_{16}" \times 6" \times 16"$	Oak	1
Rear frame stile	$^{13}/_{16}" \times 2^{1}/_{2}" \times 24^{1}/_{4}"$	Oak	2
Rear frame panel	$^{1}/_{4}" \times 16^{3}/_{8}" \times 24^{5}/_{8}"$	Plywood	1
Dust frame side	$^{3}/_{4}" \times 2" \times 18^{7}/_{8}"$	Pine	2
Dust frame front	$^{3}/_{4}" \times 2" \times 17^{5}/_{8}"$	Pine	1
Dust frame rear	$^{3}/_{4}" \times 2" \times 17^{5}/_{8}"$	Pine	1
Dust frame panel	$^{1}/_{4}" \times 15^{7}/_{16}" \times 17^{7}/_{8}"$	Plywood	1
Front apron	$^{13}/_{16}" \times 2^{7}/_{8}" \times 21"$	Oak	1

Drawers

Upper Drawer

Part	Dimensions	Material	Qty
Side	$^{1}/_{2}" \times 5" \times 18"$	Poplar	8
Rear	$^{1}/_{2}" \times 4^{1}/_{8}" \times 12^{1}/_{2}"$	Poplar	4
Sub-front	$^{1}/_{2}" \times 5" \times 12^{1}/_{2}"$	Poplar	4
Front	$^{3}/_{4}" \times 5^{3}/_{16}" \times 13^{7}/_{16}"$	Plywood	4
Bottom	$^{1}/_{4}" \times 12^{1}/_{2}" \times 17"$	Plywood	4

Lower Drawer

Part	Dimensions	Material	Qty
Side	$^{1}/_{2}" \times 10^{3}/_{8}" \times 18"$	Poplar	4
Rear	$^{1}/_{2}" \times 10^{1}/_{2}" \times 12^{1}/_{2}"$	Poplar	2
Sub-front	$^{1}/_{2}" \times 10^{3}/_{8}" \times 12^{1}/_{8}"$	Poplar	2
Front	$^{3}/_{4}" \times 11^{3}/_{8}" \times 13^{7}/_{16}"$	Plywood	2
Bottom	$^{1}/_{4}" \times 12^{1}/_{2}" \times 17"$	Plywood	2

Center Drawer

Part	Dimensions	Material	Qty
Side	$^{1}/_{2}" \times 4" \times 17^{1}/_{2}"$	Poplar	2
Rear	$^{1}/_{2}" \times 3^{1}/_{8}" \times 20"$	Poplar	1
Sub-front	$^{1}/_{2}" \times 4" \times 20"$	Poplar	1
Front	$^{3}/_{4}" \times 4^{1}/_{8}" \times 20^{15}/_{16}"$	Oak plywood	1
Bottom	$^{1}/_{4}" \times 16^{1}/_{2}" \times 20"$	Plywood	1
Drawer slide	$^{1}/_{2}" \times 2^{7}/_{16}" \times 16^{3}/_{4}"$		7
Drawer Guide	$^{7}/_{16}" \times 1^{3}/_{16}" \times 17"$		7

Other Materials

Part	Dimensions	Material	Qty
Nose and cove molding	$^{5}/_{8}" \times ^{3}/_{4}"$	Oak	45'
Lag screws	$^{5}/_{16}" \times 3"$		3
Lag screws	$^{5}/_{16}" \times 2^{1}/_{2}"$		8
Lag screws	$^{5}/_{16}" \times 2"$		3
Screws	$^{3}/_{8}"$ 6 FH		12
Screws	1" 8 RH		28
Screws	$1^{1}/_{2}"$ 10 FH		16
Finishing nail	$1^{1}/_{4}"$		1 box
Aluminum bar	$^{1}/_{8}" \times 1" \times 16^{1}/_{4}"$		2
Chippendale pull	3" centers		8
Brass knob			2
Drawerslide strip		Nylon	28
Dowels	$^{3}/_{8}" \times 2"$		70
Canvas	$18" \times 52"$	10 oz.	1
Nylon slide strip			28

Note: Full-size plan, No. 00311, is available, in addition to parts not found locally such as Chippendale pulls, nose and cove molding, knobs, canvas, dowels and nylon drawer strips. Write Armor Products.

grooves of the stiles and rails. The best way to check the size is to *dry-assemble* one end frame (assemble without glue), then use two thin sticks, telescoping them into the grooves. Tape the sticks so they won't move apart, then disassemble the frame and measure the overall length of the sticks. Do this for the length and width measurements.

Cut the plywood panels accordingly. The size of the panels should be very close to the size called for in the Materials List. Because of possible discrepancies, however, it is best to check the size.

Assembling the frame pieces must be done with care. First, size the end-grain surfaces of each of the rail pieces with glue. Simply thin some glue and brush well into the surface. You can apply glue directly from a squeeze bottle, then brush out with a brush dipped in water.

Allow the side to dry then apply full-strength glue to one end of each dowel and insert into the holes you previously drilled into each of the rail pieces. Be sure to use spiral or grooved dowels—they will allow air to escape, thus preventing the wood from splitting. Assemble the pieces with the panel in place, then clamp securely. Be sure to use sticks under the clamp jaws to prevent damage to the stile edges.

Next, cut the dadoes for the drawer dust frames. You can make them in several ways: you can use a router, table saw, or radial arm saw. If you use a router, take care to ensure that all dadoes are parallel and in perfect alignment with each other. Clamp a wood guide to the work, positioning it so the dado will be in the proper location. When using the table saw, use the fence to guide the work over the dado blade. If you use the radial arm saw, clamp stops to the fence for each set of dadoes to

be cut. The width of the dado is ¾ inch; the depth is ³⁄₁₆ inch.

Make the frame pieces next. Cut them from ¾-inch. Make 16 long pieces and 16 short ones. The width should be exactly 2 inches. After the pieces are cut, groove them to take the dust panels. Make the groove ¼ inch wide and ¼ inch deep. Center it along one edge of the long piece and on one edge and two ends of the short pieces. Use the router, table saw, or shaper to cut the grooves.

Make up 32 splines, each ¼ × ¼ × 1⅝ inches, using plywood scraps. Next, cut the plywood panels and dry-assemble one frame to check the fit. If the fit is okay, proceed to assemble the eight frames with glue. Clamp securely and be sure the frames are perfectly square before the glue sets.

You can make a simple gluing jig to clamp the assembly and assure squareness. Nail one tapered piece to the baseboard. Wedge the free taper into place using a hammer. Make sure the baseboard is flat, otherwise the frames will set with a twist.

After the frames are glued, you can assemble and glue them to the pedestal sides. This assembly consists of the two pedestal sides, four frames, and two aprons. Prepare the necessary clamps and clamp sticks or cauls, which will protect the work surfaces. If you are working alone, you might want to tape the sticks into place so you can work the clamps unhindered.

Insert the dowels into the upper and lower aprons, then apply glue to all mating surfaces. If you are good at this, you can glue the entire pedestal at one time. Otherwise, apply glue to the dadoes on one side and coat only one edge of the frame pieces. If you decide on the second method, install only one set of dowels to the aprons. You might want to install loose-fitting dowels to the dry end of the aprons to help in aligning the pieces. To make loose-fitting dowels, sand the surface of the dowels until the dowels fit the hole loosely, as was done previously. Clamp the assembly firmly and make sure that all pieces are in alignment. When the glue has set, remove the clamps, separate the dry side of the pedestal, apply glue as discussed previously, replace the loose dowels with regular dowels, then reclamp. Repeat this procedure for the second pedestal.

Cut and notch the pieces for the front frames as indicated. Then assemble them with glue to form the frame assembly. Transfer the holes made previously in the pedestals to the rear side of the front frames. Drill these holes ½ inch deep, then apply glue and clamp the frames to the pedestals.

Now join the pedestals to the rear center panel with lag screws. Be sure both pedestals are on a perfectly flat surface for this operation.

Make the drawers' sides, rear, and sub-front of ½-inch poplar. Make the front panels of ¾-inch plywood. Drill the holes for the pulls, then assemble the drawers with glue and brads. Lay out the fronts so the grain patterns match pleasingly.

To achieve the panel effect in the drawer fronts, use nose and cove moldings. Miter the moldings carefully and install with glue and brads.

Cut the drawer slides to size and groove them, then install them to the center bottom of each drawer. Accuracy is important here. Cut the center guides ¹⁄₁₆ inch narrower than the width of the groove in the slides. Install them to the top center of each dust frame. Be sure to set them back so they won't interfere with the drawer subfronts. Install with brads. Do not use glue at this time because you might need to make some adjustments. Check the drawer fit. If it is okay, remove the guide, apply glue, then reassemble in the same position.

Cut the manuscript boards as shown, using ¾-inch plywood. Face the sides and front with oak, then lay them into place.

Cut the top panel from ¾-inch oak plywood. Use either lumber core or plywood core. Edge the ends and front with nose and cove molding. Miter the corners as shown. Since most hardwood nose and cove moldings are available in 3-foot lengths, you will need to join the molding along the front edge of the top. Use either a square butt joint or miter the butt.

Fasten the top to the pedestals with flat-head screws. Countersink the heads so they are flush with the surface. The screw heads will be concealed by the roll-top unit.

The rolltop consists of the end frames fastened to two crosspieces. A ¼-inch panel closes off the rear. The top panel is fastened with dowels.

Make the end frames as shown, then cut a groove for the tambour. This groove is ⅜ inch wide and ⁵⁄₁₆ inch deep. Place it ⅝ inch from the curved section of the end frame. Cut the groove with a router fitted with a template guide. The guide screws into the router base and allows the tool to follow a template, resulting in a perfectly cut groove. Make the template of hardboard, particleboard, or other rigid material. Cut it with allowance made for the guide wall thickness and tool clearance. This allowance will differ from one manufacturer to another. You must determine the allowance for your particular tool. The template shown was made to work

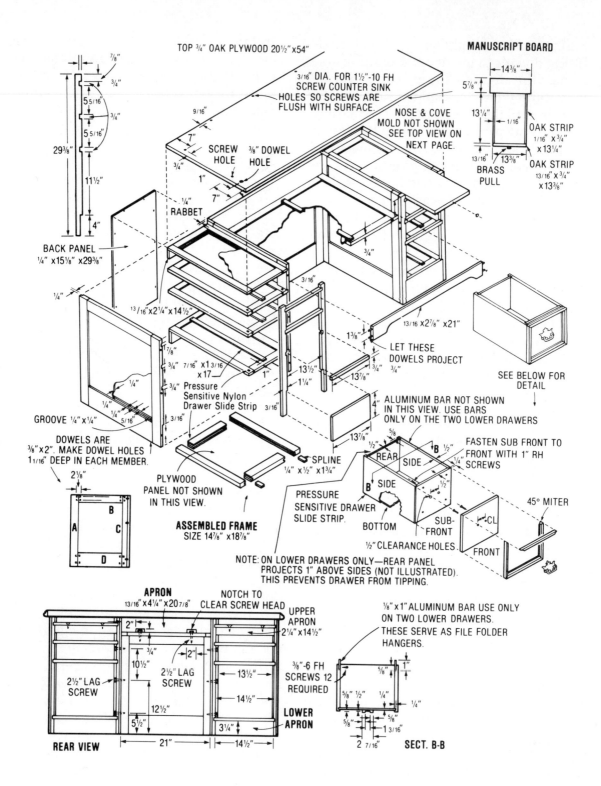

TOP ¾" OAK PLYWOOD 20½"x54"

3/16" DIA. FOR 1½"-10 FH SCREW COUNTER SINK HOLES SO SCREWS ARE FLUSH WITH SURFACE.

NOSE & COVE MOLD NOT SHOWN SEE TOP VIEW ON NEXT PAGE.

MANUSCRIPT BOARD

14⅜"
5⅞"
13¼"
1/16"
OAK STRIP 1/16" x ¾" x 13¼"
13/16"   13⅜"
BRASS PULL
OAK STRIP 13/16" x ¾" x 13⅜"

7/8"
¾"
5 5/16"
¾"
5 5/16"
29⅜"
11½"
4"

9/16"
7"
SCREW HOLE
3/8" DOWEL HOLE
¾"
1"
7"
¼" RABBET

¾"

13/16" x 2⅞" x 21"

SEE BELOW FOR DETAIL

BACK PANEL ¼" x 15⅛" x 29⅜"

¼"

13/16" x 2¼" x 14½"

3/16"

1⅜"
LET THESE DOWELS PROJECT
¾"

7/8"
¾" 7/16" x 1 3/16" x 17
¾" Pressure Sensitive Nylon Drawer Slide Strip
¼"
¼"   5/16"
3/16"

1"
13½"
1¼"
13⅞"
¾"
13⅞"

4" ALUMINUM BAR NOT SHOWN IN THIS VIEW. USE BARS ONLY ON THE TWO LOWER DRAWERS

GROOVE ¼" x ¼"

DOWELS ARE 3/8" x 2". MAKE DOWEL HOLES 1 1/16" DEEP IN EACH MEMBER.

2⅛"

A B C D

SPLINE ¼" x ½" x 1¾"

PLYWOOD PANEL NOT SHOWN IN THIS VIEW.

ASSEMBLED FRAME SIZE 14⅞" x 18⅞"

PRESSURE SENSITIVE DRAWER SLIDE STRIP.

5/8
½" ½"
REAR SIDE B
¼"
B SIDE ½"
BOTTOM SUB-FRONT
½" CLEARANCE HOLES.

FASTEN SUB FRONT TO FRONT WITH 1" RH SCREWS

45° MITER
CL
FRONT

NOTE: ON LOWER DRAWERS ONLY—REAR PANEL PROJECTS 1" ABOVE SIDES (NOT ILLUSTRATED). THIS PREVENTS DRAWER FROM TIPPING.

APRON 13/16" x 4¼" x 20⅞"
NOTCH TO CLEAR SCREW HEAD
UPPER APRON 2¼" x 14½"

2"
¾"
2"
10½"
2½" LAG SCREW
13½"
14½"
2½" LAG SCREW
12½"
5½"
3¼"
LOWER APRON

2½" LAG SCREW

REAR VIEW
21"
14½"

⅛" x 1" ALUMINUM BAR USE ONLY ON TWO LOWER DRAWERS. THESE SERVE AS FILE FOLDER HANGERS.

3/8"-6 FH SCREWS 12 REQUIRED

5/8 1"
5/8 ½" ¼" ¼"
5/8
5/8 ½"
5/8 1 3/16"
2 7/16"

SECT. B-B

68

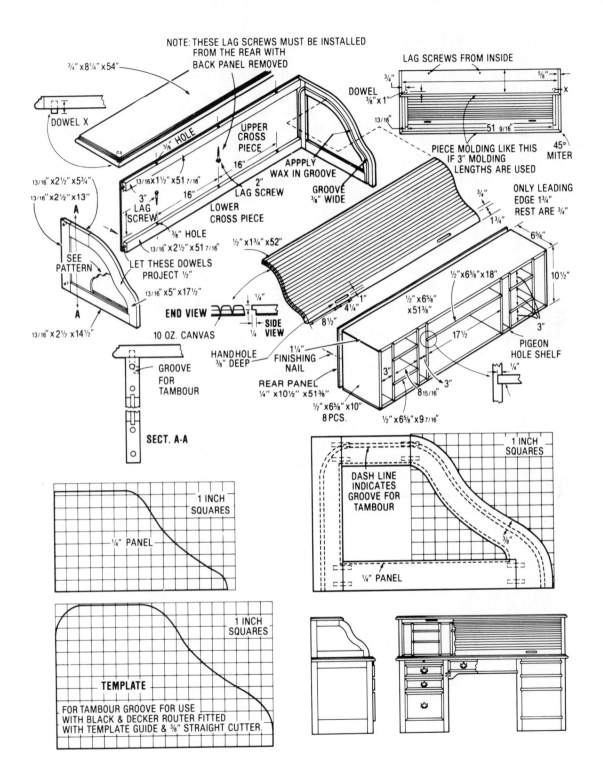

NOTE: THESE LAG SCREWS MUST BE INSTALLED FROM THE REAR WITH BACK PANEL REMOVED

3/4" x 8 1/4" x 54"

DOWEL X

HOLE

3/8" HOLE

UPPER CROSS PIECE

13/16 x 1 1/2" x 51 7/16"

16"

3"

LAG SCREW

16"

2"

LAG SCREW

LOWER CROSS PIECE

LAG SCREWS FROM INSIDE

DOWEL 3/8" x 1"

3/4"

5/8"

X

X

51 9/16"

45° MITER

PIECE MOLDING LIKE THIS IF 3" MOLDING LENGTHS ARE USED

APPPLY WAX IN GROOVE

GROOVE 3/8" WIDE

13/16" x 2 1/2" x 5 3/4"

13/16" x 2 1/2" x 13"

A

SEE PATTERN

A

13/16" x 2 1/2 x 14 1/2"

LET THESE DOWELS PROJECT 1/2"

13/16" x 5" x 17 1/2"

13/16" x 2 1/2" x 51 7/16"

3/8" HOLE

END VIEW

1/4"

SIDE VIEW

1/4"

1/2" x 1 3/4" x 52"

10 OZ. CANVAS

GROOVE FOR TAMBOUR

SECT. A-A

ONLY LEADING EDGE 1 3/4" REST ARE 3/4"

3/4"

1 3/4"

6 5/8"

10 1/2"

1/2" x 6 5/8" x 18"

1/2" x 6 5/8" x 51 3/8"

17 1/2

3"

PIGEON HOLE SHELF

1"

4 1/4"

8 1/2"

HANDHOLE 3/8" DEEP

1 1/4" FINISHING NAIL

REAR PANEL 1/4" x 10 1/2" x 51 3/8"

3"

3"

8 15/16"

1/4"

1/2" x 6 5/8" x 10" 8 PCS.

1/2" x 6 5/8" x 9 7/16"

1 INCH SQUARES

DASH LINE INDICATES GROOVE FOR TAMBOUR

3/8"

1/4" PANEL

1 INCH SQUARES

1/4" PANEL

1 INCH SQUARES

1/4" PANEL

TEMPLATE

FOR TAMBOUR GROOVE FOR USE WITH BLACK & DECKER ROUTER FITTED WITH TEMPLATE GUIDE & 3/8" STRAIGHT CUTTER.

with a Black & Decker router. Fasten the template to the work with screws, then proceed to cut the grooves.

After the grooves are cut, round the corners of the end frames. Assemble the frames to the rear crosspieces and set them aside.

Prepare the tambour by cutting the slats from ½-inch stock. You will need to use several boards for this step. Cut the boards to length. Then, before ripping into narrow strips, rabbet the ends to fit into the groove of the end panels. Make the rabbet ¼ inch wide and ¼ inch deep. Now rip the boards into strips ¾ inch wide, except for the leading strip, which should be 1¾ inches wide.

After the strips are cut, bevel them to permit the tambour to ride the groove without binding. For this step, use a table saw, with the blade set at an angle of 10 degrees.

Cut 10-ounce duck (canvas) about 18 × 52 inches. Tape it to a flat, square board. Stretch the canvas smoothly and tape the ends down securely. Cut the material slightly oversize to allow for taping; you will cut the excess away later.

Apply contact cement to the cloth and back of each slat liberally, following the manufacturer's instructions. Do not use flammable contact cement indoors. For indoor application, use a nonflammable latex type cement.

Allow the cement to set about 45 minutes, then begin to fasten the strips to the canvas. Use a side guide, consisting of a piece of 1 × 2 lumber, to ensure that the strips are installed straight and square. When all pieces are in place, trim the excess canvas with a knife or razor blade.

Move the assembled top frame forward until the grooves are off the desktop so you can install the tambour into the grooves. Roll the tambour up as far as it will go, then check it for fit. It will most likely be stiff which can be corrected later by rubbing the grooves with paraffin or candle wax. Don't use the wax before applying the finish because it will cause problems with staining and topcoats.

Fasten the top unit to the desktop with lag screws at the rear lower crosspiece. Dowel the forward ends as shown, thus allowing the upper unit to be removable. You will find it much easier to apply the stain, filler, and topcoats with the parts disassembled. Make and install the pigeonholes next, as indicated.

For a good finish, apply a paste wood filler to the oak. We use Golden Oak Filler, which fills and stains in one operation. Next, apply several coats of sanding sealer, followed by three coats of lacquer. After the lacquer has dried for about a week, rub it with rubbing compound. The results will be well worth the effort.

Colonial Canopy Bed

Fashions that are going out of style now will be back in years to come. This applies to clothes, hair styles and furniture.

This pine canopy bed is a case in point. Its dignified eighteenth Century quality is bound to please those who prefer traditional furniture to modern. Also, like so many other home-workshop projects, it can be built for a fraction of what its commercial counterpart would cost.

The four corner posts are the biggest job, so start working on them first. Since it is impossible to turn these 63⅔-inch-long posts on an ordinary lathe, you will need to make them in two sections and then join the sections.

Rip the 1 ¾-inch pieces of pine to 2-inch widths and 36-inch lengths for the upper and lower pieces. The bottom sections will be 32 inches long after they are turned, and the top sections 32 ⅔ inches. In addition, you will need to make ⅞- × - 2½-inch dowels, which will join all of the top and bottom sections.

Mark and cut both the mortises and the holes for the dowels before you turn the post sections on the lathe. The holes in the bottom sections are 1½ inches deep; those in top sections, 1 inch.

Before assembling the sections, mortise the lower halves of the posts to take the headboard and footboard crosspieces. Mortise the top of the two head posts for the headboard.

Next, turn the two sections of the footboard rail, also ripped from 1¾-inch stock. Give the rail 1⅛-inch tenons at each end. Drill holes in the posts to accept these tenons. Where these two sections are joined drill a 2-inch hole to accept half of the 4-inch dowel. Glue the turned rail and

8- × -37½-inch footboard into their respective holes and mortises.

Glue three boards together to make the headboard. To be sure of strong joints where the three boards join, use ¼-inch plywood splines set in the grooves, which you should cut with a router. Use a table saw to cut the tenons for the headboard.

When working on the bed rails, an important concern is the strength of the metal brackets, since most commercial furniture has a more elaborate system for holding the bed rails in place. By using ¼- × -1¼-inch carriage bolts and drilling through both the bed rails and the brackets (after first determining their correct position), you can solve this problem.

The next step is to position the bed rails against the completed footboard and headboard, and to make a light outline of

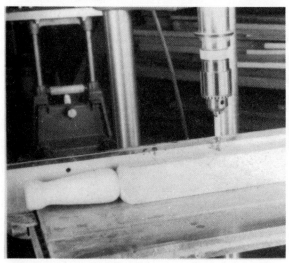

Fig. 10-1. The corner posts represent the biggest job and are made in halves. Drill holes in the lower halves for rail bracket pins.

Fig. 10-2. The footboard of bed before the top sections of corner posts are added. The rail is made in two sections.

Fig. 10-3. After you cut the bracket grooves in the posts and join the halves, cut post mortises for the headboard tenons.

Fig. 10-4. Secure bed rails to the corner posts with brackets seated in grooves with carriage bolts.

72

the brackets on the posts. This outline will mark the position of the steel pins that support the bed rails in each post. Cut the grooves in the posts for the brackets before assembling the headboard and footboard. Then drill holes in all four of the posts for the pins, drive the pins below the surface, and plug the four holes with dowels.

Now begin working on the canopy frame. By laying out a full-size view on a piece of plywood, you will find it easier to do the actual construction. For each side

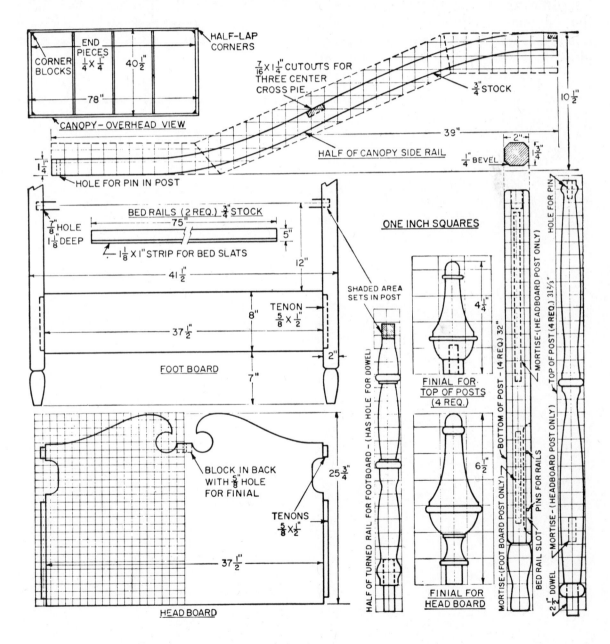

piece, use five separate cuts of wood, each 3 inches wide, splined together. Three of the crosspieces are $7/16 \times 1\frac{1}{4}$ inches, but the two end ones are larger ($1\frac{1}{4} \times 1\frac{1}{4}$ inches) for added strength. To strengthen the corners, glue in corner blocks.

After completing the canopy, turn to the last items: the finials. Mount the large one in a $5/8$-inch hole drilled into the block glued to the back center of the headboard (see drawing). The other four are smaller and fit over pins protruding from the posts.

Thoroughly sand all the pieces and spray an alcohol-base stain on the entire bed to give it that Early American look. Then apply a semigloss, alcohol-resistant lacquer. After the first coat has dried, lightly sand the entire bed with steel wool, then give it a final coat of clear lacquer.

Colonial Desk with Bookrack

THIS ATTRACTIVE DESK will enhance any room in your home. The single pedestal is an offshoot of the more common double pedestal, which was very popular in colonial days. It has four roomy drawers, with the largest one at the bottom made to hold letter-size folders. The pedestal support serves as a bookrack to hold a good supply of reading materials.

As shown in the drawing, cleats are used extensively. They greatly simplify construction and assembly, as well as eliminate the need to drive nails or screws through the top surface of the desk. Some nails are driven through the side members, but they can be replaced with nails or screws driven from the inside of the cabinet.

The pedestal and bookrack are cut from 1⅛-inch white pine. We used common lumber because it costs about one-half as much as clear. Colonial furniture should have knots, but by carefully selecting your

lumber you can eliminate the really bad ones.

You will note that fake tenons are used on the bookshelf members. The final effect looks like the real thing, but the fake method shown is easier and perhaps a little stronger.

The tools required for this project are a table saw, saber saw, router, and drill. In addition, you will need the usual hand tools, such as a hammer, screwdriver, and wrench.

Select flat boards for the top and sides. Cut the pieces to size and shape the bottom edges as shown in the drawing. After cutting the scallop design, use a router with a rounding-off cutter to round off the outside face of the cut. Do not rout the inside face.

Place the top board face down onto a flat surface. (The top of a table saw is ideal because it is exceptionally flat.) Next cut and install the cleats as indicated, using

Fig. 11-1. In assembling the colonial desk, cleats are used extensively as in most fine furniture construction. Attach with glue and nails.

Fig. 11-2. An exception is a temporary cleat in the base of the cabinet. Attach it with nails only. Remove it when you install the bottom panel.

Fig. 11-3. Installing the bottom board. Note the two blocks that are aids to positioning. Remove them after you have nailed the bottom board in the proper position.

Fig. 11-4. Use lag screws to join shaped pedestal and base sections, as well as the top section to the pedestal. Use washers under screw heads.

glue and 1¼-inch brads. Rabbet the rear cleats to accept the ¼-inch back panel. Make the rabbet either on the table saw or with the router. Note that the front cleat is 1 inch in from the front. Side cleats are 1¾ inch in from the edge.

Next, prepare the side panels. Rabbet the rear edge of both, but note that the left

upright is rabbeted at two places near the top. The smaller rabbet is to accept the rear panel of the wide drawer compartment.

To ensure proper alignment in assembly, make up a couple of temporary cleats. At this time also cut the bottom panel for the drawer compartment. Install the temporary cleats so that the bottom panel rests on them as shown. Glue up the section and nail it in place, using a square to make sure the sections are perpendicular. If necessary, nail a diagonal to hold the sections while the glue sets. Add the drawer compartment cleats and install the single drawer compartment, using a temporary spacer block to support the bottom board while nailing.

Cut the 1⅛-inch lumber for the book-rack section to size and round the edges with the router. This time round both sides to obtain a half-round effect.

Make the base piece for the upright by gluing up two pieces of ¾-inch stock. After shaping, assemble to the upright with two 3-inch lag screws.

To align the shelves, drill the dowel holes in the end piece and place it right up to the center upright. Center it and then transfer the hole centers using a pencil. Next locate and drill matching holes in the

Fig. 11-5. Attaching the scalloped base to the backup board at the front of the desk. Glue with nails only at the sides.

Fig. 11-6. Nail and glue the drawer stops to the rear of each compartment. Place them so the drawer fronts protrude ⅜ inch.

MATERIALS LIST

Purpose	Size	Description	Quantity
Top	¾″ × 17¼″ × 48″	Pine	1
Side	¾″ × 16⅛″ × 29¼″	Pine	2
End	¾″ × 5¼″ × 16⅛″	Pine	1
Bottom	¾″ × 13¼″ × 16⅛″	Pine	1
Wide bottom	¾″ × 16⅛″ × 30¾″	Pine	1
Base scallop	¾″ × 3½″ × 14¼″	Pine	1
Base backup board	¾″ × 3″ × 13¼″	Pine	1
Cleat	¾″ × 1″ × 11⅞″	Pine	8
Cleat	¾″ × 2″ × 13¼″	Pine	6
Cleat	¾″ × 2″ × 30¼″	Pine	2
Drawer, front	¾″ × 3⅝″ × 30⅛″	Pine	1
Drawer, front	¾″ × 3⅝″ × 13⅛″	Pine	1
Drawer, front	¾″ × 7¼″ × 13⅛″	Pine	1
Drawer, front	¾″ × 11½″ × 13⅛″	Pine	1
Drawer, subfront	¾″ × 3″ × 29⅜″	Pine	1
Drawer, subfront	¾″ × 3″ × 12⅜″	Pine	1
Drawer, subfront	¾″ × 6⅜″ × 12⅜″	Pine	1
Drawer, subfront	¾″ × 10⅝″ × 12⅜″	Pine	1
Drawer, rear	¾″ × 3″ × 29⅜″	Pine	1
Drawer, rear	¾″ × 3″ × 12⅜″	Pine	1
Drawer, rear	¾″ × 6⅝″ × 12⅜″	Pine	1
Drawer, rear	¾″ × 10⅞″ × 12⅜″	Pine	1
Drawer, side	⅜″ × 3⅝″ × 15″	Plywood	4
Drawer, side	⅜″ × 7¼″ × 15″	Plywood	2
Drawer, side	⅜″ × 11½″ × 15″	Plywood	2
Drawer, bottom	¼″ × 14⅜″ × 29¾″	Plywood	1
Drawer, bottom	¼″ × 12¹³⁄₁₆″ × 14⅜″	Plywood	3
Drawer stop	⅜″ × ¾″ × 8″	Pine	4
Rear panel	¼″ × 4½″ × 30¾″	Plywood	1
Rear panel	¼″ × 14³⁄₁₆″ × 25	Plywood	1
Pedestal	1⅛″ × 10¾″ × 21⅝″	Pine	1
Pedestal base	1¾″ × 2½″ × 15⁷⁄₁₆″	Pine	1
Book support, rear	1⅛″ × 4″ × 27⅜″	Pine	1
Book support, bottom	1⅛″ × 6¾″ × 27⅜″	Pine	1
Tenon	1⅛″ × 1½″ × 3½″	Pine	2
Tenon dowel	¾″ × 2⅝	Maple	2
Lag screws	⁵⁄₁₆″ × 3½″		2
Lag screws	⁵⁄₁₆″ × 2″		2
Flat washers for screws			4
Dowels	⅜″ × 2″		4
Screws	#8x2½″ FH		4
Pulls	3″ centers		5

Note: Pulls are available from Armor Products.

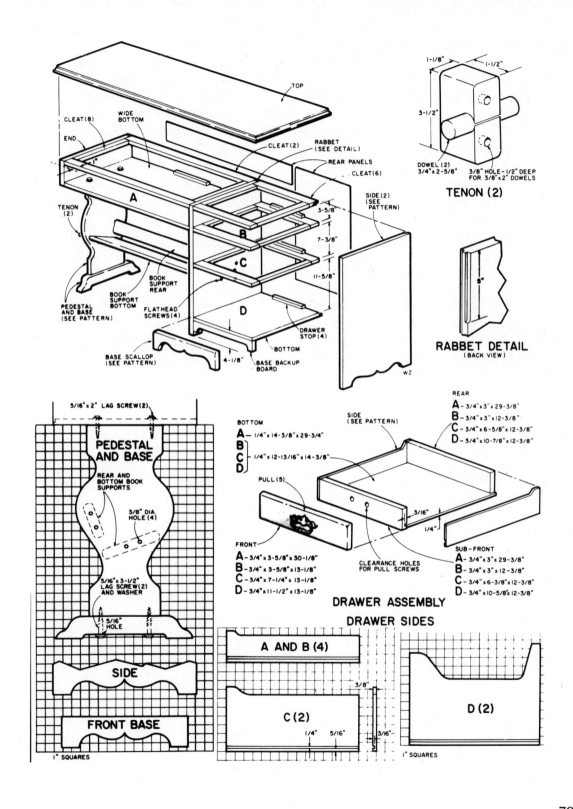

TOP

CLEAT(8)

WIDE BOTTOM

END

CLEAT(2)

RABBET (SEE DETAIL)

REAR PANELS

CLEAT(6)

A

TENON (2)

B

SIDE(2) (SEE PATTERN)

3-5/8"

·C

7-3/8"

BOOK SUPPORT REAR

BOOK SUPPORT BOTTOM

PEDESTAL AND BASE (SEE PATTERN)

FLATHEAD SCREWS(4)

11-5/8"

D

DRAWER STOP(4)

BASE SCALLOP (SEE PATTERN)

BOTTOM

4-1/8"

BASE BACKUP BOARD

WZ

1-1/8"   1-1/2"

3-1/2"

DOWEL (2) 3/4" x 2-5/8"

3/8" HOLE - 1/2" DEEP FOR 3/8" x 2" DOWELS

TENON (2)

RABBET DETAIL
(BACK VIEW)

5/16" x 2" LAG SCREW(2)

PEDESTAL AND BASE

REAR AND BOTTOM BOOK SUPPORTS

3/8" DIA. HOLE (4)

5/16" x 3-1/2" LAG SCREW(2) AND WASHER

5/16" HOLE

SIDE

FRONT BASE

1" SQUARES

BOTTOM

A— 1/4" x 14-3/8" x 29-3/4"

B
C— 1/4" x 12-13/16" x 14-3/8"
D

PULL (5)

FRONT

A— 3/4" x 3-5/8" x 30-1/8"
B— 3/4" x 3-5/8" x 13-1/8"
C— 3/4" x 7-1/4" x 13-1/8"
D— 3/4" x 11-1/2" x 13-1/8"

CLEARANCE HOLES FOR PULL SCREWS

SIDE (SEE PATTERN)

3/16"

1/4"

REAR

A— 3/4" x 3" x 29-3/8"
B— 3/4" x 3" x 12-3/8"
C— 3/4" x 6-5/8" x 12-3/8"
D— 3/4" x 10-7/8" x 12-3/8"

SUB-FRONT

A— 3/4" x 3" x 29-3/8"
B— 3/4" x 3" x 12-3/8"
C— 3/4" x 6-3/8" x 12-3/8"
D— 3/4" x 10-5/8" x 12-3/8"

DRAWER ASSEMBLY

DRAWER SIDES

A AND B (4)

3/8"

C (2)

1/4"   5/16"

3/16"

D (2)

1" SQUARES

shelves, then assemble using dowels and screws. Drive the dowels so they protrude ½ inch from the outside.

Make up two fake tenons and assemble with glue.

Drawers are made with double fronts. Sides are ⅜-inch plywood; fronts and rear are ¾-inch pine; and bottoms are ¼-inch plywood. In order to keep drawers level when they are extended, make the side panels to rise at the rear.

Cut the drawer sections to size, then dado the bottoms to accept the ¼-inch bottom panels. Drill clearance holes in the subfront panels and assemble the section with nails and glue. Do not install the front yet. Sand the edges of the ¼-inch bottom panels and slide the panels into place. A little glue in the groove will keep the bottom from rattling.

To install the fronts, center it over the drawer from side to side, raising the front ¹⁄₁₆ inch above the bottom of the drawer. This ¹⁄₁₆-inch offset at the bottom will center the front panel in the compartment opening.

Before permanently mounting the panel, tack it into place with a couple of nails and check the fit. If it is okay, apply glue and mount permanently.

The unit shown was finished in antique olive using a prepared kit. The process is simple. Apply a base color to the work. After drying, brush a glaze coat on and then wipe it off. Wiping can be done with paper, cheesecloth, or even a dry brush. You can add highlights to give the piece an authentic antique appearance.

Colonial Dry Sink

EARLY AMERICAN FURNITURE has retained its popularity from colonial days up to the present. This dry sink is a typical piece of the furniture used by the early colonists. It was found in farm kitchens that lacked plumbing connections and was used for washing dishes, etc. Because of its recessed lined well, it is extremely serviceable and can be used as a bar, a buffet server, a plant stand, or a simple storage cabinet.

The cost of this dry sink will vary depending on lumber prices in your area and the type of wood you use for construction. We recommend pine because it is easy to work with, and the end grain sands very smooth and takes paint or lacquer beautifully.

Of course, it can also be left natural or stained. There are many ways to finish the piece. Another excellent possibility is to antique it. Whatever your choice, you can bet that you'll have a great conversation piece when you're done with this one.

If you plan to paint the cabinet, you should choose lumber with a minimum of knots. To be sure of this, don't telephone in your order, but go down to the lumberyard and personally pick out the best pieces available. You will undoubtedly end up with a few pieces with glaring knots, but you can place them where they won't show up—preferably the top or bottom panels.The top panel will be covered with plastic laminate and the bottom will be concealed by the doors.

To eliminate the need for gluing up

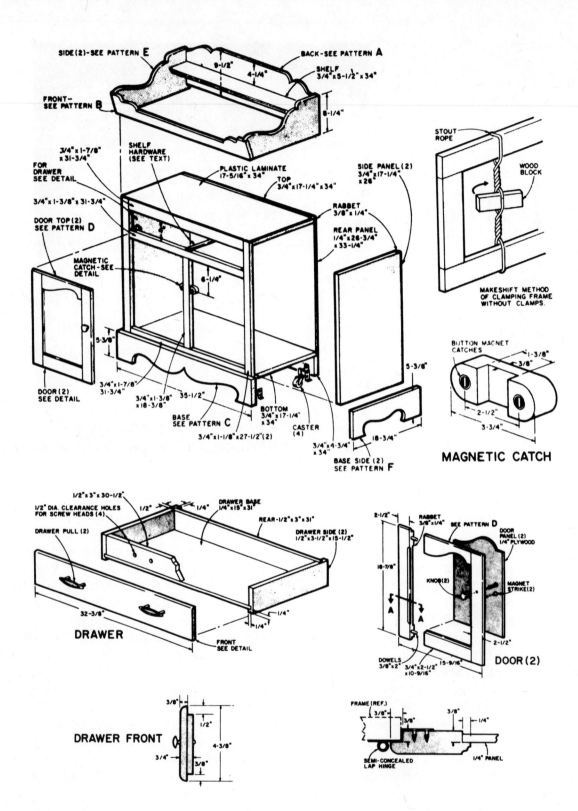

SIDE(2)-SEE PATTERN E
BACK-SEE PATTERN A
9-1/2"
4-1/4"
SHELF
3/4"x5-1/2" x 34"
FRONT-
SEE PATTERN B
8-1/4"
3/4" x 1-7/8"
x 31-3/4"
SHELF
HARDWARE
(SEE TEXT)
PLASTIC LAMINATE
17-5/16" x 34"
TOP
3/4"x17-1/4"x34"
SIDE PANEL(2)
3/4"x17-1/4"
x 26"
STOUT
ROPE
WOOD
BLOCK
FOR
DRAWER
SEE DETAIL
3/4" x 1-3/8"x 31-3/4"
DOOR TOP(2)
SEE PATTERN D
RABBET
3/8" x 1/4"
REAR PANEL
1/4"x26-3/4"
x 33-1/4"
MAGNETIC
CATCH-SEE
DETAIL
6-1/4"
MAKESHIFT METHOD
OF CLAMPING FRAME
WITHOUT CLAMPS.
5-3/8"
BUTTON MAGNET
CATCHES
1-3/8"
3/8"
DOOR(2)
SEE DETAIL
3/4"x 1-7/8"
31-3/4"
3/4"x1-3/8"
x18-3/8"
35-1/2"
BASE
SEE PATTERN C
BOTTOM
3/4"x17-1/4"
x 34"
CASTER
(4)
5-3/8"
2-1/2"
3-3/4"
3/4"x1-1/8"x27-1/2"(2)
3/4"x4-3/4"
x 34"
18-3/4"
BASE SIDE (2)
SEE PATTERN F
MAGNETIC CATCH

1/2" x 3" x 30-1/2"
1/2"
1/4"
DRAWER BASE
1/4"x19 x31
1/2" DIA. CLEARANCE HOLES
FOR SCREW HEADS (4)
REAR-1/2"x3"x31"
DRAWER PULL (2)
DRAWER SIDE (2)
1/2"x3-1/2"x15-1/2"
32-3/8"
1/4"
1/4"
DRAWER
FRONT
SEE DETAIL
2-1/2"
RABBET
3/8"x1/4"
SEE PATTERN D
DOOR
PANEL (2)
1/4" PLYWOOD
18-7/8"
KNOB(2)
MAGNET
STRIKE(2)
A
A
2-1/2"
DOWELS
3/8"x2"
3/4"x2-1/2"
x10-9/16"
15-9/16"
DOOR(2)

3/8"
1/2"
DRAWER FRONT
3/4"
4-3/8"
3/8"

FRAME (REF.)
3/8"
3/8"
3/8"
1/4"
SEMI-CONCEALED
LAP HINGE
1/4" PANEL

82

Fig. 12-1. (left) Assembled front frame. Close all sections using a hammer and a block of scrap wood.

Fig. 12-2. (above) Add the base pieces to the sides. Allow sufficient clearance for casters.

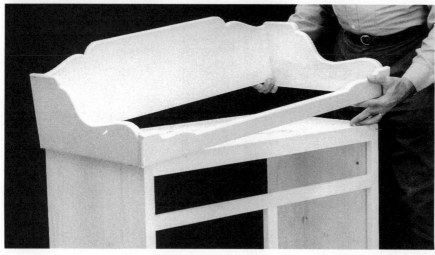

Fig. 12-3. Fasten the assembled top to the cabinet. Measure and cut plastic laminate to size.

boards, use 18-inch stock. These are glued up by the mill and the pieces are generally flat. Common pine is available up to 24 inches wide.

Start the construction by building the main case, which is really a large box. Cut the pieces to size then rabbet the rear edges to take the ¼-inch panel. Assemble the parts with glue and nails. Butt joints are used throughout. If you can temporarily install the rear panel, you can use it to square

up the case.

The front frame is of doweled construction. The dowels ensure that the frame will not separate and they add greatly to the strength of the cabinet. Follow the sequence shown to prevent difficulty in assembly. Glue up the center section first (shaped like the letter H) then follow with the side pieces. Use spiral dowels. If they are not available, use regular dowels but crimp the surface with a pair of pliers to

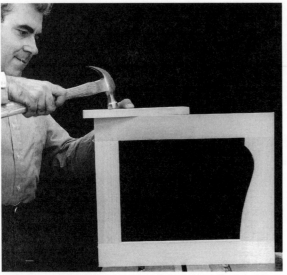

Fig. 12-4. The doors of the dry sink are of doweled construction. Cut the top before assembly.

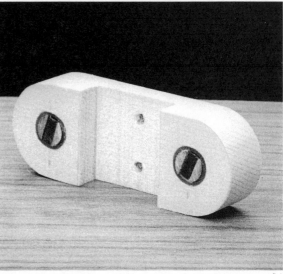

Fig. 12-5. Mount the magnets in a notched block and screw it to the center divider.

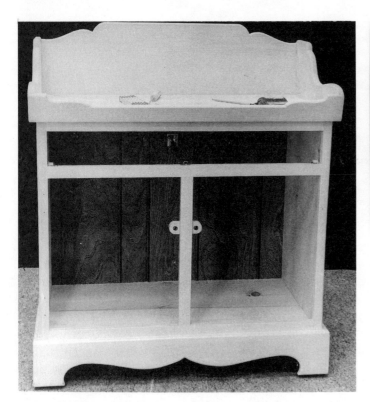

Fig. 12-6. (above) Completed cabinet with doors and drawer removed. A ¾-inch panel was used for the rear.

Fig. 12-7. (left) Self-locating casters make the unit mobile and give added strength to corners.

MATERIALS LIST

Purpose	Size	Description	Quantity
Base front	¾″ × 5⅜″ × 35½″	Pine	1
Base rear	¾″ × 4¾″ × 34″	Pine	1
Base sides	¾″ × 5⅜″ × 18″	Pine	2
Case bottom	¾″ × 17¼″ × 34″	Pine	1
Case top	¾″ × 17¼″ × 34″	Pine	1
Case sides	¾″ × 17¼″ × 26″	Pine	2
Frame upper	¾″ × 1⅞″ × 34″	Pine	1
Frame center	¾″ × 1 ⅜″ × 34″	Pine	1
Frame lower	¾″ × 1⅞″ × 34″	Pine	1
Frame sides	¾″ × 1⅛″ × 27½″	Pine	2
Frame center	¾″ × 1⅜″ × 18⅜″	Pine	1
Top front	¾″ × 3¼″ × 34″	Pine	1
Top sides	¾″ × 8¼″ × 19½″	Pine	2
Top rear	¾″ × 9½″ × 34″	Pine	1
Shelf	¾″ × 5½″ × 34″	Pine	1
Door stiles	¾″ × 2½″ × 18⅞″	Pine	4
Door rail upper	¾″ × 3½″ × 10⅝″	Pine	2
Door rail lower	¾″ × 2½″ × 10⅝″	Pine	2
Door panel	¼″ × 11⅛″ × 15″	Plywood	2
Drawer front	¾″ × 4½″ × 32½″	Pine	1
Drawer subfront	½″ × 3⅝″ × 30½″	Pine	1
Drawer sides	½″ × 3⅝″ × 15½″	Pine	2
Drawer rear	½″ × 3″ × 30½″	Pine	1
Drawer bottom	¼″ × 14⅝″ × 31″	Plywood	1
Button magnet support	¾″ × 1⅜″ × 3¾″	Pine	1
Rear panel	¼″ × 26⅜″ × 33¼″	Plywood	1
Miscellaneous			
Nails	2″	Finishing	
Glue		White	
Button catches			2
Drawer slide hardware			1
Door pulls			2
Drawer pulls			2
Decals—Meyercord 1505-A, 1505-B			
Caster and brackets			

Note: If you cannot locate the bracket casters or button magnets, write Armor Products.

form grooves. Use a hammer and block of scrap wood to drive the sections home. If clamps are available, use them. Otherwise use the rope and turnbuckle system to tighten up on the joints. (See drawing.)

Next, install the base. Use a saber saw or jigsaw to cut the scallops, then round off the edge of the scallops with a router. Place the sides and front base pieces on the outside of the case, and position the rear

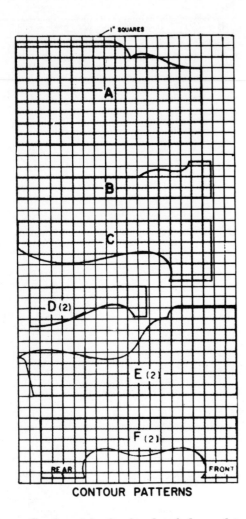

CONTOUR PATTERNS

piece flush with the back of the cabinet.

The corner bracket casters are a good idea, but not essential. They reinforce the corners and they automatically position themselves. No measuring is necessary. Just place them in the corner and drive in the screws, and the casters will protrude just the right amount. Mounted on casters, the dry sink will be easy to move about the room when you are cleaning or redecorating.

Assemble the top section as a unit and then install it onto the cabinet using 2-inch finishing nails. Before assembling the top

pieces, round off all top edges with the router. Be sure to stop short of the ends at the rear side of the front where it joins the sides.

The drawer is of simple construction. The front is ¾-inch pine; the sides and rear are of ½-inch pine; the bottom is ¼-inch plywood. Follow the drawing details for construction. The center bottom drawer slide makes for quick and easy installation. They are available at hardware shops and lumberyards.

The recessed panel doors are easier to make than they seem. Cut all pieces to size then assemble them with dowels. Cut the scroll at the top of the doors and sand it before assembly. Shape the inside edge of the door (face side) with a router fitted with a small beading bit. Do the back side next with a square rabbeting bit to take the ¼-inch panel. The depth of the rabbet should be ⅜ inch to allow the panel to set below the surface about ⅛ inch.

To operate efficiently, the magnetic catches should be placed as near as possible to the door pull. The button magnetic catches shown are ideal because they can be mounted on a small block of wood, which fastens to the center divider.

The plastic laminated top is recommended because it will take plenty of wear and cleans easily. If you plan to spray the cabinet, mask the top surface of the laminate and install it in the usual manner. If you are painting, paint the cabinet first, then install the laminate.

The colorful decals (fruits, flowers, birds, etc.) add greatly to the appearance of the finished piece. The corner piece at the upper part of the door is not available in the shape shown. It was made by simply cutting apart several of the ready-made decals and rearranging them as shown.

Colonial Hutch

HERE IS A FAIR-SIZED HUTCH dimensioned so that it can be constructed by using a single panel of 4- × -8-foot lumber-core plywood for the main assembly. Pleasantly proportioned, the basic colonial design has been cleverly reworked to permit the piece

to blend with a wide range of decor, enabling you to use it in the dining area, living room, or den.

The upper section features two good-sized shelves and a wide single drawer. This drawer front is made to appear as a double, simply for purposes of design, by cutting a partial saw kerf down the center and adding two drawer pulls. The delightful deceit is repeated on the lower section. A horizontal saw kerf across both door panels and a pair of pulls relieves the otherwise heavy look of the lower cabinet, while ample storage space is provided behind the doors. If an actual set of drawers are your preference, you can, of course, easily make the substitution.

Two professional tricks are used in the construction. The cabinet door trim appears to be carved right out of the panel, but it is actually created by adding on ready-made straight and curved molding, which is available as a stock item at most lumber supply dealers. Additionally, molded accent edges are shaped separately, cut into strips, and also added on.

This project was made of birch lumber-core plywood, with solid birch for trim and base. Many fine hardwoods are available in lumber core form, so the choice is yours.

Construction begins with layout. The first step is one that you should carry out with care because one wrong cut could prove quite costly. The reason is that lumber core is quite generally sold only as an entire 4- × -8-foot panel so you can't go back to buy an additional small piece should the need arise. Thus, it is advisable to carefully measure and mark off the

Fig. 13-1. (left) Use finishing nails to hold the glued sections together until the clamps can be applied. Note the novel use of the parallel clamps to hold each of the sections securely in place while nailing.

Fig. 13-2. (above) Large bar clamps are a big help to provide gluing pressure. If not available, you can use flat-head wood screws instead.

Fig. 13-3. (middle left) Use a spokeshave to smooth over curved sections that have been cut to the plan. Contour with band or jigsaw.

Fig. 13-4. (middle right) After the base is assembled, use a plane to contour the cross section, then sand the assembly thoroughly.

Fig. 13-5. (bottom left) Use glue and small finishing nails to apply the molding trim. Set the nails, then fill all holes with plastic wood.

Fig. 13-6. (above left) Before applying molding on cabinet doors, predrill holes for ⅝-inch brads, which you should leave protruding a little bit.

Fig. 13-7. (above right) Cover the molding's back surface with glue, and press the molding down on protruding brad points.

Fig. 13-8. (left) View of the completed base. Plan dimensions allow for the cabinet to set into the base. Add the molding trim later.

various pieces right on the panel. Use a hard-leaded pencil and mark lightly. Be sure to make allowance for the thickness of the saw kerf at all cuts.

The radial arm saw is, by far, the most useful power tool for such construction, but a table or portable circular saw also can be used. If yours is a small shop and the handling of a full 4- × -8-foot panel presents a problem, allow for several rough cuts in your layout (there'll be sufficient waste for this purpose). Use a saber or even a hand saw to cut the panel into four bite-size pieces, which will handle easily.

Use a planer or plywood blade on your saw to obtain clean, smooth cuts, which will not require finish sanding. Cut all the main pieces and follow up by marking them for dado and rabbet cuts. Use of a dado cutter simplifies the operation, but a

regular saw blade can do the job if necessary. In the latter case, make twin cuts ¾ inch apart, then a series of passes to clean out between.

Dado the upper and lower side pieces ¾ inch wide and ⅜ inch deep to receive the horizontal members and drawer shelves. Make a ¼-inch rabbet cut at the inside back of the top, bottom, and side pieces. The drawer shelves and top of the lower cabinet are not rabbeted because they were cut ¼ inch narrower at the onset to allow the back panel to set in flush.

Note: The bottom member of the cabinet is ¾-inch fir plywood. The front edge is faced with a 1-inch length of birch.

Although some craftsmen like the effect of the exposed raw edge of lumber core, the trick used by professionals to conceal the edge is to simply add on a thin

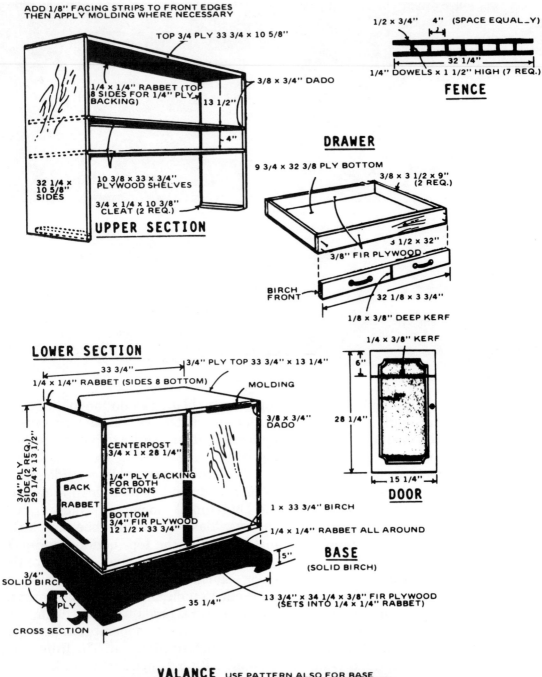

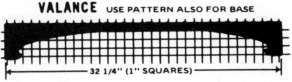

MATERIALS LIST

Purpose	Size	Description	Quantity
	¾″ × 10⅝″ × 33¾″	Birch lumber	1
	¾″ × 10⅝″ × 32¼″	Core plywood	2
	¾″ × 10⅜″ × 33″	Core plywood	2
	¾″ × 4″ × 32¼″	Core plywood	1
	¾″ × ½″ × 32¼″	Core plywood	2
	¾″ × 3¾″ × 32⅛″	Core plywood	1
	¾″ × 13¼″ × 33¾″	Core plywood	1
	¾″ × 13½″ × 29¼″	Core plywood	2
	¾″ × 1″ × 28¼″	Core plywood	1
	¾″ × 1″ × 33¾″	Core plywood	1
	¾″ × 15¼″ × 28¼″	Core plywood	2
	¾″ × 1¼″ × 10⅜″	Core plywood	2
	ALL ABOVE BIRCH LUMBER CORE PLYWOOD (from 4′ × 8′ panel)		
	¾″ × 12½″ × 33¾″	Fir plywood	1
	⅜″ × 9¾″ × 32″	Fir plywood	1
	⅜″ × 3½″ × 32″	Fir plywood	2
	⅜″ × 3½″ × 9″	Fir plywood	2
	⅜″ × 13¾″ × 34¼″	Fir plywood	1
	⅛″ × 33″ × 62½″	Birch plywood	1
	¾″ × 5″ × 35¼″	Solid birch	1
	¾″ × 5″ × 13½″	Solid birch	2
	¼″ × 2″	Round dowel	7
Molding	½″	Curved corner	8
Molding	½″	To match above	12 ft.
Solid birch edging	⅛″ × ¾″	Cut to size	30 ft.
Birch molding	¾″ × ¾″	Cut to size	20 ft.
Butt hinges	1½″	Brass	4
Door pulls			2
Drawer handles			4
Finishing nails	1½″		

strip of solid stock about ⅛-inch thick. After all panels are cut to size, rip up a supply of such strips and glue onto all the front edges of the panels. Sand flush to the sides.

Assembly and gluing are the next steps. Use of white glue is recommended because of its good holding, quick setting, and nonstaining characteristics. Use 1½-inch finishing nails to hold the parts while clamping. In a number of places, the nails eventually will be concealed by the molding trim; elsewhere countersink them and fill the holes with plastic wood or similar material. If you don't have large clamps to handle the job, you'll need to resort to the use of flat-head wood screws to provide gluing pressure. Here again, holes will require filling after the screws have been countersunk.

The base of the unit is made of ¾-inch solid stock—birch or maple are equally suitable. If you prefer to use a less expensive wood, try bass or poplar for both the base and the trim.

Cut the parts for the base, noting that the dimensions allow for the cabinet to set into the base. Thus, the inside dimensions of the base wall are equal to the outside dimensions of the cabinet. Cut a ⅜-inch dado ¼ inch deep and ¼ inch from the top of the three pieces (two sides and front) before gluing. Because the ⅜-inch set-in panel will add much strength, ordinary butt joints will suffice between the front and sides. To achieve the curved cross section of the base, hand-plane to shape. If a planer jointer is available, so much the better.

Fancy treatment of the cabinet doors is next. This is a rather simple operation. Position the curved molding at each corner, 2 inches in from each edge, and mark the outline lightly in pencil. Nail a couple of ⅝-inch brads about two-thirds into the panel. Then clip the heads off with a diagonal cutter or pliers to form a point of sorts. Again put the molding into place and press lightly to get an impression of the nail positions for drilling. Drill same-size holes, apply a few small beads of glue, and finally press the corner firmly into place. The protruding nail points usually will suffice to hold the molding in place while the glue

sets. If not, apply clamp pressure.

Inasmuch as the ends of the corner molding are precut to a 45-degree angle, you will need only to cut matching 45-degree angles on the straight lengths and apply, following the same procedures as for the corners.

Set butt hinges into mortised recesses in the door so they will lay almost flush with the edge. This method will eliminate the need to mortise on the cabinet side. Position the doors so they will set back ⅛ inch from the cabinet front and measure and mark for hinge screw holes. Before finally attaching doors, make the partial saw cut ⅜ inch deep across both doors, 6 inches from the top to simulate the set of drawers.

The upper drawer is a simple box construction. Use ⅜-inch plywood and attach the front panel to it. Make accent molding by cutting the pattern on a shaper or saw with shaper cutters. Rip down the lengths required using 45-degree miters for corner joints, then nail and glue into place. Set all nails and fill the holes.

The addition of the decorative fence and valance on the upper shelf completes construction. Screw the three sections together for rigidity, glue in the back panel (⅛-inch birch plywood) and smooth-sand the unit thoroughly. Take your time to do a complete job. Now that you've spent all that time constructing the piece, it's worth it to spend a little more on the sanding. Then stain the hutch to your liking and surface it with several coats of satin brushing lacquer for a fine, lasting finish.

Colonial Hutch Table

HUTCH TABLES WERE COMMON in the eighteenth and nineteenth centuries. They were usually made of pine boards and were very functional. When not used as a table, they were placed against a wall with the top open, thus serving as a seat. Also, the seat lid was hinged so the space below could be used for storage. Those colonists were very practical.

The table is a standard height, and the top is a generous 42 inches in diameter. It is styled somewhat like the original, which is exhibited at the Morgan Museum in Hartford, Connecticut. To add a little distinction and color, we stenciled a colorful duck on the front and rear panels of the seat compartment.

The entire table is made of ⁵⁄₄ (1⅛-inch) pine. Choose flat boards with tight knots if you are using common lumber. You can use clear pine, but at about double the price of common stock.

To make the top (A), glue up a series of narrow boards. They may vary in width, but none should be more than 8 inches wide. The grain should be matched and the annular rings must be alternated to ensure that the top remains flat. The number of pieces you use will depend on the widths of each piece. Ten pieces were used in the table shown.

Use butt joints with dowels to join the top. Because of the number of joints involved, it is best to glue up the top in two stages. If done in one step, the glue applied to the first joints will start to set before you reach the last joint. We glued up the boards in three groups: a center section of four boards, and two end groups of three boards each. After the glue sets, join the three sections to make up the top. You will need to glue only two joints in the final step.

Use dowels as indicated in the drawing, spacing them about 10 inches apart. A dowel jig and dowel centers will simplify the doweling operation. When clamping the boards, be sure to use cauls under the clamp jaws to protect the work.

Fig. 14-1. Propped on a couple of 2 × 4s, the top is transformed into a circle with a saber saw.

Fig. 14-2. The close up shows the router fitted with a carbide trimming bit mounted to a circle board.

Fig. 14-3. A stout nail serves as a pivot when dressing up the circle. Router will remove saw marks, leaving a smooth circle.

Fig. 14-4. Fasten the end panels to the compartment members with screws. Do not use glue at this joint.

Fig. 14-5. Space the cleats ⅛ inch from pedestal ends. Mark the pilot holes for screws as shown.

Fig. 14-6. Install the feet with lag screws. Do not use glue. Be sure to use a flat washer under the screw head.

Fig. 14-7. Close up of the tilting mechanism. Rear pins have been locked in with stops at ends of dowels.

Fig. 14-8. Stenciling is done after staining and sealing. The sealer coat permits you to wipe away paint if an error is made.

The final clamping of the top requires 48-inch clamps. If these are not available, you can use an alternate means. One method uses a flat board with cleats and sliding wedges. Glue only one joint at a time.

After you have glued the top, remove the clamps, sand the surfaces smooth, and then proceed to draw the 42-inch-diameter circle. Use a strip of thin wood containing two small holes drilled 21 inches apart. Use a push pin at the center as a pivot, then place a pencil in the other hole and scribe the 42-inch circle. Do this on the underside of the top if one surface is better than the other.

MATERIALS LIST

Purpose	Size	Description	Quantity
Top	1⅛″ × 42″		1
Cleat	1⅛″ × 3″ × 34½″		2
Ball	½″ Dia.		4
Dowel	⅝″ × 3″		2
Dowel	⅝″ × 3¾″		2
Dowel	¼″ × 1⅛″		2
End	1⅛″ × 14″ × 25⅜″		2
Feet	2¼″ × 2½″ × 23″		2
Seat	1⅛″ × 10⅝″ × 16⅞″		1
Seat rear	1⅛″ × 5⅝″ × 17″		1
Front	1⅛″ × 8½″ × 17″		1
Rear	1⅛″ × 8½″ × 17″		1
Bottom	1⅛″ × 10¾″ × 17″		1
Glue dowel	⅜″ × 2″		40
Hinge		Nonmortise	2
Finishing nail	2″		6
Screw	2½″ 12 FH		16
Lag screw	⅜″ × 3½″		4
Washer	⅜″ Flat		4
Plug	½″	Maple	24
Stencil with paints			1 set
Stain		Minwax #211	1 pint

Note: The balls, dowels, hinges and stencil are available from Armor Products.

Trim the circle on the band saw or with a saber saw. Stay to the outside of the line, then true-up the circle with a router fitted with a pivoted circle guide. You can make the guide easily using a piece of ¼-inch plywood. Remove the base of the router and replace it with the plywood into which a 1-inch hole has been bored at one end. Drill the four bolt holes into the plywood, then mount the router with the trimming bit in place. Rotate the cutter so the cutting edge is facing the opposite end of the plywood, then measure 21 inches over to locate the pivot center. Drill this hole to match a 10d or 12d nail, then drive the nail into the center of the circle made when drawing the circle.

To trim the circle, raise the plywood with router on the pivot so the cutter clears the work. Turn on the power, then bring the plywood and router down slowly, allowing the cutter to engage the work. Now in a counterclockwise direction feed the router slowly around the work. To lessen the load on the trimmer, you might want to round the edges with a ¼-inch rounding bit before trimming. After trimming, however, you will need to use the rounding bit again.

Cut the cleats (B) from straight pieces

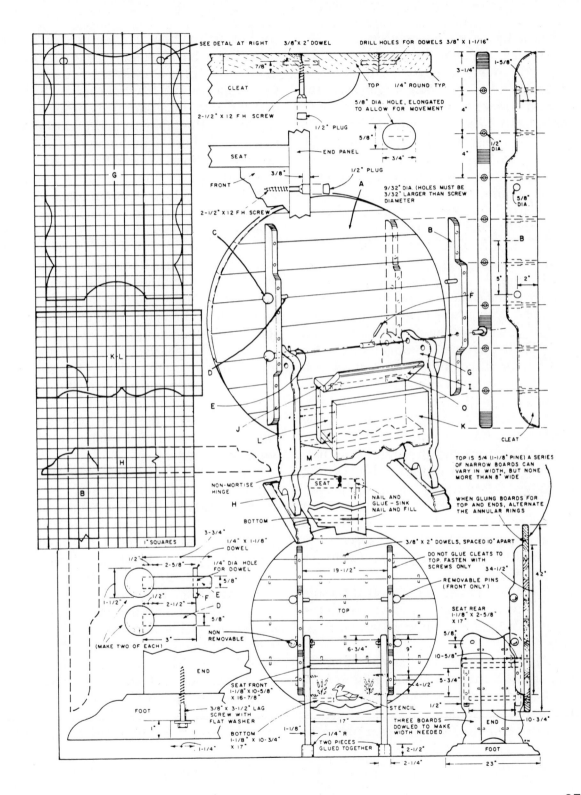

of stock 3 inches wide. Locate and drill the two ⅝-inch-diameter holes, then cut the shape and round the edges. Drill the screw clearance holes ³⁄₃₂ inch larger than the screw diameter to allow for movement of the tabletop. Use a ½-inch drill bit to countersink so the screws will project ⅞ inch into the top. The ½-inch diameter will accept the wood plugs to conceal the screws. Do not mount the cleats at this time.

To make the pedestal ends (G) glue up two or three boards to make up the required 14-inch width. Cut the lengths several inches oversize, then dowel and glue as usual. When locating the dowels, be sure to place them away from the cutting lines. You must place the elongated holes very carefully because they must line up with the holes in the cleats. Elongate the holes to allow for movement caused by humidity and temperature changes. Use a saber saw to elongate them to the ¾-inch width. Next, drill and countersink the four screw holes or the compartment. Round the edges of the sides, top, and the arch at the bottom with a ¼-inch rounding bit. Do not round the bottom where it joins to the feet.

The compartment consists of a front (K) and rear (L) member, as well as a top (I,J) and bottom (M). The top serves as a seat, and it is hinged to gain access to the compartment.

Cut the parts to length on the table saw, placing a stop at 17 inches. Recut the seat to 16⅞ inches to allow clearance at the ends.

Shape the front and rear members at the bottom, then round them. Round only the shaped parts at the bottom, leaving the tops and ends square.

Assemble the front and rear pieces to the bottom member using glue and 2-inch finishing nails. Next, add the top seat rear, again using glue and finishing nails. Sink the nailheads and fill, then screw the pedestal ends to the assembled compartment.

Invert the tabletop and pedestal, and insert four short ⅝-inch dowels (D) in the appropriate holes to align the pedestal with the cleats. Now center the entire assembly onto the 42-inch circle, then place ⅛-inch spacers between the pedestal and the cleats. Drop screws into the holes in the cleat and gently tap them to locate the screw pilot holes. Remove the assembly and drill ⅛-inch holes ⅞ inch deep. Install the cleats without glue, then apply a little glue around the edge of the holes and install the ½-inch plugs.

Make the feet (H) by gluing two pieces of 1⅛-inch stock to make up the 2¼-inch thickness. After gluing, cut the outline then drill and counterbore the holes for the lag screws. Fasten the feet to the end panels without glue, using flat washers under the lag screw heads.

Make the pivot and locking pins using ⅝-inch dowels (E) and 1½-inch-diameter balls (C). Drill the balls as shown, then insert the dowels after applying a little glue around the sides of the holes. Drill the two longer pins to take a ¼-inch dowel, which serves to prevent the pivot from being removed accidentally.

Do the stenciling after you have stained the table and given it a coat of sealer. We used Minwax #211 Provincial Stain followed by a thin coat of shellac.

The stencil and paints are available as a kit. Simply follow the instructions. After the stencil design has dried, give the entire table two coats of semigloss lacquer.

Console
Cabinet Mirror

THIS BEAUTIFUL SET was made with just one machine: a Sears 10-inch table saw. All routing or shaping was eliminated by the use of standard stock moldings. Another outstanding feature is that by using common pine for the construction, the cost was kept to a minimum.

The construction is not difficult. If you haven't had much experience cutting angles on the table saw, you most certainly will after this project. Both blade tilting and miter gauge angle cutting are used extensively.

The only tricky cutting involves the crown molding at the base of the cabinet and top of the mirror. You must cut the crown molding at the angle in which it will be used. Therefore, it must rest against the miter gauge at this angle. In addition, the miter gauge must be set at either 22½ or 45 degrees. The 45-degree cut is made for the mirror, but the console requires 22½-degree cuts. Note how the crown is held for cutting. If you don't already possess one, you should fit your miter gauge with an auxiliary back stop. The back stop facilitates the cutting of moldings, and it also makes for more accuracy, because it prevents any "give" in the workpiece.

Before starting work, check the calibration on the miter gauge and the blade tilt. If it is off, make the necessary adjustments.

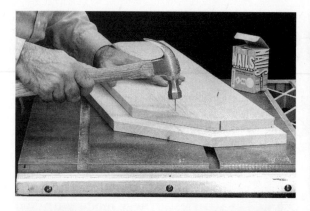

Fig. 15-1. (top left) Use a table saw for the top and bottom board diagonal cuts. Check the miter gauge for accuracy. Before beginning work, check the calibration on the miter gauge and blade tilt. To check, make two 45-degree cuts on scrap wood: one set using the miter gauge, the other with the blade tilt. When joined, each set should make a 90-degree corner which you can easily check with a try square.

Fig. 15-2. (top right) Cut the rabbets on a saw using the rip fence as shown. Make the vertical cut first. You'll have experience cutting angles on a saw with this project.

Fig. 15-3. (middle left) Use a base molding to frame the panels. A temporary gauge block facilitates assembly. Reverse the moldings—low side out, high edge toward the center.

Fig. 15-4. (bottom left) Toe-nail the panels when assembling for greater strength, using nails generously. When assembling the end and diagonal panels together, drive a couple of nails along the edges to close the joint while the glue sets.

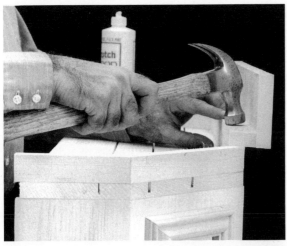

Fig. 15-5. Add the bottom step as shown. The lumber we used was badly warped, so the kerf cuts were made to straighten the board. When assembled, the sections flattened out perfectly.

Fig. 15-6. When cutting the crown molding, support it in the angle in which it will be used.

Fig. 15-7. Greek-key molding adds the finishing touch to the cabinet. Check the miters before gluing.

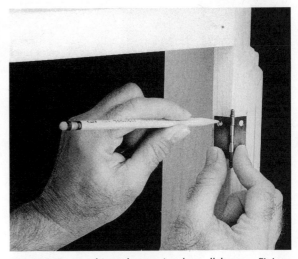

Fig. 15-8. Position hinges by opening them all the way. Fit into a corner and locate the screw holes.

To check for accuracy, make two sets of 45-degree cuts on scrap wood. Make one set using the miter gauge and the other with the blade tilt. When joined, each set should make a perfect 90-degree corner, which you can easily check with a try square.

Cut the lumber to size and, where possible, cut between knots. If the knots must be included, try to locate them where they will be covered with panels or moldings later. The lumber we used for the subtop and bottom was badly warped, but rather than waste it, we cut a few longitudinal grooves on the hidden side. When assembled, the sections flattened out perfectly.

Use 1- × -12-inch lumber (actual size ¾ × 11¼ inches). The depth of the top measures 11⅝ inches, so you must glue up a strip to make this piece or buy a wider board.

The subtop is not an essential piece, but it greatly simplifies assembly. The same results are possible using nailing cleats, but the assembly is more difficult. When nailing the subtop to the top, set the back edge in ⅜ inch, thus forming a rabbet for the rear panel. Rabbet the end panels on one edge and miter it on the other. Note that the miters are 22½ degrees because the

shape of the cabinet is actually half an octagon.

To achieve the raised-panel effect, use beveled boards framed with base molding. Note that you will use the moldings in reverse, low side out, and high edge toward the center.

Assemble all parts with white glue and nails. When gluing mitered moldings, be sure to apply the glue to the miters and wipe off the excess before glue sets. When assembling the end and diagonal panels to-

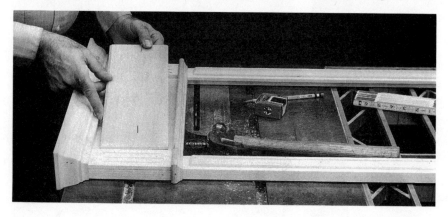

Fig. 15-9. The mirror panel is cut from ½-inch pine lumber. Center the carved appliqué in the panel. The decorative oval in the top panel of the mirror is available at most lumberyards that carry carvings.

Shown here are the detailed drawings of door, diagonal and mirror ornament.

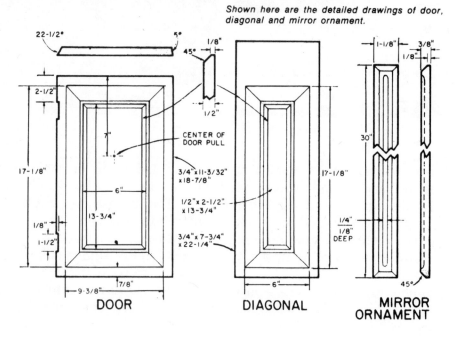

DOOR   DIAGONAL   MIRROR ORNAMENT

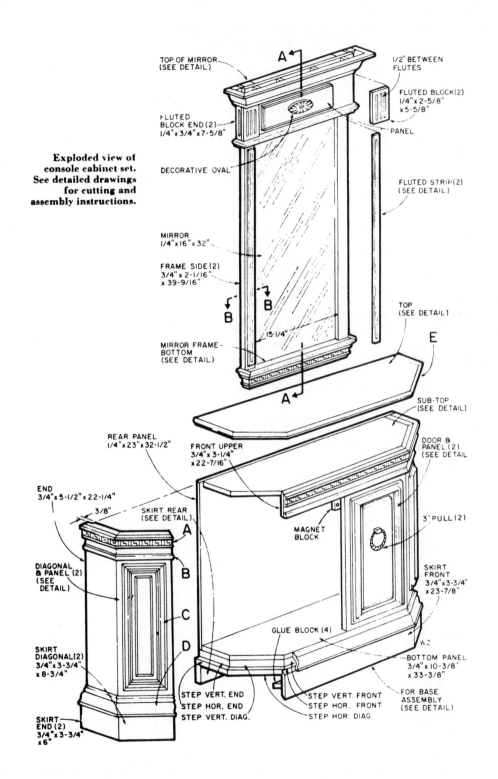

TOP OF MIRROR
(SEE DETAIL)

A

1/2" BETWEEN
FLUTES

FLUTED BLOCK(2)
1/4" x 2-5/8"
x 5-5/8"

PANEL

FLUTED
BLOCK END(2)
1/4" x 3/4" x 7-5/8"

DECORATIVE OVAL

FLUTED STRIP(2)
(SEE DETAIL)

MIRROR
1/4" x 16" x 32"

FRAME SIDE(2)
3/4" x 2-1/16"
x 39-9/16"

B

B

B

TOP
(SEE DETAIL)

E

15-1/4"

A

MIRROR FRAME
BOTTOM
(SEE DETAIL)

A

SUB-TOP
(SEE DETAIL)

REAR PANEL
1/4" x 23" x 32-1/2"

FRONT UPPER
3/4" x 3-1/4"
x 22-7/16"

DOOR 8
PANEL (2)
(SEE DETAIL)

END
3/4" x 5-1/2" x 22-1/4"

3/8"

SKIRT REAR
(SEE DETAIL)

A

MAGNET
BLOCK

3" PULL (2)

DIAGONAL
8 PANEL (2)
(SEE
DETAIL)

B

C

SKIRT
FRONT
3/4" x 3-3/4"
x 23-7/8"

SKIRT
DIAGONAL(2)
3/4" x 3-3/4"
x 8-3/4"

D

GLUE BLOCK (4)

W.Z.

BOTTOM PANEL
3/4" x 10-3/8"
x 33-3/8"

SKIRT
END (2)
3/4" x 3-3/4"
x 6"

STEP VERT. END
STEP HOR. END
STEP VERT. DIAG.

STEP VERT. FRONT
STEP HOR. FRONT
STEP HOR DIAG

FOR BASE
ASSEMBLY
(SEE DETAIL)

Exploded view of console cabinet set. See detailed drawings for cutting and assembly instructions.

MATERIALS LIST

Purpose	Size	Description	Quantity
Top	¾″ × 11⅝″ × 35⅛″	Pine	1
Sub-top	¾″ × 9¾″ × 31⅞″	Pine	1
Front upper	¾″ × 3¼″ × 22⁷⁄₁₆″	Pine	1
End	¾″ × 5½″ × 22¼″	Pine	1
Diagonal	¾″ × 7¾″ × 22¼″	Pine	2
Door	¾″ × 11³⁄₃₂″ × 18⅞″	Pine	2
Diagonal panel	½″ × 2½″ × 13¾″	Pine	2
Door panel	½″ × 6″ × 13¾″	Pine	2
Magnet block	¾″ × 3¼″ × 3½″	Pine	1
Rear panel	¼″ × 23″ × 32½″	Plywood	1
Bottom panel	¾″ × 10⅜″ × 33⅜″	Pine	1
Skirt end	¾″ × ¾″ × 6″	Pine	2
Skirt diagonal	¾″ × 3¾″ × 8¾″	Pine	2
Skirt front	¾″ × 3¾″ × 23⅞″	Pine	1
Skirt rear	¾″ × 5″ × 34½″	Pine	1
Step horizontal end	¾″ × 1¼″ × 5⅝″	Pine	2
Step horizontal diagonal	¾″ × 1¼″ × 8¼″	Pine	2
Step horizontal front	¾″ × 1¼″ × 23¼″	Pine	1
Step vertical end	¾″ × 1¼″ × 5⅛″	Pine	2
Step vertical diagonal	¾″ × 1¼″ × 7½″	Pine	2
Step vertical front	¾″ × 1¼″ × 22½″	Pine	1
Molding	⅜″ × 48″	Nose and cove	
Molding	¾″ × 60″	Nose and cove	
Greek key	1¾″ × 60″		
Base molding	¾″ × 20′		
Crown molding	2½″ × 60″		
Butts	1½″		2 pr.
Pulls			2
Magnet catches			2
Screws			
Nails			
Glue			
Mirror			
Frame upper	¾″ × 8⅜″ × 15¼″	Pine	1
Frame side	¾″ × 2¹⁄₁₆″ × 39⁹⁄₁₆″	Pine	2
Filler strip	¼″ × 2″ × 20″	Pine	1
Frame bottom	¾″ × 7⅞″ × 19¾″	Pine	1
Panel	½″ × 4¾″ × 14″	Pine	1
Fluted block	¼″ × 2⅝″ × 5⅝″	Pine	2
Fluted block end	¼″ × ¾″ × 7⅝″	Pine	2
Fluted strip	⅜″ × 1⅛″ × 30″	Pine	2
Crown molding	2½″ × 36″		
Molding	¾″ × 60″	Nose and cove	
Greek key	1¾″ × 24″		
Decorative oval	2½″ × 5″		

Note: If you cannot locate oval carving at local lumberyard, it can be obtained from Armor Products.

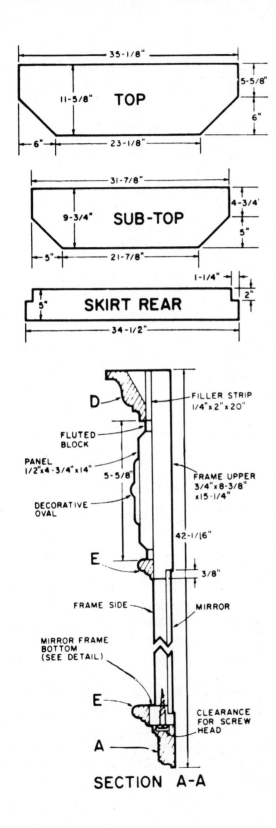

TOP
35-1/8"
11-5/8"
5-5/8"
6"
6"
23-1/8"

SUB-TOP
31-7/8"
9-3/4"
4-3/4"
5"
5"
21-7/8"

SKIRT REAR
1-1/4"
2"
5"
34-1/2"

D — FILLER STRIP 1/4"x2"x20"

FLUTED BLOCK

PANEL 1/2"x4-3/4"x14"

5-5/8"

FRAME UPPER 3/4"x8-3/8" x15-1/4"

DECORATIVE OVAL

42-1/16"

E

3/8"

FRAME SIDE

MIRROR

MIRROR FRAME BOTTOM (SEE DETAIL)

E

A

CLEARANCE FOR SCREW HEAD

SECTION A-A

gether, drive a couple of nails along the edges to close the joint while the glue sets.

Before cutting and adding the step for the set-out at the base, check the *altitude* of the 2½-inch crown molding, which is the vertical measurement taken when the molding is resting on a horizontal surface. (See drawing.) The moldings will vary in size between manufacturers, so check carefully. You must cut the step so that when the moldings rest on it, the top of the molding will be flush with the top edge of the bottom panel.

Cut doors with about ¹⁄₁₆-inch clearance all around. Cut all of the gain for the hinges on the doors to eliminate the need for cutting into the door frame. Before assembling the doors, drill the holes for the pull screw. Note the clearance for the screw head.

The addition of the moldings completes the base. Use ¾-inch nose and cove at the top and set it down ¹⁄₁₆ inch to form a step. Add the Greek key next, followed by the miniature nose and cove just above the door line. The crown molding takes care of the bottom.

The mirror frame is not as difficult to build as it might seem. Moldings again play an important part in construction. As for the console, all lumber is pine.

Make the fluted pieces on the table saw using a molding head. We used the groove part of a tongue-and-groove set. The tip of the cutters was ground round to form the half-round groove, but you could leave it square to achieve the same effect. To determine where to start and stop the cut, it is best to make trial cuts on scrap wood.

There are two ways to make the cut; in each case the fence is used to guide the work. You can elevate the blade to the proper height (³⁄₁₆ inch), then carefully

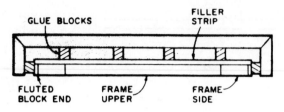

GLUE BLOCKS FILLER STRIP

FLUTED BLOCK END FRAME UPPER FRAME SIDE

TOP OF MIRROR

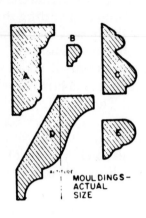

MOULDINGS—ACTUAL SIZE

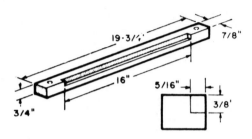

19-3/4" 7/8"

16" 5/16" 3/8'

3/4"

MIRROR FRAME BOTTOM REAR VIEW

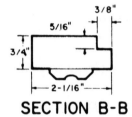

3/8"

5/16"

3/4"

2-1/16"

SECTION B-B

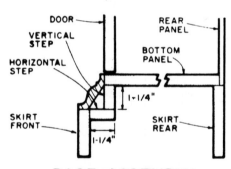

DOOR REAR PANEL

VERTICAL STEP

BOTTOM PANEL

HORIZONTAL STEP

1-1/4"

SKIRT FRONT SKIRT REAR

1-1/4"

BASE ASSEMBLY

lower the work onto it; or you can place the work in position, hold it firmly, then raise the blade to its 3/16-inch protrusion and feed the work until you reach a predetermined stop marked on the table.

To make the built-up columns at the top add blocks as indicated in the drawings. The decorative oval in the top panel of the mirror is available at most lumberyards that carry carvings. Most carved wood moldings are bowed slightly. To remedy this problem simply moisten the back with water and flatten. Apply with glue and a couple of brads.

When the construction is completed, fill all nail holes, then sand thoroughly. Dust and finish as desired. We used antique green, highlighting the high spots and letting the corners go dark. Antiquing kits are readily available in a variety of colors with easy-to-follow instructions.

Drop-leaf Movable Server

THIS ELEGANT SERVER measures 48 inches long, but stretches to 78 inches when the leaves are extended. There is ample room for any occasion, whether it be a banquet or family gathering.

The three roomy drawers can be used for storage of linens and silver. The two compartments will hold plenty of tableware and appliances and, if necessary, they can be fitted with shelves. The original was made without shelves. Sturdy lid supports fold flat when not in use, and the hidden casters allow the large piece to be moved about with ease.

Construction is basic, with butt joints used throughout. The raised panel is easily accomplished on the table saw, and the shaped edges are done with a router.

The lumber used is common Idaho pine, which is available in most lumberyards in glued-up stock to 24 inches wide. This server requires 18-inch material. Choose flat board and avoid boards with loose knots. The knots are not objectiona-ble, but they should be sound and free of sap.

You will find that 18-inch stock actually measures 17¼ inches, so don't be confused when looking over the Materials List. Likewise, 1-inch stock measures ¾ inch. Therefore, 1- × -18-inch stock really measures ¾ × 17¼ inches.

In looking over the drawings, you will note that the top is doubled. This design makes for a sturdier piece and it also facilitates assembly. Cleats are eliminated and you won't need to drive nails or screws through the top surface.

Cut the boards to size as per the specifications. If you purchased long boards, it would be best to rough-cut them to size with a portable saw, or you might want to use a saber saw to part the large sections. It's a little slower, but much safer. If a board sags toward the end of the cut and you are using a portable saw, the tool could kick and this could be dangerous. The saber saw will not kick. This doesn't

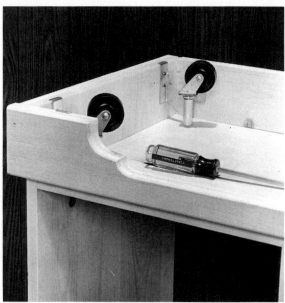

Fig. 16-1. (left) Assemble the drawer divider as a separate unit. Check for squareness after you complete the assembly.

Fig. 16-2. (above) The drop-leaf support is mounted with sufficient space to clear the strip hinge.

Fig. 16-3. Drawer bottoms of ¼-inch plywood slide into the side panel dadoes. Cut sides from a medium-density overlay.

Fig. 16-4. The positioning of the self-aligning casters will give the drop-leaf server its mobility.

Fig. 16-5. The panel raising is done by setting the saw blade at 15 degrees, and then feeding the work slowly and carefully. Give the saw blade plenty of time to make the cut.

Fig. 16-6. Rabbet the door frames after they are assembled. Make the rabbet groove deep enough so that the back of raised panel will fit flush with the back of the door frame.

Fig. 16-7. Fit the panels to the door frames from the rear. You can round the corners of the panels to match rabbeted corners, or you can chisel the frame corners square.

109

MATERIALS LIST

Purpose	Size	Description	Quantity
Sides	¾" × 16¼" × 29¼"	Pine	2
Bottom and subtop	¾" × 16¼" × 46"	Pine	2
Top	¾" × 17¼" × 48⅞"	Pine	1
Top ends	¾" × 14¾" × 17¼"	Pine	2
Uprights	¾" × 16" × 24⅛"	Pine	2
Front and rear shelf supports	¾" × 2⁵⁄₁₆" × 16½"	Pine	4
Side shelf supports	¾" × 1⅜" × 11⅜"	Pine	4
Apron side	¾" × 3¾" × 16¼"	Pine	2
Apron front	¾" × 3¾" × 48¾"	Pine	1
Apron cleat	¾" × 1" × 42"	Pine	1
Rear panel	¼" × 24¾" × 46⅝"	Plywood	1
Drop leaf spacer	¾" × ⅞" × 11⅝"	Pine	2
Drawer front	¾" × 7⁹⁄₁₆" × 16⁷⁄₁₆"	Pine	3
Drawer subfront and rear	½" × 7⅜" × 15⅜"	Plywood	6
Drawer sides	½" × 7⅜" × 14"	Plywood	6
Door frame sides	¾" × 2⅛" × 24"	Pine	4
Door frame top and bottom	¾" × 2⅛" × 9¾"	Pine	4
Door panel	¾" × 10" × 20"	Pine	2
Continuous hinge	1" × 16¼"		2
Door hinge	1⅜" × 2"		4

Note: Also needed are casters, catches, pulls, knobs, drop leaf brackets, and finishing materials.

mean that the portable saw should not be used, but use it only when necessary. As a matter of fact, the saw is ideally suited to trim boards after they have been rough cut, if you do not have a radial arm saw. If you use the portable saw, clamp a guide strip on your work to ensure a smooth, straight cut.

If you use the radial arm saw, chances are that it will not cut the full width of your boards, but with a little ingenuity you can do it. Set the fence to the rearmost position, then make the cut. Draw the arm forward as far as it will travel, then if the cut is not completed, carefully raise the leading edge of the panel slowly until the board separates. Keep your fingers clear of the blade.

After the boards are cut to size, rabbet the rear edges to take the ¼-inch plywood panel. Use a table saw or router. If you are using a table saw, set the height of the blade ¼ inch above the table and the fence ⅜ inch from the blade. Make the first pass holding the work vertically. For the second pass, readjust the blade and hold the work horizontally to remove the stock forming the rabbet.

Assemble the parts with glue and nails. The nails will be concealed by the drop leaf at the top and the apron at the bottom. Before assembly, it would be wise to

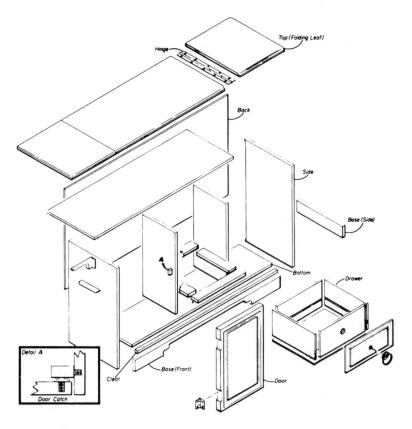

Top (Folding Leaf)

Hinge

Back

Side

Base (Side)

Bottom

Drawer

Detail A

Base (Front)

Cleat

Door Catch

Door

cut the rear panel, which can then be used to keep the cabinet case square while the glue sets. Simply insert it temporarily with a few brads, then remove it after the glue has set.

Build up the drawer compartments as a separate modular unit, then inserted into the previously assembled case. Be sure to keep the unit square during assembly. Bar clamps are useful to hold the parts, but not essential. If you use nails to hold the sections, try cement-coated finishing nails. They hold very well and will not work loose. The best combination, however, is the use of screws and glue, especially if you lack the bar clamps.

Install the drawer compartment, centering it within the main case. Use glue on all joints and again fasten with nails or screws.

Next add the apron at the base of the cabinet. Use a saber saw or jigsaw to cut the scallop in the front piece. When the two side pieces and front have been cut, run a router fitted with a rounding cutter over the edges to break the sharp corners. Assemble the side pieces by driving screws from the inside of the side panels. To fasten the front apron, use a cleat.

The top board and drop leaves should be cut from the same board, if possible, to ensure continuity in the grain pattern. Continuity is especially important if the unit is to be stained. Cut the parts, then shape the edge with a suitable router cutter. Follow with a good sanding, especially at the

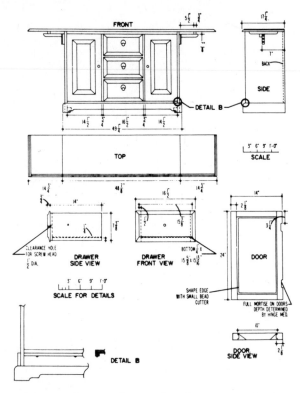

square edges where the leaves and top meet.

To apply the piano hinges, place the top and leaf sections upside down on a clean flat surface. Pull sections together and mark the location of the screw holes. Install a few screws and check the fit. If okay, add the rest of the screws. Now add the wood spacer to the underside of each leaf, then fasten the top to cabinet.

Next install the drop-leaf hinges. With the leaf in open position (the leaf up), locate the mounting holes for the hinge. Drill pilot holes, then install the hinge. Repeat for other side. Note that the drop-leaf hinges come in a set—one left and one right one.

The doors are simple to construct. Cut the frame pieces and assemble with dowels and glue. Use one dowel per corner and be sure to keep the surfaces flat when gluing. When the glue has set, rabbet the back of the frame to take the raised panel. Perhaps it would be best to wait until you cut the panels before proceeding with this step.

Cut the door panels to size then tilt the saw blade 15 degrees and raise it 1¼ inches. Set the fence so that the saw leaves a $\frac{1}{16}$-inch step on the surface of the board (see drawing). To ensure a proper fit, cut a trial piece on scrap wood before cutting the doors. When the panels have been cut, rabbet the door frame so that the back of the panel is flush with the door frame.

The rabbeting of the frame will leave a radius at each corner. You can leave this as is and round the raised panels to match, or you can cut the rounded corners square with a chisel. Apply a bead of glue in the rabbet, then insert the panel and clamp.

Mortise the doors to accept the full depth of the hinges. Then flush-mount the hinges on the side panels.

Make the drawers as per drawing. Raise the front panels, as for the door pieces. Before adding the front piece to the drawers, drill ½-inch clearance holes to allow clearance for the drawer hardware. Fasten the fronts with 1-inch round-head screws and glue. Place stops at the rear of the drawer compartments to limit the travel of the drawers.

Sand the entire cabinet, then add the casters and door catch hardware. Finish as desired. This server was finished with two coats of a latex antique-base paint.

Dry Sink/ Bar Combo

WHEN THE LID of this novel dry sink/bar is raised, it reveals a rack of stemware neatly stored and ever handy. The piece also features four roomy drawers and three compartments. The door of the upper compartment swings downward to provide additional top space. The material used is pine plywood and solid pine. The use of plywood eliminates the need for gluing up boards and more important, it is stable and will not expand and contract with weather conditions. Expansion and contraction can be quite a problem when solid lumber is used, especially when large panels are involved.

Construction is not at all complicated. Most pieces are straight and assembled with butt joints. Wood buttons conceal the screw heads and add a decorative touch to the piece. Mounted on concealed swivel casters, the bar is easily moved about.

Make the base first. Choose flat boards and rip to the necessary width. If you use pine, knots are not objectional. Do be sure, however, that they are good and tight. The sides and front are 4¼ inches wide, but the rear piece is only 3¼ inches wide. You will note that the top edge is set down to permit the rear edge of the cabinet bottom to rest on it.

The cabinet sides and front rest on cleats, as shown. The cleats stop short of the corners to allow clearance for the casters. If you do not plan to use the casters, you can run the cleats full length to the corners.

Cut the cleats to size, then bore the screw holes. Countersink the heads if you use flat-head screws.

Assemble the base using glue and 2-inch finishing nails. Because end grain is absorbent, apply a thin coat to the end grain and allow it to dry. Then apply full-strength glue and assemble the parts. Make sure the frame is square while the glue sets. Install the cleats, then set aside.

Next make the case. It consists of a boxlike structure with sides, top, bottom, and shelf. You will make the front frame as a separate piece and add it later. Cut the panels to size and remove any splinters that have been left by the saw blade. You won't

Fig. 17-1. (left) The cabinet box must be kept square as the glue sets. One method is to use a square and clamps.

Fig. 17-2. (above) The mid stiles and rails are glued section by section. Use one dowel pin for each joint, and clamp the joints while the glue sets.

Fig. 17-3. After the frame is glued, sand the joints. Then attach the frame to the cabinet and trim the overhang flush with the plane.

Fig. 17-4. Glue the corner post of the drawer frame. Also shown is the positioning of the drawer's guides.

have this problem if you use a plywood blade, which cuts smooth and clean. Following the same procedure used for the base pieces, apply a sizing coat of glue to the top and bottom edges of the side pieces. Recoat with glue, then fasten with nails.

Sink the nailheads slightly, but you do not need to fill the holes because they will be covered by the base and upper sections.

Cut the center shelf to size and fasten it to cleats attached to the side members. Use 1¼-inch screws to mount the cleats to

Fig. 17-5. Shape the top piece with a router and sand before assembly. Install the rear panel with a set-back at the bottom.

Fig. 17-6. The front panel has been cut but not shaped. Check the fit, and if it's okay drill the holes for the screws and buttons.

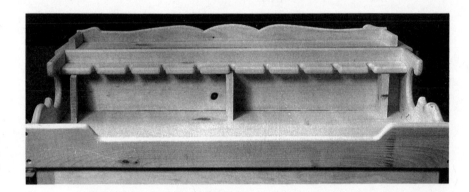

Fig. 17-7. Use temporary blocks to support the glass rack. Then fasten it in place with screws at the back.

Fig. 17-8. The simplicity of the construction of the drawer is shown. Large holes in the subfront allow clearance for pull screws.

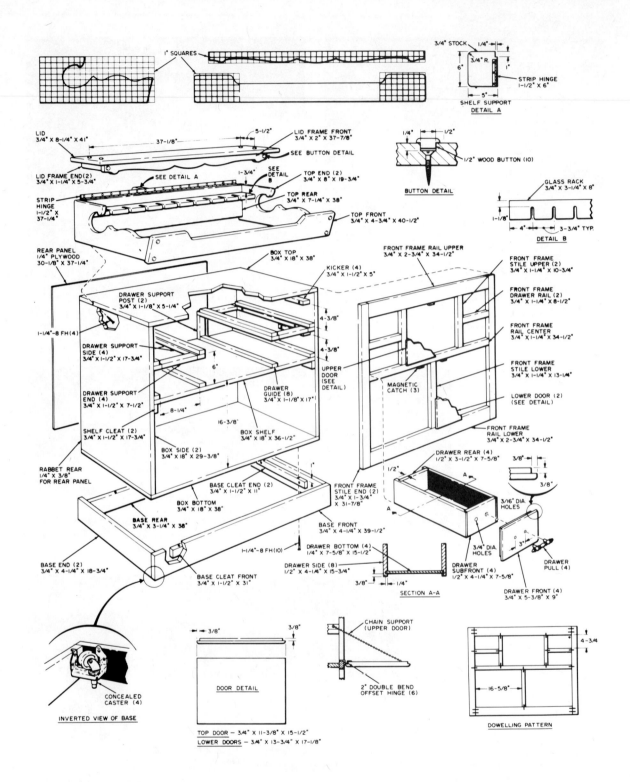

1" SQUARES

3/4" STOCK
1/4"
3/4" R.
6"
STRIP HINGE
1-1/2" X 6"
5"
SHELF SUPPORT
DETAIL A

LID
3/4" X 8-1/4" X 41"
37-1/8"
5-1/2"
LID FRAME FRONT
3/4" X 2" X 37-7/8"
SEE BUTTON DETAIL

LID FRAME END (2)
3/4" X 1-1/4" X 5-3/4"
SEE DETAIL A
1-3/4"
SEE DETAIL B
TOP END (2)
3/4" X 8" X 19-3/4"

STRIP HINGE
1-1/2" X 37-1/4"
TOP REAR
3/4" X 7-1/4" X 38"
TOP FRONT
3/4" X 4-3/4" X 40-1/2"

1/4"
1/2"
1/2" WOOD BUTTON (10)
BUTTON DETAIL

GLASS RACK
3/4" X 3-1/4" X 8"

1-1/8"
4"
3-3/4" TYP.
DETAIL B

REAR PANEL
1/4" PLYWOOD
30-1/8" X 37-1/4"

BOX TOP
3/4" X 18" X 38"

KICKER (4)
3/4" X 1-1/2" X 5"

FRONT FRAME RAIL UPPER
3/4" X 2-3/4" X 34-1/2"

FRONT FRAME STILE UPPER (2)
3/4" X 1-1/4" X 10-3/4"

DRAWER SUPPORT POST (2)
3/4" X 1-1/8" X 5-1/4"

4-3/8"

4-3/8"

FRONT FRAME DRAWER RAIL (2)
3/4" X 1-1/4" X 8-1/2"

1-1/4"-8 FH (4)

FRONT FRAME RAIL CENTER
3/4" X 1-1/4" X 34-1/2"

DRAWER SUPPORT SIDE (4)
3/4" X 1-1/2" X 17-3/4"

6"

DRAWER GUIDE (8)
3/4" X 1-1/8" X 17"

UPPER DOOR (SEE DETAIL)

FRONT FRAME STILE LOWER
3/4" X 1-1/4" X 13-1/4"

DRAWER SUPPORT END (4)
3/4" X 1-1/2" X 7-1/2"

8-1/4"

16-3/8"

MAGNETIC CATCH (3)

LOWER DOOR (2) (SEE DETAIL)

SHELF CLEAT (2)
3/4" X 1-1/2" X 17-3/4"

BOX SHELF
3/4" X 18" X 36-1/2"

FRONT FRAME RAIL LOWER
3/4" X 2-3/4" X 34-1/2"

RABBET REAR
1/4" X 3/8"
FOR REAR PANEL

BOX SIDE (2)
3/4" X 18" X 29-3/8"

1"

DRAWER REAR (4)
1/2" X 3-1/2" X 7-5/8"

3/8"

3/8"

1/2"

BASE CLEAT END (2)
3/4" X 1-1/2" X 11"

FRONT FRAME STILE END (2)
3/4" X 1-3/4" X 31-7/8"

3/16" DIA. HOLES

BOX BOTTOM
3/4" X 18" X 38"

BASE REAR
3/4" X 3-1/4" X 38"

BASE CLEAT FRONT
3/4" X 1-1/2" X 31"

1-1/4"-8 FH (10)

BASE FRONT
3/4" X 4-1/4" X 39-1/2"

DRAWER BOTTOM (4)
1/4" X 7-5/8" X 15-1/2"

3/4" DIA. HOLES

3"

DRAWER PULL (4)

BASE END (2)
3/4" X 4-1/4" X 18-3/4"

DRAWER SIDE (8)
1/2" X 4-1/4" X 15-3/4"

DRAWER SUBFRONT (4)
1/2" X 4-1/4" X 7-5/8"

DRAWER FRONT (4)
3/4" X 5-3/8" X 9"

3/8"

1/4"

SECTION A-A

CONCEALED CASTER (4)

INVERTED VIEW OF BASE

3/8"

3/8"

DOOR DETAIL

TOP DOOR — 3/4" X 11-3/8" X 15-1/2"
LOWER DOORS — 3/4" X 13-3/4" X 17-1/8"

CHAIN SUPPORT (UPPER DOOR)

2" DOUBLE BEND OFFSET HINGE (6)

4-3/4

16-5/8"

DOWELLING PATTERN

Purpose	Size	Description	Quantity
Base end	$\frac{3}{4}'' \times 4\frac{1}{4}'' \times 18\frac{3}{4}''$	Pine	2
Base front	$\frac{3}{4}'' \times 4\frac{1}{4}'' \times 39\frac{1}{2}''$	Pine	1
Base rear	$\frac{3}{4}'' \times 3\frac{1}{4}'' \times 38''$	Pine	1
Base cleat end	$\frac{3}{4}'' \times 1\frac{1}{2}'' \times 11''$	Pine	2
Base cleat front	$\frac{3}{4}'' \times 1\frac{1}{2}'' \times 31''$	Pine	1
Box bottom	$\frac{3}{4}'' \times 18'' \times 38''$	Pine	1
Box side	$\frac{3}{4}'' \times 18'' \times 29\frac{3}{8}''$	Pine	2
Box shelf	$\frac{3}{4}'' \times 18'' \times 36\frac{1}{2}''$	Pine	1
Box top	$\frac{3}{4}'' \times 18'' \times 38''$	Pine	1
Shelf cleat	$\frac{3}{4}'' \times 1\frac{1}{2}'' \times 17\frac{3}{4}''$	Pine	2
Drawer support side	$\frac{3}{4}'' \times 1\frac{1}{2}'' \times 17\frac{3}{4}''$	Pine	4
Drawer support end	$\frac{3}{4}'' \times 1\frac{1}{2}'' \times 17\frac{1}{2}''$	Pine	4
Drawer guide	$\frac{3}{4}'' \times 1\frac{1}{8}'' \times 17''$	Pine	8
Drawer support post	$\frac{3}{4}'' \times 1\frac{1}{8}'' \times 5\frac{1}{4}''$	Pine	2
Kicker	$\frac{3}{4}'' \times 1\frac{1}{2}'' \times 5''$	Pine	4
Rear panel	$\frac{1}{4}'' \times 30\frac{1}{8}'' \times 37\frac{1}{4}''$	Plywood	1
Front frame stile end	$\frac{3}{4}'' \times 1\frac{3}{4}'' \times 31\frac{7}{8}''$	Pine	2
Front frame stile lower	$\frac{3}{4}'' \times 1\frac{1}{4}'' \times 13\frac{1}{4}''$	Pine	1
Front frame stile upper	$\frac{3}{4}'' \times 1\frac{1}{4}'' \times 10\frac{3}{4}''$	Pine	2
Front frame rail upper	$\frac{3}{4}'' \times 2\frac{3}{4}'' \times 34\frac{1}{2}''$	Pine	1
Front frame rail center	$\frac{3}{4}'' \times 1\frac{1}{4}'' \times 34\frac{1}{2}''$	Pine	1
Front frame rail lower	$\frac{3}{4}'' \times 2\frac{3}{4}'' \times 34\frac{1}{2}''$	Pine	1
Front frame drawer rail	$\frac{3}{4}'' \times 1\frac{1}{4}'' \times 8\frac{1}{2}''$	Pine	2
Top end	$\frac{3}{4}'' \times 8'' \times 19\frac{3}{4}''$	Pine	2
Top front	$\frac{3}{4}'' \times 4\frac{3}{4}'' \times 40\frac{1}{2}''$	Pine	1
Top rear	$\frac{3}{4}'' \times 7\frac{1}{4}'' \times 38''$	Pine	1
Glass rack	$\frac{3}{4}'' \times 3\frac{1}{4}'' \times 38''$	Pine	1
Lid support	$\frac{3}{4}'' \times 5'' \times 6''$	Pine	1
Lid	$\frac{3}{4}'' \times 8\frac{1}{4}'' \times 41''$	Pine	1
Lid frame end	$\frac{3}{4}'' \times 1\frac{1}{4}'' \times 5\frac{3}{4}''$	Pine	2
Lid frame front	$\frac{3}{4}'' \times 2'' \times 37\frac{7}{8}''$	Pine	1
Door upper	$\frac{3}{4}'' \times 11\frac{3}{8}'' \times 15\frac{1}{2}''$	Pine	1
Door lower	$\frac{3}{4}'' \times 13\frac{3}{4}'' \times 17\frac{1}{8}''$	Pine	2
Drawer front	$\frac{3}{4}'' \times 5\frac{3}{8}'' \times 9''$	Pine	4
Drawer subfront	$\frac{1}{2}'' \times 4\frac{1}{4}'' \times 7\frac{5}{8}''$	Pine	4
Drawer side	$\frac{1}{2}'' \times 4\frac{1}{4}'' \times 15\frac{3}{4}''$	Pine	8
Drawer rear	$\frac{1}{2}'' \times 3\frac{1}{2}'' \times 7\frac{5}{8}''$	Pine	4
Drawer bottom	$\frac{1}{4}'' \times 7\frac{5}{8}'' \times 15\frac{1}{2}''$	Plywood	4
Strip hinge	$1\frac{1}{2}'' \times 37\frac{1}{4}''$		1
Strip hinge	$1\frac{1}{2}'' \times 6''$		1
Hinge	$2''$	Double-bend offset	6
Magnetic catch		MC type	3
Wood buttons			10
Concealed casters			4

the sides and 2-inch screws to fasten the shelf to the cleats.

The front frame consists of rails and stiles cut from solid pine. The *rails* are the horizontal members and the *stiles*, the verticals. The joints of the frame require reinforcement, such as mortise-and-tenon, lap, or dowel joints. The dowel joint used here is the easiest of the three. Regardless of the joint used, accuracy is of the utmost importance.

Cut the stiles and rails to size as shown in the Materials List. It's a good idea to make the side stiles about 1/16 inch wider than the size given to allow for some discrepancy and ensure a good, clean joint at the sides. You can trim the excess with a plane after you fasten the frame to the cabinet. Because they are so narrow, the intermediate stiles and rails will take one dowel per joint. Use two dowels at each of the wider upper and lower rail pieces.

Assemble the cut pieces on a flat surface the way they will appear on the cabinet. Draw gauging lines at each point where a dowel will be used. Square over these lines to the edges of each piece, then mark the center and bore the 3/8-inch-diameter dowel hole. If you use a doweling jig, the device will automatically center the hole. Standard dowels for this purpose are 2 inches long so bore the holes 1 inch deep in each section. In some cases, this is not practical, especially when the part is rather narrow. In such cases, simply make the holes 3/4 inch deep into the narrow piece and 1 1/4 inches deep into the mating piece.

It is impossible to glue, assemble, and clamp the entire frame in one operation. You can check this out by installing undersized dowels dry. The problem is that dowels at 90 degrees to each other will not assemble as a unit. Even if these steps could be done in one shot, it would be quite tricky to clamp such a setup.

The best way to handle this problem is as follows. Glue and clamp the short drawer rails to the short stiles. Be sure to use blocks under the clamp jaws to protect the work edges. Also glue up the lower rail and center still in this manner. When the glue has set, clamp the subassemblies in the vertical plane with three short bar clamps. For the final assembly, insert the 12 horizontal dowels into the rails, then fasten and clamp the two outer stiles to complete the frame. If all the parts were cut square and all holes properly aligned, the frame will be square and true.

Before mounting the frame to the cabinet, sand all joints to remove any unevenness between the pieces. Use a sanding block or a power sander. Start with a coarse grit, working down to a fine one. You now can fasten the frame to the cabinet. Use nails and glue along the top and bottom edge. Use screws installed diagonally from the inside to draw the frame stiles tightly against the cabinet sides.

Cut the drawer supports and guides and assemble them with screws. Make the upper unit as a frame and secure it to the side panel, as well as the front drawer compartment rail. Attach a corner piece vertically at the outside rear corner of the upper drawer support. You should also install the side guides at this time. To keep the drawers from tipping downward when extended, place a kicker above the drawer and fasten it to the side panel. Only one kicker per drawer is necessary, as shown in the drawing.

Cut the shaped pieces for the top with

a band saw, jigsaw, or saber saw. If you use a saber saw, be sure to work with a fine blade to minimize the sanding operations.

Use a router fitted with a rounding-off cutter to round the edges of the front, sides, and top. Do not round the lower rear edge of the front piece because it will bear against the upper rail of the front frame. When the routing is completed, sand all edges smooth. Pay particular attention to the ends of the front and top pieces.

Bore and countersink the screw holes and assemble with glue at all joints. When installing the buttons, do not apply glue to the button. Place a small amount of glue around the edge of the hole to prevent squeeze-out.

Attach the glass rack with screws driven through the back piece. To simplify the finishing operations, you might want to leave this piece off until after you have applied stain and topcoats.

Hinge the top shelf at the rear so it will open 180 degrees. To support it in the open position, install a hinged lid support. When the top is in the closed position, the support is swung flush against the back piece. A piece of thin felt glued to the top edge will prevent the top shelf from being marred.

Lip the doors with a ⅜-inch rabbet. The sizes shown will allow the use of double-bend nonmortise type hinges. The ones shown have a decorative finial at the top and bottom. The only part showing on them is the knuckle and finial. The other parts are concealed. If you decide to use surface-mounted or mortise-type hinges, be sure to make the necessary allowances.

The drawers are made of ½-inch plywood, except for the fronts, which are ¾-inch thick. We used ½-inch fir, but you could substitute solid pine. Make up the drawer sections as a unit, then add the fronts. Dado the side panels at the rear and rabbet them at the front. Cut a ¼-inch groove for the bottom piece into the lower part of the side and front panels. If you use a thinner material such as ⅛-inch wall paneling for the bottoms, be sure to change the width of the grooves accordingly.

Assemble the drawers with glue and brads. Do not use glue for the bottom panel, however. You can nail or staple it along the rear edge into the back panel of the drawer.

Dust off the entire cabinet, then give a final sanding to all exposed surfaces. Dust again, then apply stain as desired. Allow the stain to dry overnight, then apply topcoats of varnish or lacquer. If you use varnish or one of the slow-drying plastic finishes, be sure to work in a dust-free area. Dust is not much of a problem when using lacquer because it is fast drying.

Install the casters after the finishing operation is completed. If you have difficulty locating the casters or nonmortise hinges, write to Armor Products.

Early American Dowry Chest

THIS DOWRY CHEST is an excellent example of Early American furniture. It is made of pine and its many drawers provide ample storage for linens, towels, etc. Except for a few mitered moldings, all joints are butts, thus keeping construction simple. The top and backboard are made of ⁵⁄₄ stock (1⅛-inch dressed size). Otherwise the cabinet is of 1-inch stock (¾-inch dressed size). The addition of brass pulls and scalloped backboard make it a beautiful, decorative piece of furniture.

Although it is possible to obtain wide boards at most lumberyards, you will save considerably on costs by gluing up your own. You can also economize by using common lumber instead of clear. Just be sure to choose boards with good, sound knots. Loose knots will not do and should be avoided.

Basic tools are used for this piece: table saw, router, drill, and band saw or saber saw (for the backboard). Another tool you should have is a doweling jig. Although not essential, it makes easy work of gluing up the boards and butt joints for the front frame.

Choose good, flat boards for the top. Use 6-inch stock and arrange the boards so the knots are not too close to the ends of edges. Cut the boards slightly longer than needed. After gluing, they can be trimmed to the final length.

Place the boards on a pair of sawhorses and mark the locations of the dowels. Identify each board so you will know how each piece goes together during assembly. If you have a doweling jig, align it with the marks and drill the ⅜-inch-diameter holes 1¹⁄₁₆ inches deep. You can do this with a portable drill or a drill press. The doweling jig automatically centers the drill on the board. Apply a little glue to the dowels and drive them in with a hammer. Use spiral dowels; smooth dowels might split the boards because there is no way for the air to escape from the holes when they are driven in.

Prepare your clamps by opening them to the proper size, then apply glue to all surfaces to be joined. Be sure to include the protruding dowels. Bring the parts together and clamp securely. Do not wipe the glue droplets that ooze from the joints. When the glue has hardened, remove the excess droplets with a chisel. This step is especially important if you plan to stain the piece. Wiping the excess will spread the glue on the wood surface and tend to size the wood, resulting in uneven and spotty staining later on.

While the glue is setting for the top, you can prepare the sides. The procedure is the same as for the top except that the lumber used is ¾ inch thick. After the glue has set, trim the sides to the proper length and width. If you have a jointer, use it to plane the front and rear edges. At this time

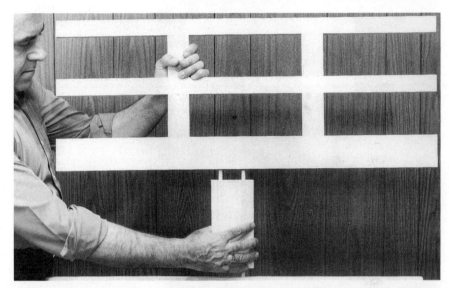

Fig. 18-1. Assemble the front frame with dowels. Glue and clamp the upper section first.

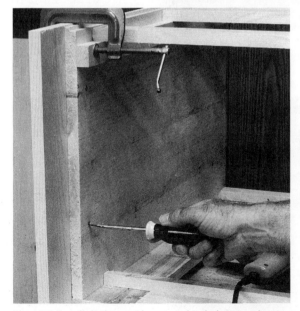

Fig. 18-2. Install the base with screws driven from inside. Use clamps to hold the base.

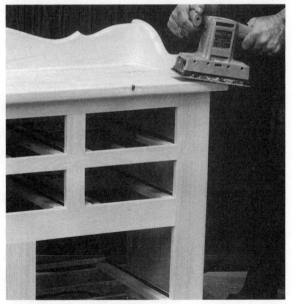

Fig. 18-3. To make the corners look worn, use a sander. Rock the sander back and forth for a round look.

Fig. 18-4. Drawers are made of ½-inch pine except for fronts. Drive nails through sides.

you can also cut the rabbet at the rear edges. Make the rabbet ¼-inch deep.

Choose clear lumber for the front frame, especially for the narrower pieces. Cut these pieces to the sizes shown then drill the dowel holes, following the procedure used for the sides and top.

The assembly sequence of the front frame is important. Note that the upper grid is glued up as a unit. This is the part that contains the six drawer openings. After the glue has set, remove the clamps and install the lower rail and center stile. When the assembly is completed, mark the dowel locations for the end stiles. Again use the dowel jig to align the holes.

With the front frame completed, sand the surface so that all joints are smooth and flush. Then assemble the front frame to the side panels. Note that dowels are used here also. Since the front frame is only ¾ inch thick, the dowels can penetrate only about ½ inch. Use care when drilling these holes.

As an alternative, you can use nails to join the front to the sides. If you do, use 2-inch finishing nails and be sure to sink the heads. Use protective cleats under the clamps when assembling the front frame

Fig. 18-5. This rear view shows the drawer guides and the kicker. Note the stops at the rear of each guide set.

MATERIALS LIST

Purpose	Size	Description	Quantity
Top	1⅛″ × 18¼″ × 46½″	Pine	1
Backboard	1⅛″ × 4¾″ × 41¾″	Pine	1
Sideboard	1⅛″ × 4¾″ × 14¼″	Pine	2
Side	¾″ × 16¼″ × 26¹¹⁄₁₆″	Pine	2
Base side	¾″ × 5¼″ × 16¼″	Pine	2
Base front	¾″ × 5¼″ × 45¼″	Pine	1
Front side	¾″ × 3⅞″ × 26¹¹⁄₁₆″	Pine	2
Stile	¾″ × 2¹⁄₁₆″ × 4″	Pine	4
Stile center	¾″ × 4⅛″ × 8¹⁄₁₆″	Pine	1
Upper rail	¾″ × 1½″ × 36″	Pine	2
Center rail	¾″ × 3″ × 36″	Pine	1
Lower rail	¾″ × 4⅝″ × 36″	Pine	1
Top cleat, front	¾″ × 1¼″ × 42¼″	Pine	2
Drawer support	¾″ × ¾″ × 42¼″	Pine	3
Front vertical cleat	¾″ × 1½″ × 26¹¹⁄₁₆″	Pine	2
Drawer support rear	¾″ × 1⁹⁄₁₆″ × 42¼″	Pine	3
Rear base	¾″ × 3″ × 43¾″	Pine	1
Kicker, upper	¾″ × 1½″ × 14¼″	Pine	3
Kicker, center	¾″ × 1¹⁄₁₆″ × 15¾″	Pine	3
Kicker, lower	¾″ × 2⁹⁄₁₆″ × 15¾″	Pine	3
Drawer guide	¾″ × 1¾″ × 16″	Pine	16
Drawer guide strip	¼″ × ¾″ × 16″	Plywood	16
Drawer stop	½″ × ½″ × 10½″	Pine	6
Drawer stop	½″ × ½″ × 15½″	Pine	2
Drawer upper front	¾″ × 3¹⁵⁄₁₆″ × 10½″	Pine	6
Drawer upper rear	½″ × 3⁵⁄₁₆″ × 10″	Pine	6
Drawer upper, side	½″ × 3¹⁵⁄₁₆″ × 15½″	Pine	12
Drawer upper, bottom	¼″ × 9¹⁵⁄₁₆″ × 15″	Plywood	6
Drawer lower, front	¾″ × 8″ × 15⅞″	Pine	2
Drawer lower, rear	½″ × 7⅜″ × 15⅜″	Pine	2
Drawer lower, side	½″ × 8″ × 15½″	Pine	4
Drawer lower, bottom	¼″ × 15″ × 15⁵⁄₁₆″	Pine	2
Molding	⅝″ × ¾″	Nose and cove	15′
Dust cover	¼″ × 26¹⁵⁄₁₆″ × 42¼″	Plywood	1
Screws	1¼″ × 8 FH		36
Screws	2½″ × 10 FH		13
Nails	2″	Finishing	
Brads	1″	Finishing	
Wood buttons			8
Pulls			8
Casters with bracket			4

Note: Doweling jig and casters are available from Armor Products.

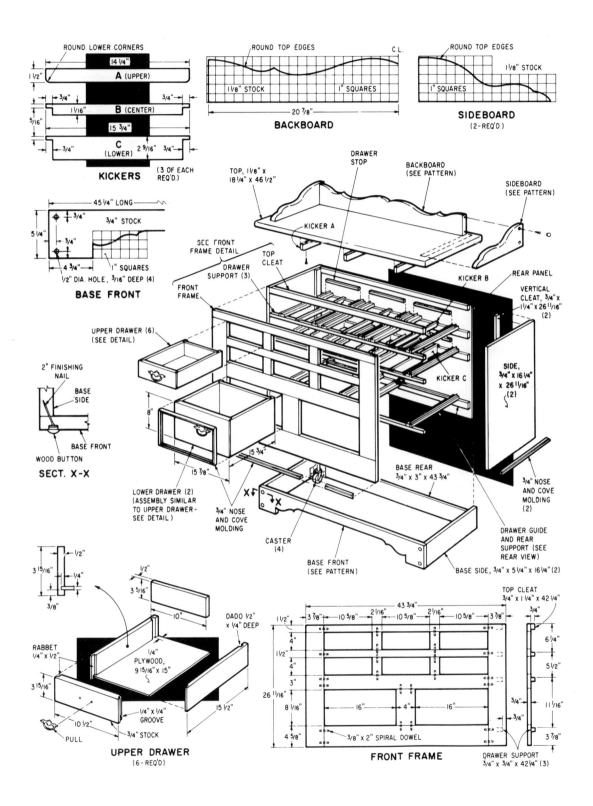

ROUND LOWER CORNERS

14 1/4"

A (UPPER)

1 1/2"

3/4" 3/4"

1 1/16" B (CENTER)

5/16"

15 3/4"

C (LOWER)

3/4" 2 9/16" 3/4"

KICKERS

(3 OF EACH REQ'D.)

ROUND TOP EDGES

C.L.

1 1/8" STOCK 1" SQUARES

20 7/8"

BACKBOARD

ROUND TOP EDGES

1 1/8" STOCK

1" SQUARES

SIDEBOARD

(2-REQ'D.)

45 1/4" LONG

3/4"

5 1/4"

3/4"

3/4" STOCK

4 3/4"

1" SQUARES

1/2" DIA. HOLE, 3/16" DEEP (4)

BASE FRONT

DRAWER STOP

TOP, 1 1/8" x 18 1/4" x 46 1/2"

BACKBOARD (SEE PATTERN)

SIDEBOARD (SEE PATTERN)

KICKER A

SEE FRONT FRAME DETAIL

TOP CLEAT

DRAWER SUPPORT (3)

FRONT FRAME

KICKER B

REAR PANEL

VERTICAL CLEAT, 3/4" x 1 1/4" x 26 11/16" (2)

UPPER DRAWER (6) (SEE DETAIL)

2" FINISHING NAIL

BASE SIDE

BASE FRONT

WOOD BUTTON

SECT. X-X

KICKER C

SIDE, 3/4" x 16 1/4" x 26 11/16" (2)

8"

15 3/4"

15 7/8"

LOWER DRAWER (2) (ASSEMBLY SIMILAR TO UPPER DRAWER - SEE DETAIL)

3/4" NOSE AND COVE MOLDING

X

X

CASTER (4)

BASE FRONT (SEE PATTERN)

BASE REAR 3/4" x 3" x 43 3/4"

3/4" NOSE AND COVE MOLDING (2)

DRAWER GUIDE AND REAR SUPPORT (SEE REAR VIEW)

BASE SIDE, 3/4" x 5 1/4" x 16 1/4" (2)

1/2"

3 15/16"

1/4"

3/8"

1/2"

3 5/16"

10"

DADO 1/2" x 1/4" DEEP

RABBET 1/4" x 1/2"

1/4" PLYWOOD, 9 15/16" x 15"

3 15/16"

1/4" x 1/4" GROOVE

3/4" STOCK

15 1/2"

10 1/2"

PULL

UPPER DRAWER

(6-REQ'D)

TOP CLEAT 3/4" x 1 1/4" x 42 1/4"

43 3/4"

3/4"

1 1/2"

3 7/8" 10 5/8" 2 1/16" 10 5/8" 2 1/16" 10 5/8" 3 7/8"

1 1/2"

4"

3"

8 1/16"

4 5/8"

26 11/16"

6 1/4"

5 1/2"

3/4"

3/4"

11/16"

3 7/8"

16" 4" 16"

3/8" x 2" SPIRAL DOWEL

DRAWER SUPPORT 3/4" x 3/4" x 42 1/4" (3)

FRONT FRAME

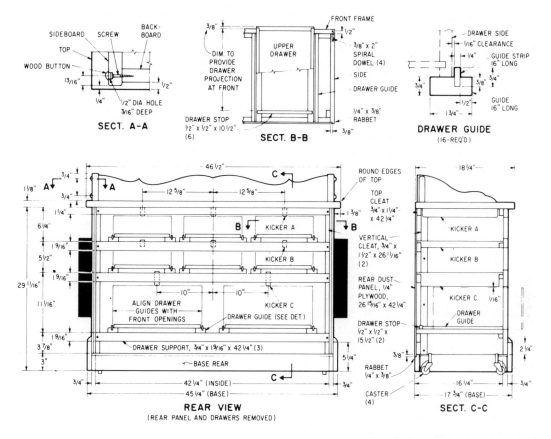

SECT. A-A

SECT. B-B

DRAWER GUIDE
(16-REQ'D)

REAR VIEW
(REAR PANEL AND DRAWERS REMOVED)

SECT. C-C

to the sides. Be sure the sides are square to the front frame. Check with a large square. If necessary, use braces to hold the assembly square while the glue sets.

Cut the base pieces to the sizes indicated. Trace the scallop design on the front piece, then round off all outer edges with a router or sandpaper. Drill the button holes at each end of the front piece ¾ inch from the edge. The buttons will conceal the nailheads. Drive the nails into the side pieces at an angle, as shown in the drawing.

After the base is completed, fasten it to the cabinet with glue and 1¼-inch screws.

The drawers ride on corner guides. To keep the drawers from tipping when ex-

tended, use a *kicker* above each drawer. The kicker is a strip of wood placed so the top rear of the drawer rides against it.

Cut all the necessary strips and install them as indicated in the drawing. Drill screw clearance holes and install with screws. The two vertical strips at the rear must be set back to allow for the horizontal crosspieces. Although the crosspieces are different widths, you must install them with the top edges aligned.

Cut the 16 corner guides from flat stock. Make the lengths uniform, then cut the groove for the thin plywood strip. This task is best done on the table saw with a blade of proper thickness. Apply a little glue to the plywood strips, then insert them into the grooves. Clamping is not necessary. Do not install this piece onto the assembly yet.

Drawers are rabbeted with flush sides, and they are rather simple to make. The two larger drawers are similar to the smaller ones, except that moldings are added to the face. Note that the drawer fronts are ¾ inch thick. The sides are ½-inch and the bottoms are ¼-inch plywood.

Cut all pieces to size according to the Materials List. If you find that the wide side and rear members of the larger drawers are bowed, you can relieve them by sawing narrow grooves as shown. The grooves will not affect the operation of the drawers. Cut the rabbets and dadoes using either a table saw with a dado blade or a router. If you lack a dado blade or router, you can make several passes with a regular blade. This method is not easy, but it does work.

After all parts are cut, drill the clearance holes for the pulls, sand each piece, and then assemble with glue and finishing nails. To keep the assembly square, the bottoms should be ready to insert. Place a little glue in the grooves and slide the bottom into place. Fit the two large drawers with ¾-inch nose and cove molding. Miter the corners and install as shown, using glue and brads. Round the edges of the six small drawers.

Next install the drawer guides. Do each drawer individually. Just in case there is some discrepancy between drawers, number each drawer and the corresponding opening. Dab a little glue at the points where the bottoms of the guides contact the crosspieces. Insert a drawer and position the guides so that the drawer front is flush with the front frame. This assembly will indicate that the guides are perpendicular to the front. Allow a little play between the drawer sides and the guide.

Repeat this procedure for the remaining drawers. Be careful not to move the guides while the glue is setting. After the glue has set, you can drive a couple of finishing nails into the joint. Actually, the glue should suffice.

Cut the kickers and install them next. Note that there are three different sizes. Fasten the uppermost ones to the underside of the cabinet top. Add the drawer stops. Position them so the drawers project ⅜ inch from the front.

Trim the cabinet top to size and round all corners. "Wear" the top front corners by using a file or plane. File until the corners slant downward. Finish with sandpaper.

Cut the backboard and side pieces according to the drawing. Round the top edges, then assemble with screws and glue. Conceal screw heads with wood buttons.

Attach the backboard to the top with screws from the underside. Next attach the top to the cabinet with screws through the front and rear cleats.

Mount the concealed casters at each corner. Then install the rear dust panel.

Finish the piece as desired. If you plan to use stain, apply a thin coat of penetrating sealer and allow it to dry before you apply the stain.

End Table Cellarette

THIS ELEGANT END TABLE made of cherry lumber features a compartment for storing your favorite refreshment, complete with glasses. At first glance, this piece looks like an ordinary table with three drawers; however, a tug at the decorative pull on the side reveals the hidden compartment. The door drops down in drop-leaf fashion so it can be used as a serving surface. The three drawers are reduced in width to make room for the compartment. Full-width drawer fronts help conceal the subterfuge.

This cabinet is right-handed. If you want to make a pair of tables for use at both ends of a sofa or chair, simply reverse the dimensions and assembly, mirror fashion,

for one table. The cabinet is made of solid cherry. This is an ideal cabinet wood because it handles well and is easy to finish.

Note that hardwoods are generally thicker than softwoods. For example, 1-inch cherry has a dressed or actual size of $13/16$ inch. A piece of 1-inch pine, however, has a *dressed*, or actual, size of $3/4$ inch. To add to the confusion, a piece of $1/2$-inch hardwood or softwood measures $1/2$ inch. If you want to substitute softwoods, you would need to alter the dimensions accordingly.

When you construct a piece of furniture such as this, it is important that all fastenings should be invisible. A study of the drawings shows how this is accom-

Fig. 19-1. The four front frame members are the last sides to be glued in the final assembly. Use clamps with protective strips.

Fig. 19-2. This view shows the partition. Place the screws in the front panel so they will be hidden by front framework.

plished. You will also note that a considerable amount of dowels are used. They are needed to ensure strong tight joints. Wide boards are hard to come by and even if available, they seldom can be used because of cupping. They would have to be cut into 3- or 4-inch widths, then glued to make up the wide boards. All framing members are also doweled.

Gluing the boards takes place after you have decided where to use the various grain patterns. For example, you should use the most attractive pattern for the top, and the least attractive for the rear or side that is not exposed. When gluing boards, make the lengths and widths slightly larger than the finish size. Leave some stock for trimming.

The dowels used should be the spiral type, preferably oak. This type has a good gripping surface and the spiral groove allows air to escape as the dowel is driven. Dowels used for this project are $3/8 \times 2$ inches. The doweling jig is indispensable in this type of project. It automatically centers on the board to ensure perfect alignment. The jig can be used with a portable drill or a drill press. It works equally well on both.

Use a fast-setting nonstaining type of glue. When gluing hardwood, allow the glue to air-dry a few moments before you join the pieces. When wide boards are required, alternate the growth rings to eliminate cupping.

Glue up the necessary pieces to make the top, then clamp and allow the glue to set. Trim to size, then shape the edge as desired. The shaping can be done with a router or shaper. Before shaping the edges, sand the top surface so it is flat and smooth. A belt sander is ideal for this operation. Sand with the grain of the wood. You can

Fig. 19-3. This photo shows drawer construction. Place glides on the drawer guides to allow the drawer to open and close smoothly.

Fig. 19-4. The nearly completed cabinet is ready for the installation of hardware like hinges and chain. Note the dummy extension drawer front.

wait to do finish sanding until all the parts are completed. When shaping, do the end grain first, then follow with the longer sides.

Dado the left side to accept the front frame as well as the drawer guides. Use *blind dadoes*, which are dadoes cut to stop short of the rear edge of the panel. You can cut the dado on a table or radial arm saw fitted with a dado blade. Otherwise, you can use a router. If the router is used, tack a guide strip onto the work surface.

Cut the dado so the parts will fit snugly. In addition to the dadoes, the side piece will require two grooves: one for a splined joint at the rear, and one for the top fasteners. These are cut best on a table saw. Use a regular saw blade for the ⅛-inch groove at the top. For the spline, you can use a dado blade or make several passes with the regular blade. When making the spline groove, check the fit on scrap wood before cutting the actual workpiece. Scrap paneling makes good spline stock.

Note: Do not cut the grooves for the spline and fasteners until after you make the rear and right panel. These grooves must be cut with the saw at the same setting as for those panels. Set the fence and blade height to correspond to the dimensions shown on the drawing. For the spline cut, pass the rear panel through the blade with the work held vertically. Pass the sides through horizontally.

The right side panel must be the same overall size as the left one after trimming; however, it must be cut as indicated. Glue the piece so it is slightly oversize. After glue sets, make cuts 1 and 2 as indicated by the dotted lines in the drawing. Set the two narrow strips aside and from the large piece make cuts 3 and 4. Retain the center piece for the door and glue up parts A, B, C, and D to make up the side frame. Be sure to match up the grain patterns in the four narrow pieces and the door. Dowel the frame members and glue up. Use one dowel at each joint. After the glue sets, trim

129

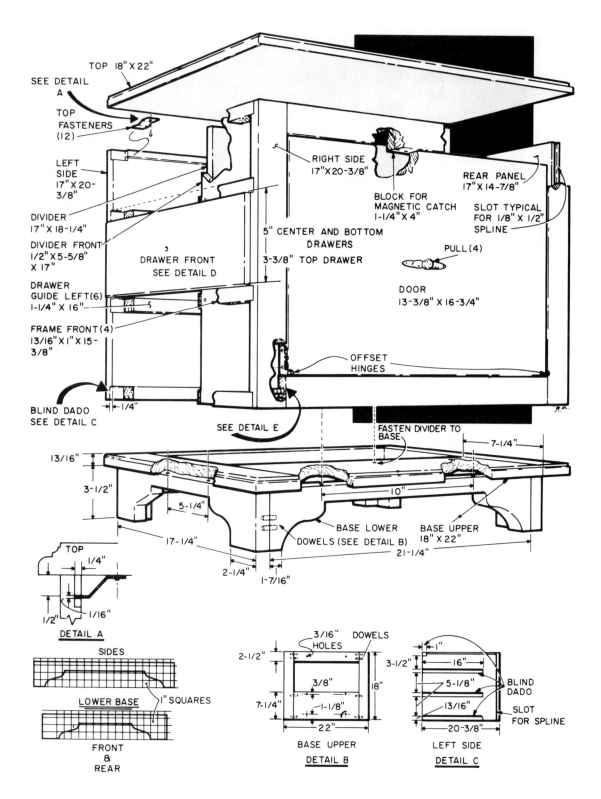

TOP 18" X 22"

SEE DETAIL A

TOP FASTENERS (12)

LEFT SIDE 17" X 20-3/8"

DIVIDER 17" X 18-1/4"

DIVIDER FRONT 1/2" X 5-5/8" X 17"

DRAWER GUIDE LEFT(6) 1-1/4" X 16"

FRAME FRONT(4) 13/16" X 1" X 15-3/8"

BLIND DADO SEE DETAIL C

1/4"

DRAWER FRONT SEE DETAIL D

RIGHT SIDE 17" X 20-3/8"

BLOCK FOR MAGNETIC CATCH 1-1/4" X 4"

REAR PANEL 17" X 14-7/8"

SLOT TYPICAL FOR 1/8" X 1/2" SPLINE

PULL(4)

5" CENTER AND BOTTOM DRAWERS
3-3/8" TOP DRAWER

DOOR 13-3/8" X 16-3/4"

OFFSET HINGES

SEE DETAIL E

FASTEN DIVIDER TO BASE

13/16"

3-1/2"

5-1/4"

17-1/4"

2-1/4"

1-7/16"

7-1/4"

10"

BASE LOWER
DOWELS (SEE DETAIL B)

BASE UPPER 18" X 22"

21-1/4"

TOP

1/4"

1/2"   1/16"

DETAIL A

SIDES

LOWER BASE   1" SQUARES

FRONT & REAR

3/16" HOLES   DOWELS

2-1/2"

3/8"

7-1/4"

1-1/8"

22"

18"

BASE UPPER
DETAIL B

3-1/2"

1"

16"

5-1/8"

13/16"

20-3/8"

BLIND DADO

SLOT FOR SPLINE

LEFT SIDE
DETAIL C

130

Purpose	Size	Description	Quantity
Top	$13/16'' \times 18'' \times 22''$	Cherry	1
Left side	$13/16'' \times 17'' \times 20\frac{3}{8}''$	Cherry	1
Rear	$13/16'' \times 17'' \times 14\frac{7}{8}''$	Cherry	1
Right side	$13/16'' \times 17'' \times 20\frac{3}{8}''$	Cherry	1
Door	$13/16'' \times 13\frac{3}{8}'' \times 16\frac{3}{4}''$	Cherry	1
Divider	$13/16'' \times 17'' \times 18\frac{1}{4}''$	Cherry	1
Divider front	$\frac{1}{2}'' \times 5\frac{5}{8}'' \times 17''$	Cherry	1
Frame front	$13/16'' \times 1'' \times 15\frac{3}{8}''$	Cherry	4
Drawer guide left	$13/16'' \times 1\frac{1}{4}'' \times 16''$	Cherry	6
Base upper front	$13/16'' \times 2\frac{1}{2}'' \times 18''$	Cherry	1
Base upper rear	$13/16'' \times 2\frac{1}{2}'' \times 18''$	Cherry	1
Base upper left	$13/16'' \times 2\frac{1}{2}'' \times 17''$	Cherry	1
Base upper right	$13/16'' \times 7\frac{1}{4}'' \times 17''$	Cherry	1
Base lower front	$13/16'' \times 3\frac{1}{2}'' \times 17\frac{1}{4}''$	Cherry	1
Base lower rear	$13/16'' \times 3\frac{1}{2}'' \times 17\frac{1}{4}''$	Cherry	1
Base lower side	$13/16'' \times 3\frac{1}{2}'' \times 19\frac{5}{8}''$	Cherry	2
Drawer front	$\frac{1}{2}'' \times 3\frac{3}{8}'' \times 14\frac{3}{4}''$	Cherry	1
Drawer side	$\frac{1}{2}'' \times 3'' \times 19''$	Cherry	2
Drawer subfront	$\frac{1}{2}'' \times 2\frac{1}{2}'' \times 8\frac{1}{2}''$	Cherry	1
Drawer rear	$\frac{1}{2}'' \times 5'' \times 14\frac{3}{4}''$	Cherry	1
Drawer front	$\frac{1}{2}'' \times 4\frac{1}{2}'' \times 8\frac{1}{2}''$	Cherry	1
Drawer side	$\frac{1}{2}'' \times 4\frac{1}{2}'' \times 8\frac{1}{2}''$	Cherry	2
Drawer subfront		Cherry	2
Drawer rear	$\frac{1}{2}'' \times 4'' \times 8\frac{1}{2}''$	Cherry	2
Drawer bottom	$\frac{1}{4}'' \times 8\frac{1}{2}'' \times 18\frac{3}{8}''$	Cherry	3
Spline	$\frac{1}{4}'' \times \frac{1}{2}'' \times 48''$	Cherry	1
Screws	$1\frac{3}{4}''$ 8 FH		18
Screws	$\frac{1}{2}''$ 8 RH		12
Top fasteners			12
Chain	24''		
Offset hinges			2
Magnetic catch (PM)			1
Pulls			4

the frame so length and width match the left side panel. Also, trim the door so there will be a clearance of $\frac{1}{16}$ inch all around it and the frame opening.

Make the compartment divider or partition with a frontal piece of $\frac{1}{2}$-inch stock. This piece serves to close off the compartment and also provides a neat appearance behind the dummy part of the drawers. The dadoes on the divider can be cut full length. When joining the front piece to the divider, place the screws so they will be concealed by the front frame pieces. Install the drawer guides into the dadoes with glue. Cut the front framing members at this time, then set aside.

The base consists of two parts, upper and lower. The upper base is made with

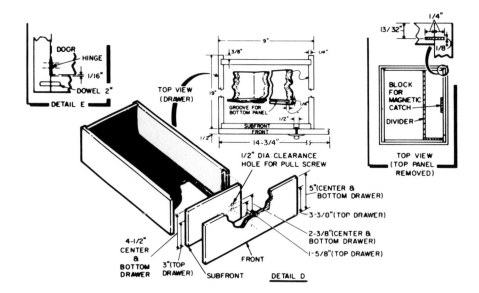

DETAIL E

TOP VIEW (DRAWER)

GROOVE FOR BOTTOM PANEL

SUBFRONT
FRONT

1/2" DIA CLEARANCE HOLE FOR PULL SCREW

BLOCK FOR MAGNETIC CATCH

DIVIDER

TOP VIEW (TOP PANEL REMOVED)

5"(CENTER & BOTTOM DRAWER)

3-3/8"(TOP DRAWER)

2-3/8"(CENTER & BOTTOM DRAWER)

1-5/8"(TOP DRAWER)

4-1/2" CENTER & BOTTOM DRAWER

3"(TOP DRAWER)

SUBFRONT

FRONT

DETAIL D

one side wider than the other. The wider section serves as the bottom of the compartment. Lay out the pieces and glue up with dowels. After the glue sets, surface the joints if necessary, then shape the edges. Follow the same procedure as for the top. Drill the mounting holes as shown.

Make the lower base with splined joints. Cut the pieces to exact size, then groove for the spline. Trace the outline for the cutout and cut with a saber saw. Use a router to round off the edges of the cutout. Before gluing the pieces, drill the two mounting holes in each piece. Countersink the holes so the flat-head screws will lay flush.

Before final assembly, sand all exposed surfaces. Sand until all surfaces are as smooth as glass.

Cut splines and check fit before applying glue. Work on a flat surface and install the splines into the rear panel. Apply the glue to the glue line and fasten the sides. Use strips of wood under the clamps to distribute the pressure and to prevent marring of the cabinet surfaces.

Next apply glue and add the front frame members. Check that the assembly is square. Adjust if necessary. When glue has set, insert the partition, then turn the unit upside down and install the top. Use top fasteners, which are designed to pull the top down tight when the screws are tightened. With the unit still upside down, install the two screws into the bottom of the divider. Follow with the upper base then the lower base. It is not necessary to use glue at these joints.

The door is hinged to the lower part of the frame opening. Use offset hinges to locate them so the door will be centered in the opening. Use a chain to contain the door. Also, install a magnetic catch at the top of the frame.

The top drawer is not as tall as the other two, but all the parts are cut for the larger drawers. After rabbeting and dadoing, you can trim the upper drawer to size. Drill the screw clearance hole in the subfronts before assembling. Note that this hole is off-center so it coincides with the center of the drawer front. When fastening the subfront to the front, raise the front about 1/16 inch. Use a shim to ensure accuracy.

Because cherry wood is close-grained, finishing is simple. Stain as desired, then apply several top coats of clear lacquer or varnish.

Note: The doweling jig, hinges, and catches are available from Armor Products.

Gossip Bench

THIS WELL-DESIGNED GOSSIP BENCH is ideal for use in almost any room in the house. It provides a place for the telephone and directory above, and ample storage in two compartments below. The smaller compartment has a door at the front. The other uses the seat as a lift-up door.

The spindles are ready made so if you don't have a lathe you can still make the piece. Butt joints have been used throughout, so construction is not difficult. The basic tools needed are a table saw, router, drill, and saber saw. The raised panels were made on the table saw, but the radial saw also may be used for this operation. The lumber used is pine in both ¾- and 1⅛-inch thicknesses.

Begin construction with the base. Rip four pieces of ¾-inch stock to 4-inch widths, then cut the lengths as indicated. The ends are of equal length, but the front and rear sections are not. After you have

cut the lengths, check the ends for squareness then proceed to cut the splines. The kerf of the spline will depend on the spline used. You can use steel splines or ¹⁄₁₆-, ⅛-, or ¾-inch plywood splines. After you have made the splines, cut the contour in the front piece.

Next, assemble the base. Apply a thin coat of glue to the end grain of the rear piece and the front ends of the side pieces. Allow the glue to dry (about 15 minutes), then recoat with glue and assemble. Follow this procedure for all end-grain gluing. Fit the splines carefully. Check the assembly for squareness, then clamp securely and set aside while the glue sets.

Prepare the four base cleats and bore the screw-clearance holes. Be sure the vertical and horizontal holes are offset so the screws will clear. Install the cleats to the upper inside edge of the base with glue and flat-head screws.

Next, make the bottom frame using flat lumber. After cutting the five pieces to size, lay them on a flat surface to mark the location of the dowels. Use two dowels per joint. To prevent errors in assembly, mark each joint with matching numbers or letters, such as A-A, B-B, etc. Use $3/8$- × -2-inch dowels and bore each hole about $1\frac{1}{16}$

inches deep. Glue and clamp in the usual manner.

Use a router fitted with a rabbeting bit and make a rabbet along the top rear edge of the bottom frame to take the rear panel. Use it also to cut the clearance in the bottom frame for the $1/4$-inch panels. You also need to use the router to shape the end and

Fig. 20-1. After the bottom frame is completely assembled, use a router fitted with a rabbeting bit to make a rabbet along the top rear edge of the bottom frame to accept the plywood panels, which will be inset a bit later.

Fig. 20-2. The bottom of the bench. Note how the base is fastened to the bottom frame with wood screws through cleats.

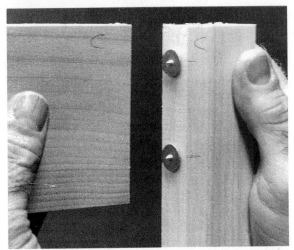

Fig. 20-3. Use dowel centers to transfer the location of the holes from the stile to the rail. This method will ensure an aligned fit between pieces.

Fig. 20-4. Top cleats being installed. The horizontal member shown forms the great support. Strengthen top member joints with dowels.

135

Fig. 20-5. Assemble the front frame to the end panel. You can use splines or finishing nails, countersunk.

Fig. 20-6. The top cleats are completely preassembled and shaped before mounting on frame. A rounding tool breaks sharp corners.

Fig. 20-7. After aligning the two pieces, transfer the hole locations from the backrest to the rear of the top frame with pencil marks.

Fig. 20-8. You can easily cut the curved end of the bench's armrest on a band saw. If you don't have one, you can use a coping saw.

Fig. 20-9. The raised effect of the door panel is accomplished with a table saw. A sharp blade and care are required for this operation.

front edges of the frame. Use a suitably shaped cutter and if necessary, use two or more cutters in several passes to achieve the desired shape.

To make the left and right end pieces and the divider, glue two or three narrow boards (preferably three). This method will prevent cupping. Be sure to reverse the annual rings in adjacent pieces. Use dowels or, if you have a shaper, you might want to use a glue joint instead. Of course, you will require a glue-joint cutter for this operation. Regardless of the joint used, be sure the glue line is straight and clean. Make the width of the boards oversize so the boards can be trimmed after gluing. Trim the divider ¼ inch narrower than the end pieces to allow clearance for the rear panel and align it with rabbets cut in the end pieces.

Trim the three pieces to the length and width required, then cut ¼- × -⅜-inch rabbets along the rear edge of the end pieces.

Fig. 20-10. Assemble the telephone shelf separately with screws and glue and fasten to the bench top with screws from beneath.

Make the front frame with doweled joints. Follow the same procedure used for making the bottom frame. After the glue has set, trim the height to match that of the end pieces, then use the router to round off the face of the opening. Rabbet the back edge to take the raised panel.

137

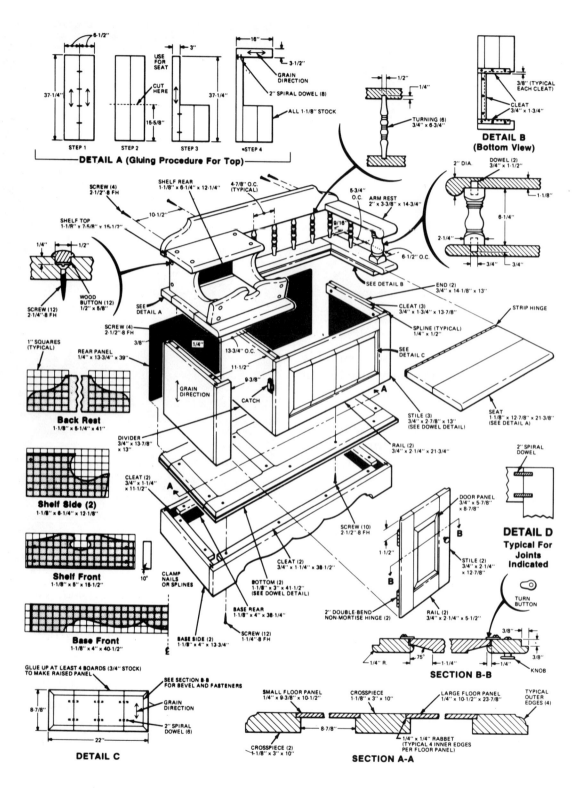

DETAIL A (Gluing Procedure For Top)

6-1/2"

37-1/4"

STEP 1

USE FOR SEAT

CUT HERE

STEP 2

3"

STEP 3

37-1/4"

15-5/8"

16"

3-1/2"

GRAIN DIRECTION

2" SPIRAL DOWEL (8)

ALL 1-1/8" STOCK

STEP 4

1/2"

1/4"

TURNING (6)
3/4" x 6-3/4"

DETAIL B
(Bottom View)

3/8" (TYPICAL EACH CLEAT)

CLEAT
3/4" x 1-3/4"

2" DIA.

DOWEL (2)
3/4" x 1-1/2"

1-1/8"

6-1/4"

2-1/4"

3/4"   3/4"

SCREW (4)
2-1/2"-8 FH

SHELF REAR
1-1/8" x 6-1/4" x 12-1/4"

4-7/8" O.C.
(TYPICAL)

5-3/4"
O.C.

ARM REST
2" x 3-3/8" x 14-3/4"

SHELF TOP
1-1/8" x 7-5/8" x 15-1/2"

10-1/2"

9/16"

6-1/2" O.C.

1/4"   1/2"

WOOD
BUTTON (12)
1/2" x 5/8"

SCREW (12)
2-1/4"-8 FH

SEE DETAIL A

SCREW (4)
2-1/2"-8 FH

3/8"

1/4"

SEE DETAIL B

END (2)
3/4" x 14-1/8" x 13"

CLEAT
3/4" x 1-3/4" x 13-7/8"

SPLINE (TYPICAL)
1/4" x 1/2"

SEE
DETAIL C

STRIP HINGE

1" SQUARES
(TYPICAL)

REAR PANEL
1/4" x 13-3/4" x 39"

13-3/4" O.C.

11-1/2"

9-3/8"

GRAIN
DIRECTION

CATCH

Back Rest
1-1/8" x 5-1/4" x 41"

SEAT
1-1/8" x 12-7/8" x 21-3/8"
(SEE DETAIL A)

STILE (3)
3/4" x 2-7/8" x 13"
(SEE DOWEL DETAIL)

DIVIDER
3/4" x 13-7/8"
x 13"

RAIL (2)
3/4" x 2-1/4" x 21-3/4"

2" SPIRAL
DOWEL

Shelf Side (2)
1-1/8" x 6-1/4" x 12-1/8"

CLEAT (2)
3/4" x 1-1/4"
x 11-1/2"

A

A

DOOR PANEL
3/4" x 5-7/8"
x 8-7/8"

DETAIL D
Typical For
Joints
Indicated

Shelf Front
1-1/8" x 5" x 15-1/2"

10°

CLAMP
NAILS
OR SPLINES

SCREW (10)
2-1/2"-8 FH

CLEAT (2)
3/4" x 1-1/4" x 38-1/2"

BOTTOM (2)
1-1/8" x 3" x 41-1/2"
(SEE DOWEL DETAIL)

1-1/2"

B

B

STILE (2)
3/4" x 2-1/4"
x 12-7/8"

TURN
BUTTON

Base Front
1-1/8" x 4" x 40-1/2"

BASE REAR
1-1/8" x 4" x 38-1/4"

BASE SIDE (2)
1-1/8" x 4" x 13-3/4"

SCREW (12)
1-1/4"-8 FH

2" DOUBLE-BEND
NON-MORTISE HINGE (2)

RAIL (2)
3/4" x 2-1/4" x 5-1/2"

3/8"

3/8"

KNOB

1/4" R.   75°   1-1/4"   1/4"

SECTION B-B

GLUE UP AT LEAST 4 BOARDS (3/4" STOCK)
TO MAKE RAISED PANEL

SEE SECTION B-B
FOR BEVEL AND FASTENERS

8-7/8"

GRAIN
DIRECTION

2" SPIRAL
DOWEL (6)

22"

DETAIL C

SMALL FLOOR PANEL
1/4" x 9-3/8" x 10-1/2"

CROSSPIECE
1-1/8" x 3" x 10"

LARGE FLOOR PANEL
1/4" x 10-1/2" x 23-7/8"

TYPICAL
OUTER
EDGES (4)

8-7/8"

1/4" x 1/4" RABBET
(TYPICAL 4 INNER EDGES
PER FLOOR PANEL)

CROSSPIECE (2)
1-1/8" x 3" x 10"

SECTION A-A

138

MATERIALS LIST

Purpose	Size	Description	Quantity
Base front	¾" × 4" × 40½"	Pine	1
Base end	¾" × 4" × 14⅛"	Pine	2
Base rear	¾" × 4" × 39"	Pine	1
Base cleat	¾" × 1¼" × 11½"	Pine	2
Base cleat	¾" × 1¼" × 38½"	Pine	2
Bottom front/rear	1⅛" × 3" × 41½"	Pine	2
Bottom crosspiece	1⅛" × 3" × 10"	Pine	3
End	¾" × 14⅛" × 13"	Pine	2
Divider	¾" × 13⅞" × 13"	Pine	1
Stile	¾" × 2⅞" × 13"	Pine	3
Rail	¾" × 2⅞" × 21¾"	Pine	2
Cleat	¾" × 1¾" × 13⅞"	Pine	3
Rear panel	¼" × 9⅜" × 10½"	Plywood	1
Floor panel	¼" × 10½" × 23⅞"	Plywood	1
Floor panel	¼" × 13¾" × 39"	Plywood	1
Seat cleat, rear	¾" × 1¾" × 20⅞"	Pine	1
Seat cleat, side	¾" × 1¾" × 13⅞"	Pine	2
Top front	1⅛" × 13" × 37¼"	Pine	1
Top rear	1⅛" × 3" × 37¼"	Pine	1
Top end piece	1⅛" × 3½" × 16"1	Pine	1
Back rest	1⅛" × 5¼" × 41"	Pine	1
Shelf rear	1⅛" × 6¼" × 12¼"	Pine	1
Shelf top	1⅛" × 7¾" × 15½"	Pine	1
Shelf end	1⅛" × 6¼" × 12¼"	Pine	2
Shelf front	1⅛" × 5" × 15½"	Pine	1
Arm rest	1⅛" × 3⅜" × 14¾"	Pine	1
Arm rest end	1⅛" × 3⅜" × 2"	Pine	1
Door stile	¾" × 2¼" × 12⅞"	Pine	2
Door rail	¾" × 2¼" × 5½"	Pine	2
Door panel	¾" × 5⅞" × 8⅞"	Pine	1
Seat panel	¾" × 8⅞" × 22"	Pine	1
Spline	¼" × ½" × 6'	Pine	
Spindle	¾" × 6¾"	Pine	6
Post	2¼" × 2¼" × 6¼"	Pine	1
Post dowel	¾" × 1½"	Pine	2
Button	½" × ⅝"	Pine	12
Dowel	⅜" × 2"	Pine	52
Screws	1¼" 8 FH		
Screws	2½" 8 FH		
Turn button retainer			12
Non-mortise double bend hinge			2
Strip hinge	1" × 21⅜"		1
Knob			1
Magnetic catch			1

Note: Spindles, buttons, and hinges are available at hardware stores or from Armor Products.

Sand the face of the front frame, then prepare to assemble it to the divider and end pieces. Use a spline or, if you do not want to go to the trouble, assemble with nails. In any event, use glue to ensure a good tight joint. Assemble the front member for the left end panel in the same way.

You can now assemble the front frame with side members to the bottom frame. Place the frame with sides onto the bottom piece. Align the rear of the divider and right side with the rear edge of the bottom piece. Set in the right side $7/8$ inch from the edge of the bottom frame. Let the frame rest in this position, then locate the left side piece with its front member. Set in the left side the same amount as the right end. The front edge of this piece should be in a straight line with the front frame. If required, make the necessary adjustments, then gauge a light pencil line around the frame and side members. Draw the line inside and out. Now remove the frame pieces and bore screw-clearance holes through the bottom frame. Center the holes between the lines and space them two over the side pieces and three along the front.

After the holes are bored, place the vertical members on a flat surface upside down. Then lay the bottom frame (also upside down) onto the verticals. Align the pieces using the pencil marks as a guide. Mark the centers for the screw holes, bore pilot holes, then assemble with glue and screws. Use the glue sparingly to keep it from squeezing out along the outer edges of the base. You can now fasten the assembly to the base by means of the cleats.

The top is made of $1\frac{1}{8}$-inch stock. The procedure is a bit unusual because of the hinged seat and grain direction in the right end piece. (See drawing.)

First, dowel and glue two boards, each $7\frac{1}{2}$ inches wide and 38 inches long (Detail A). After the glue has set, trim both ends to $37\frac{1}{4}$ inches long. Then make one cut $15\frac{5}{8}$ inches from the left end to form the seat (Detail B). Allowing for the kerf cuts, the seat should measure $21\frac{3}{8}$ inches. If there is a discrepancy, trim it to this size.

Set the seat aside, and dowel and glue the remaining piece to the rear strip (Detail C). Trim the L-shaped piece to size, then cut a rabbet for the rear panel. Place the rabbet along the bottom rear edge. Add the right end piece, securing it with two dowels as indicated (Detail D). Trim the seat in length so it has about $1/8$-inch clearance at each end.

Cut and install the seat cleats along the ends and rear of the seat opening. Allow the cleats to project into the seat area $3/8$ inch all around. Then cut and install the fastening cleats to hold the frame and side members to the top. Secure the members with flat-head screws.

Cut the backrest to size and shape it at the ends with a saber saw. Carefully lay out the spindle spacing along the bottom edge of the backrest. Then transfer the marks to the rear edge of the top frame. Bore the blind holes to take the spindle tenons. The hole diameter and depth will depend on the spindles used.

To give the armrest thickness at the end, glue a piece of stock as indicated. After gluing, round it with a coping saw or band saw if one is available. A saber saw won't work because of the width of the piece.

The corner post should be on hand before you bore its mounting holes. When installed, the corner post and spindles should be exposed equally.

Cut the parts for the telephone holder from 1⅛-inch stock. Counterbore the ½-inch-diameter button holes ¼ inch deep, then bore the screw-clearance holes clear through. Bevel the bottom edge of the front panel to an angle of 10 degrees. Use a table saw for this step and be sure to do it before you shape the top edge.

When it is assembled, fasten the telephone shelf to the bench top with screws driven from the underside of the top and through the lower edge of the backrest.

Dowel and glue the door frame, then cut the rabbets for the door frame and raised panel with a router. Cut the door frame rabbets only along the sides. Do not rabbet the top and bottom edges of the door.

Make the raised panels on the table saw by tilting the blade 15 degrees. Let the blade project 1⅜ inches and make a trial cut on scrap lumber before raising the panels.

The panels should be made from glue-up stock to prevent them from cupping.

Make them with a ⅛-inch clearance at the ends to allow for expansion. To hold them, use turn button retainers only, not glue. The retainers will hold the panels securely but permit movement resulting from weather conditions. (The panels will be shorter in cool, dry weather and longer in hot humid weather.)

Fasten the door with double-bend non-mortise hinges, which are especially designed for cabinet doors and do not require mortising. The door catch is a novel magnetic type. It is fully adjustable and simply snaps into two predrilled holes in the divider.

Cut the strip hinge to size and install it with the top edge flush with the seat top. Install all other hardware at this time, then remove and sand the work thoroughly.

Finish the piece as desired. We used walnut stain and three topcoats of lacquer. We followed with a final application of rubbing compound.

Grandfather Clock

IF YOU HAVE WANTED a grandfather's clock, but have been deterred from buying one because of the expense, try building one yourself. This design can be executed for much less than a comparable store model. It has all of the traditional styling of a grandfather's clock and yet is designed with economy and simplicity of construction in mind.

You can choose almost any kind of wood for this clock—either solid lumber or birch, maple, pine, or mahogany plywood. The moldings are stock items found in lumberyards everywhere.

Construction is much simpler than it might seem from the appearance of the finished item. The major tool used is a table saw, but a router is helpful if you have one.

Start with the back panel, which can be considered the backbone of the clock. It is a simple rectangle that measures 10½ × 69 inches, and it is cut from ¾-inch stock. Attach the top and bottom back panel tabs as shown in the drawing. Use finishing nails, and coat the mating surfaces with glue. Be sure to sink nailheads below the surface.

Cut out the lower shelf and lower sides, and nail and glue them in place. Then install the floor, floor cleats, and base sides. With the exception of the lower shelf, these pieces are all simple rectangles.

Be sure all mating parts are square with each other as you go along.

Make up the front panel, rabbeting the edges as shown in the drawing. Next cut out the base front, mortise its edges, and glue and nail it in place. Install the nosing molding using miter joints at the corner. This completes the lower section of the clock.

Next cut out and install both the waist sides. Use screws to attach them to the back panel, and to the lower shelf. Use glue, of course, on all mating surfaces.

Cut out and install the upper sides and upper shelf. You can glue and nail the roof cleats in place at this time. Note that the side roof cleats do not extend to the forward edges of the upper side panels. Cut out and install the upper and lower waist headers.

Next, cut out the upper front. Trace the opening from a full-size pattern or use the dial itself as a guide. Since there are slight

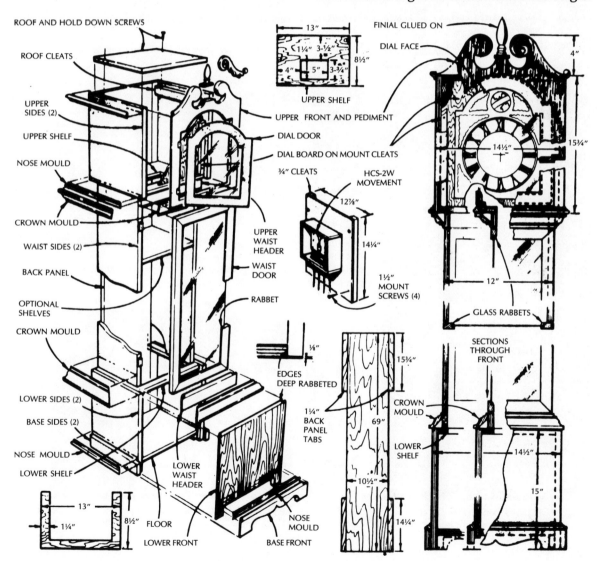

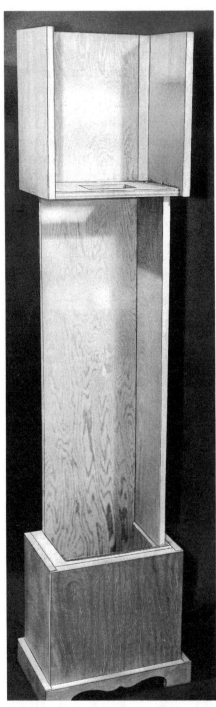

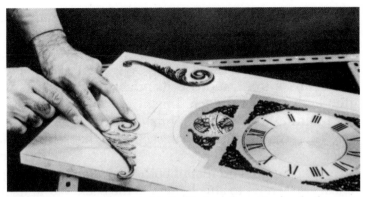

Fig. 21-2. You can use the dial plate itself to trace the cutting line for the opening. Because of slight variations in carvings, trace the form of the top from pediment carvings.

Fig. 21-3. All of the pieces making up the lower section are simple rectangles, except for the lower shelf, which is a U shape. Rabbet the front piece, and butt-join the rest.

Fig. 21-1. The back panel is the backbone on which the other sections are built. Note the deep rabbeting of the lower front panel.

Fig. 21-4. Slip the dial board with clock mechanism into place from the top of the clock. This movement is operated by weights, although electric movement will work equally well.

144

MATERIALS LIST

Purpose	Size	Description	Quantity
Back panel	$\frac{3}{4}'' \times 10\frac{1}{2}'' \times 69''$	Lumber of choice	1
Upper back panel tabs	$\frac{3}{4}'' \times 1\frac{1}{4}'' \times 15\frac{3}{4}''$	Lumber of choice	2
Lower back panel tabs	$\frac{3}{4}'' \times 1\frac{1}{4}'' \times 15''$	Lumber of choice	2
Base sides	$\frac{3}{4}'' \times 2\frac{5}{8}'' \times 10\frac{11}{16}''$	Lumber of choice	2
Base front	$\frac{3}{4}'' \times 2\frac{5}{8}'' \times 16''$	Lumber of choice	1
Lower sides	$\frac{3}{4}'' \times 9\frac{15}{16}'' \times 15''$	Lumber of choice	2
Lower front	$\frac{3}{4}'' \times 14\frac{1}{2}'' \times 15''$	Lumber of choice	1
Upper front	$\frac{3}{4}'' \times 14\frac{1}{2}'' \times 19\frac{9}{16}''$	Lumber of choice	1
Upper sides	$\frac{3}{4}'' \times 9\frac{15}{16}'' \times 15\frac{3}{4}''$	Lumber of choice	2
Waist sides	$\frac{3}{4}'' \times 8'' \times 38\frac{1}{4}''$	Lumber of choice	2
Waist headers	$\frac{3}{4}'' \times 2\frac{1}{16}'' \times 12''$	Lumber of choice	2
Shelves, roof and floor	$\frac{3}{4}'' \times 8\frac{1}{2}'' \times 13''$	Lumber of choice	4
Roof side	$\frac{3}{4}'' \times 1\frac{1}{2}'' \times 5\frac{3}{4}''$	Cleats	2
Roof rear	$\frac{3}{4}'' \times 1\frac{1}{2}'' \times 13''$	Cleats	1
Dial board	$\frac{3}{4}'' \times \frac{3}{4}'' \times 14\frac{1}{4}''$	Cleats	2
Floor, rear	$\frac{3}{4}'' \times 1\frac{1}{2}'' \times 13''$	Cleats	1
Floor, side	$\frac{3}{4}'' \times 1\frac{1}{2}'' \times 7\frac{3}{4}''$	Cleats	2
Dial board	$\frac{3}{8}'' \times 12\frac{7}{8}'' \times 14\frac{1}{4}''$	Lumber of choice	1
Dial door	$\frac{3}{4}'' \times 12'' \times 15''$	Lumber of choice	1
Waist door	$\frac{3}{4}'' \times 12'' \times 34''$	Lumber of choice	1
Dial door	$\frac{1}{8}'' \times 9\frac{1}{8}'' \times 12\frac{3}{8}''$	Glass	1
Waist door	$\frac{1}{8}'' \times 9\frac{1}{8}'' \times 31\frac{1}{8}''$	Glass	1
Crown molding	$2\frac{1}{2}'' \times 7'$	As needed	
Nosing molding	$\frac{3}{4}'' \times 9'$	As needed	
Final	$1''$ dia. $\times 3\frac{1}{2}''$		
Final base	$\frac{1}{4}'' \times 1'' \times 1\frac{5}{8}''$		
Dial	$10'' \times 13''$		

Note: Also need clock movement, pediment carvings, base carving, hardware, glue, etc.

variations in carvings, use the pediment carvings themselves to establish your cutting line. When you have cut out the front and sanded it smooth, glue the carvings to the front. Be sure to allow the outer edges of the carvings to extend beyond the sides slightly so they will blend with the upper nosing molding when it is installed.

Now you can mount the front of the clock, nailing it and gluing it in place. Install upper and lower crown molding next, then the finial at the top of the clock. These corners must be mitered at a 45-degree angle.

With the addition of the upper nosing molding, the basic clock structure is complete. At this time, however, you can add shelves, if you are using an electric clock movement.

Now make up the dial board. Be sure the hole for the hands is centered exactly. Glue the dial itself on the front of the panel, and mount the movement on the back. Slip the dial board into place from the top of the clock, and fasten it in place with four 1½-inch screws. Then fasten the roof in place. Use screws but not glue, since this will be the only access to the clock works.

Next, make up the dial and waist doors. They can be of ¾-inch stock, with the inner edges rabbeted as shown in the detail drawing or with two layers of ⅜-inch stock. If you use the latter method, cut one piece to full size for each door. For the waist door, cut the second piece to the full outside dimension, but ¼ inch narrower around the inside. For the dial door, cut the second piece so that it fits easily inside the upper front panel. Its inner cutout should be ¼ inch narrower than the first door piece.

When the two pieces of each door are glued together, you will have a ¼-inch lip running around the inside edge, against which the door glass rests. It is recommended that you have the glass cut to the proper shape by a glass dealer, unless you are experienced in this type of work. When the glass is installed, use ¼-inch quarter-round stock to hold it in place.

Next, mortise for the hinges and install the doors so they fit flush against the waist and upper front. Finally, check all the joints, and set any nailheads that protrude. Fill the depressions with wood putty, and you are ready to apply the finish. If you have an open-grained wood, use a paste wood filler before staining. Your local paint dealer is your best source on fillers, stains, and coatings.

Hutch Bookcase

THIS ELEGANT BOOKCASE is easily made with ordinary tools. No lathe is needed, since the two gracefully turned legs are store bought. This unit is made of ash wood, but any wood may be substituted. Ash is similar to oak. Both are hardwoods and take a beautiful finish.

The base and upper hutch top are made as two separate pieces to facilitate

construction and make the piece more mobile. The front apron is not a drawer; the pull is merely decorative.

Start with the base piece. Cut the boards for the top and lower shelf. They must be glued up to obtain the necessary width. If you have a shaper, you can use a glue-joint cutter to form the sections; otherwise use butt joints and dowels. Reverse every other piece to prevent warping of the large, flat surfaces. If you use dowels, they should be the spiral-grooved type 2 inches long.

Use a good furniture glue and clamp the parts securely until the glue sets. Cut the lower shelf with square edges. Shape the upper piece on three edges with a router. Before shaping, however, sand the surface to remove any unevenness at the glue line. A belt sander is ideal for this operation. If you are using a hardwood, start with a medium-grit paper then finish with a fine grit. If you are working with a softwood such as pine, use care not to gouge out the surface. Raise and lower the tool squarely.

Cut the apron pieces next, grooving them as shown. You can cut the groove square by using a table saw. Set the blade to protrude ⅛ inch above the table and adjust the fence ¾-inch from the blade. If you use a router, use the router fence to locate the groove. Use a V-cutter.

Miter the lower front aprons at the corners. There are several ways to join the miters. The spline is the most practical, and can be steel or wood. Wood splines can be cut from a piece of ⅛-inch plywood.

147

Steel splines called *clamp nails* are readily available. They are driven into 22-gauge kerf cuts and are designed to tightly close the joint since they are driven with a hammer. Clamps are not required.

After the lower apron pieces have been mitered, cut the rabbet along the top inner edge. This rabbet will support the lower shelf. You can make the rabbet using a router or by making two passes on the table saw. Either method works well.

Fasten the shelf to the apron using tabletop fasteners. These Z-shaped steel brackets pull the joints tightly because they are screwed into place. They simply rest in a groove cut ½-inch from the apron edge. Normally they are used to pull the top down tightly. In this instance, however, they are also used to draw the rabbet joint tightly against the edge of the shelf. To accomplish this, cut a second groove on the underside of the top. (See drawing.)

Assemble the lower apron first, using dowels at the rear and clamp nails at the front on the mitered corners. Apply glue into the rabbet cut, then lower the shelf into place. Install the fasteners and draw them tight with round head screws.

Now cut the legs. Make the turned legs of 3-inch stock. If you purchase them ready-made, be sure to use 24-inch lengths. They have sufficient blocks at the ends, which can be trimmed. Make the rear legs from square or glued-up blocks. Rabbet one corner in each block to take the ¼-inch rear panel. Cut the turned legs so there will be 5 inches at the top block and 5 inches at the lower end.

Drill ⅜-inch-diameter holes into the ends of all the apron pieces. Drill corresponding holes into the legs. This task is easily done with the use of dowel centers. Drill the corresponding holes into the legs. Join the legs to the short aprons. Use a

Fig. 22-1. The two front corners of the base require miter joints. Use clamp nails, which will close the joint tightly. Use a hammer to drive the clamp nail into the 22-gauge saw-cut slot, which is ⁹⁄₃₂-inch deep.

Fig. 22-2. With the base and post assembly upside down, drill the lag screw holes through the base and into the post ends. Then insert the lag screws and, with a socket wrench, screw the lower shelf tightly to the corner posts.

Fig. 22-3. (left) The top and bottom of the bookshelf side have curves. Trace them from kraft paper with a grid of 1-inch squares. You can use either a band saw or saber saw to make these cuts.

Fig. 22-4. (bottom left) The blind dadoes in the bookcase sides can be made with either a router or a table saw with cutter head. If you use a table saw, lower the work onto the revolving blade, tilting the board as shown.

Fig. 22-5. Detail of a blind dado: If you use a router, make the cut with several passes, instead of attempting the full cut in one pass. The two spiral dowels will join the bookshelf side to the backboard. (bottom right)

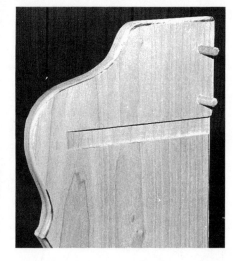

block of wood under the hammer to protect the surface of the leg. Use ⅜- × -2-inch spiral dowels.

Clamp till the glue sets, then repeat for the longer apron pieces. Fasten the top with the Z brackets. The lower shelf to the legs with 2-inch lag screws using a washer under each lag screw head. Sand the assembly.

Make the bookcase from solid stock. If you cannot obtain good, flat lumber of sufficient width, glue up two or more pieces. Lay out the outline for the shape at the top and bottom, then cut with a band saw or saber saw. Use a router to round off the outer edges, and follow with the dado cuts. Cut the two lower dadoes full length, but blind-cut the top dadoes.

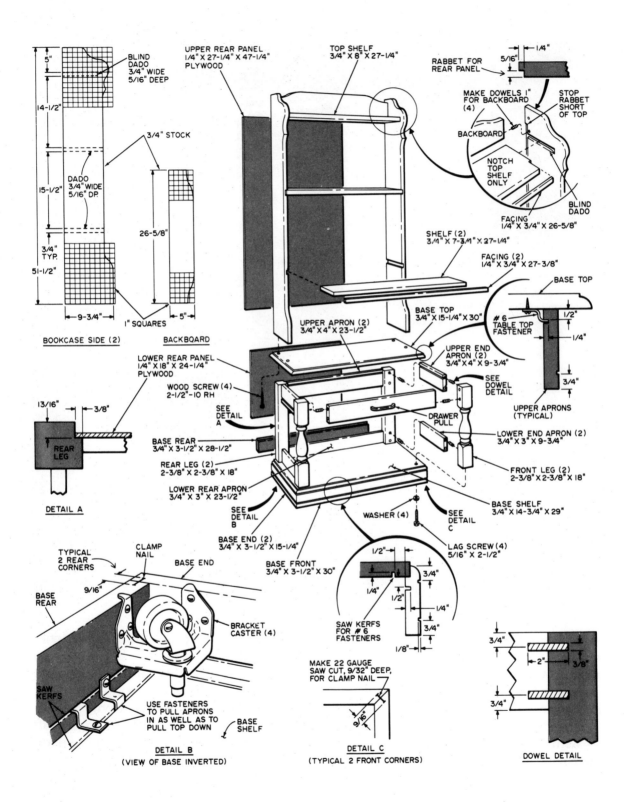

MATERIALS LIST

Purpose	Size	Description	Quantity
Bookcase side	¾" × 9¾" × 51½"	Ash	2
Backboard	¾" × 5" × 26⅝"	Ash	1
Top shelf	¾" × 8" × 27¼"	Ash	1
Center and lower shelf	¾" × 7¾" × 27¼"	Ash	2
Facing	¼" × ¾" × 27¼"	Ash	2
Base, top	¾" × 15¼" × 30"	Ash	1
Apron, upper	¾" × 4" × 23½"	Ash	2
Apron, upper end	¾" × 4" × 9¾"	Ash	2
Leg, front	2⅜" × 2⅜" × 18"		2
Leg, rear	2⅜" × 2⅜" × 18"		2
Apron, lower rear	¾" × 3" × 23½"	Ash	1
Apron, lower end	¾" × 3" × 9¾"	Ash	2
Base shelf	¾" × 14¾" × 29"	Ash	1
Base end	¾" × 3½" × 15¼"	Ash	2
Base front	¾" × 3½" × 30"	Ash	1
Base rear	¾" × 3½" × 28½"	Ash	1
Rear panel, upper	¼" × 27¼" × 47¼"	Plywood	1
Rear panel, lower	¼" × 18" × 24¼"	Plywood	1
Clamp nails			4
Bracket casters	⅜" × 2"		44

Note: Should you have difficulty in obtaining the legs and casters locally, write to Armor Products.

You can make the dadoes on a table saw fitted with a dado blade, or you can use a router. If you use a router, do not attempt to cut the full depth of the dado in one pass. Take several shallow cuts until the full depth is achieved. You will need to use side guides to keep the router "on course."

If you use a table saw, cut the blind dado by lowering the work on the revolving blade. Tilt the board as shown. Make several trial cuts on scrap pieces to determine where to start the cut.

When all the dadoes have been cut, make the shelf pieces and install them by gluing. Also dowel and install the backboard at this time. While the glue sets, clamp the assembly, making certain that it is perfectly aligned. Check with a square, and add a couple of diagonal cleats at the rear edge to keep it square while the glue sets.

Cut the shelves so that they are flush with the sides (except for the top one). After they are in place, add the face strip to each shelf. Make the two lower strips to extend past the length of the shelf, but make the top face strip the same length as the shelf.

Cut the rear panels for the upper and lower sections and install with panelling nails, which are ring grooved and will hold tightly.

If you wish to make the unit mobile, add concealed casters with self-locating corner brackets. If you use a prefinished panel for the rear, apply finish material to the pieces before you install the rear panel. We used Beverly's provincial satin stain and several coats of clear lacquer.

Library Wall Cabinet

LIBRARY UNITS ARE ALWAYS USEFUL, whether they are used in single or double units, or to line an entire wall. They are attractive and functional pieces, offering shelves above for books and curios, and storage cabinets below. Each unit is easily constructed and butt joints are used throughout. With the exception of the door panels and decorative arched valance, all cutting is straight and simple. Some router work is involved and some ready-made molding is used.

We kept the cost of building this cabinet way down by using common pine and Lauan paneling. The Lauan was used for the rear of the cabinet and also as a backup for the doors. Finished in antique green, the unit couldn't look any better even if it had been made of rock maple.

Start by cutting the sides, top, and bottom as indicated. Before assembling the parts, cut the rabbet along one edge to form the recess for the back panel. Size the edge grain of the top and bottom sections by thinning the glue slightly with water. Let the glue dry about 15 minutes, then apply glue in the normal manner and assemble the sections. Use galvanized finishing nails and clamps, if available. Be sure to work on a level floor and keep the frame square as the glue sets. If necessary, temporarily fasten diagonal cleats to hold the frame plumb.

You can now cut and install the shelves. Treat the edge grain as outlined previously. Round the front edges of the

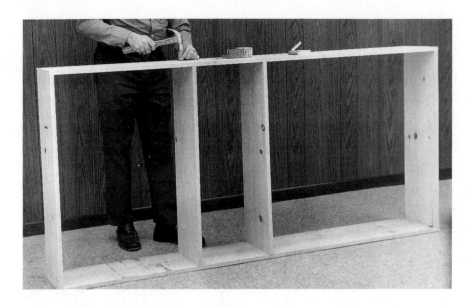

Fig. 23-1. Assemble the cabinet frame using butt joints, which greatly simplify the construction. Use glue and galvanized nails.

Fig. 23-2. Assemble the door stiles and rails with dowels, then attach them to ¼-inch panel, along with the raised center piece.

Fig. 23-3. Make the valance by blocking up a piece of 1-×-12 stock. Use a saber saw to cut the curves and shape the edge with a router.

153

three upper shelves after you install them. The cabinet sides serve as a stop for the router, thus allowing the rounding off to stop short of the front frame.

Add the front framing next. Attach one vertical first, then the crosspieces, followed by the second vertical. This method will ensure a good tight joint.

You can add the door divider at this time. Be sure to center it accurately.

To make the valance, we blocked up a piece of 1- x -12-inch stock, although it could have been cut from a single 1- x -18-inch piece. For economy, it is wiser to block up the ends. Leave the length of the valance oversize and cut it to fit after

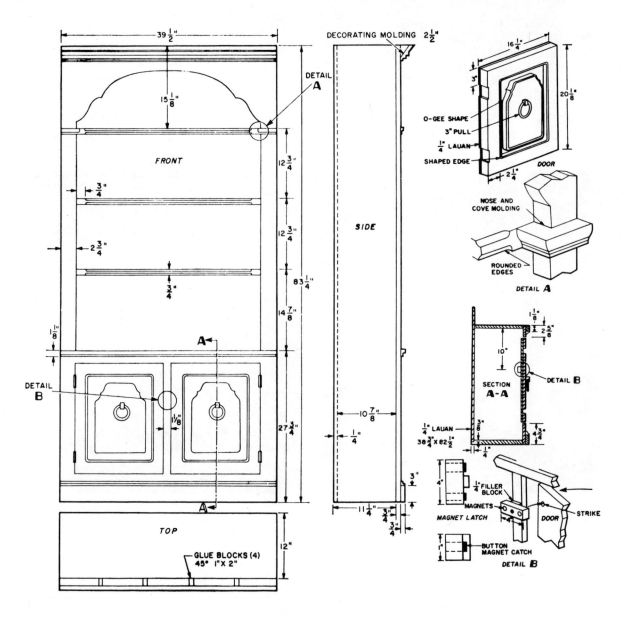

the blocks have been glued. Use a saber saw to cut the arched curve, then shape the edge with a router.

To build out the main shelf (above the doors) add a filler strip and the front overhang. Cut the overhang $1\frac{1}{8}$ inches deep to give the shelf a heavy look. Next, add moldings; apply it with glue and brads. Miter the small molding (at the top shelf) at the inside corners. Mount the top molding (cornice) at an angle. To support it, install small glue blocks.

Doors are of simple construction. Cut stiles and rails to size and assemble them with dowels, using two dowels per corner. Clamps must be used here for a good glue joint. When the frame is glued, shape the inner edges, then attach the back board, which is cut from a piece of $\frac{1}{4}$-inch plywood. Glue the center section of the door to the $\frac{1}{4}$-inch panel. To prevent the cen-

ter from shifting, drive a few small brads into it from rear.

Set hinges into the door, but mount them flush on the side panels. You can cut hinge clearance in the doors several ways. You can use a chisel, router, or table saw. The table-saw method is fast and the results are very good. Measure the thickness of the hinge when closed, the allow the saw blade to protrude $\frac{1}{16}$ inch less than the hinge thickness. For example, if the hinge measures $\frac{3}{16}$ inch thick when closed, let the table-saw blade protrude $\frac{1}{8}$ inch. Mark the hinge positions on the door, and using the miter gauge, make a series of cuts between the marks to clean out the area. Install magnetic door catches or bullet catches, as desired.

Cut the rear panel to size, but do not install it until after applying the finish material, since it is much easier to work this

MATERIALS LIST

Purpose	Size	Description	Quantity
Shelves	$\frac{3}{4}" \times 10\frac{7}{8}" \times 38"$	Pine	6
Sides	$\frac{3}{4}" \times 10\frac{7}{8}" \times 83\frac{1}{4}"$	Pine	2
Valance	$\frac{3}{4}" \times 15\frac{1}{8}" \times 39\frac{1}{2}"$	Pine	1
Base	$\frac{3}{4}" \times 3" \times 39\frac{1}{2}"$	Pine	1
Vertical	$\frac{3}{4}" \times 2\frac{3}{4}" \times 68\frac{1}{8}"$	Pine	2
Filler	$\frac{3}{4}" \times 2\frac{5}{8}" \times 34"$	Pine	1
Overhang	$\frac{3}{4}" \times 1\frac{1}{8}" \times 39\frac{1}{2}"$	Pine	1
Bottom	$\frac{3}{4}" \times 4\frac{3}{4}" \times 34"$	Pine	1
Door divider	$\frac{3}{4}" \times 1\frac{1}{8}" \times 20\frac{3}{8}"$	Pine	1
Rear panel	$\frac{1}{4}" \times 38\frac{3}{8}" \times 82\frac{1}{2}"$	Luan	1
Door rear	$\frac{1}{4}" \times 16\frac{1}{4}" \times 20\frac{1}{8}"$	Luan	2
Door rail	$\frac{3}{4}" \times 2\frac{1}{4}" \times 11\frac{3}{4}"$	Pine	4
Door panel	$\frac{3}{4}" \times 9\frac{7}{8}" \times 13\frac{1}{2}"$	Pine	2
Catch block	$\frac{3}{4}" \times 1" \times 4"$	Pine	1
Catch block	$\frac{1}{4}" \times 1" \times \frac{1}{8}"$	Luan	1
Molding	$\frac{3}{4}" \times 8"$	Nose and cove	8
Molding	$2\frac{1}{2}" \times 39\frac{1}{2}"$	Decorative	1

Note: Also need filler, glue, dowels, hardware, and finish coating.

way. Be sure to sink and fill all nailheads, then sand all surfaces until smooth.

When antiquing a large piece such as this, you might find it easier to work with an antiquing kit that has a latex base material. Latex will dry in a couple of hours, as opposed to the overnight dry required by oil-based materials.

Of course, you might want to stain or even leave the wood natural, with several coats of varnish or shellac. However you finish your library unit, we are sure you will be greatly pleased with it. Its design allows for expansion later if desired.

Mini Office

$\mathbf{H}$ERE'S A COMPACT MINI-OFFICE that packs a lot of punch. It's small enough to fit most anywhere and yet it holds a typewriter, office supplies, and a file drawer for all your important papers. When open, the top measures a full 22 × 36 inches. The cabinet stands 30¼ inches high and is 22 inches deep and 18 inches wide. The upper compartment serves as the storage area for the typewriter. A pull-out shelf supports the typewriter in use. The compartment door and drawers below have matching fronts with raised panels, which are easily made on the table saw. The drawers ride on double-track hardware, which eliminates sticking and ensures smooth, quiet operation.

Common pine was used for the prototype, but you can substitute whatever species you desire. Select boards that have a

pleasant grain and knot pattern. Unless you use plywood, you will need to glue up boards to make the necessary widths. Use dowels to strengthen the joints. A doweling jig will ensure accuracy in locating and drilling the dowel holes. Drill the ⅜-inch-diameter holes 1⅛ inches deep to allow sufficient clearance so that the joint will close tightly. Apply glue to half the length of the dowels, then drive them into the edge of the board. Apply a thin coat to both mating edges as well as the protruding dowels, then bring the parts together. Clamp securely and allow the glue to set. If you cut the boards slightly oversize in width, you won't need blocks under the clamps. Simply trim to size after removing the clamps.

Cut the rabbets and dadoes next. You can use a router or table saw for this operation. If you decide on the router, you will need to clamp guides on the workpiece. Use the widest router bit you have and make successive cuts until you achieve the proper depth and width. For cutting the dadoes and rabbets on the table saw, use a dado blade and bolt a ¾-inch wood strip to the fence. The wood strip keeps the dado blade safely away from the metal fence. Most fences are provided with holes for this purpose. Use flat-head bolts or round-head screws to fasten the board.

Cut the sides to their proper length (assuming you left them slightly oversize when gluing), then cut the dadoes. Make a trial cut on scrap to check the size. If it is all right, proceed to cut the dadoes. Cut the matching dadoes and rabbets for each fence setting.

Next cut the four horizontal sections. These are also made up of glued stock. Since they won't show, you can use stock of lesser quality. Be sure to cut the pieces square. Plane the front edge of each piece,

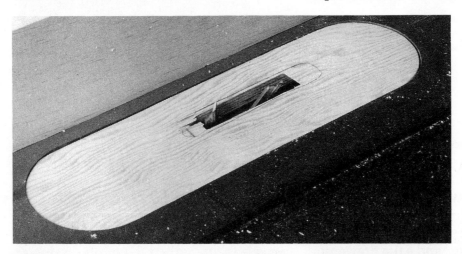

Fig. 24-1. Attaching a wood strip to a saw fence keeps the blade from the fence when rabbeting the ends. When hammering the dowel joints, use a piece of scrap wood to avoid marring the edges.

Fig. 24-2. Nail the subtop into place. It fits into the rabbets in side pieces.

Fig. 24-3. Fasten the strip hinge with flat-head screws.

MATERIALS LIST

Purpose	Size	Description	Quantity
Top	¾" × 18" × 18"	Pine	2
Subtop	¾" × 15½" × 21¾"	Pine	1
Side	¾" × 22" × 29½"	Pine	2
Crosspiece	¾" × 15½" × 21¾"	Pine	3
Base side	¾" × 3½" × 22"	Pine	2
Base front	¾" × 3½" × 18"	Pine	1
Drop leaf cleat	¾" × 1¼" × 16¾"	Pine	1
Molding	24"	Nose and cove	4 pcs.
Sliding shelf	¾" × 14⅞" × 20¾"	Pine	1
Shelf cleat	¾" × ¾" × 20¾"	Pine	2
Rear panel	¼" × 15½" × 26"	Plywood	1
Door front	¾" × 9" × 15⅜"	Pine	1
Door subfront	½" × 8⅜" × 14¾"	Pine	1
Drawer front	¾" × 4¼" × 15⅜"	Pine	1
Drawer subfront	½" × 3¼" × 12⅞"	Pine	1
Drawer side	½" × 3¼" × 20"	Pine	2
Drawer rear	½" × 2¾" × 12⅞"	Pine	1
Drawer front	¾" × 11⅜" × 15⅜"	Pine	1
Drawer subfront	½" × 10⅜" × 12⅞"	Pine	1
Drawer side	½" × 10⅜" × 20"	Pine	2
Drawer rear	½" × 9⅞" × 12⅞"	Pine	1
Drawer bottom	¼" × 12⅞" × 19¾"	Plywood	2
Strip hinge	1" × 22"		1
Buttons			4
Magnetic catch			1
Offset hinges			1 pair
Drawer slides			2 pair
Pulls			3
Knob			1
Screws	1½" 10 RH (stops)		4
Screws	1¼" 8 FH (cleats)		8

then check the fit with the dadoes cut in the side panels. If the pieces are badly bowed, you might need to cut a groove through the center to straighten them. Cut the groove on the table saw and make it about ½ inch deep. This groove will weaken the piece until it is assembled but once in place, the groove will have no effect on the strength of the piece. Be sure to keep the groove on the underside. Apply a thin coat of glue to the edge grain of the compartment dividers (horizontal pieces) and allow to dry.

If you have sufficient clamps, you can glue up the assembly without nails or screws. Otherwise you can use nails or screws to hold the parts while the glue sets. Drive nails or screws diagonally from the underside of each divider, except for the top one, which can be fastened through the top as shown.

Make the top by gluing up several pieces of stock with a pleasing grain appearance. Knots are permissible, but they should be tight and not too large. The length of the pieces should be at least 38 inches so you have sufficient stock for trimming later. Use dowels, as for the other sections. If you use a doweling jig, be sure to always align the tool from the same side to ensure perfect alignment and accuracy

Fig. 24-4. Make the drawers of ½-inch stock, except for the bottoms which are ¼-inch plywood. Cut the pieces to size, and assemble with glue and finishing nails. Drill the screw and clearance holes before assembly.

of the holes even if there is a slight variation in the lumber thickness.

After you have glued the top, cut the piece in half then trim the ends so that each piece will be 18 inches wide. Plane or join all edges. Do not mount the top at this time.

Construct the door and drawer fronts next. Cut them with a raised panel edge. First cut the doors to size, then bevel the edges on the table saw. Set the blade to a 15-degree tilt, then adjust the fence to produce the bevel. Make trial cuts on scrap the same thickness as the fronts. A planer blade is recommended for this cut. It will leave a smooth clean bevel. The saw blade will leave a small triangular edge, which you should remove by recutting the pieces with the blade tilt set to 0 degrees and projecting about ⅛ inch. Set the fence as required and trim each piece. Again, make trial cuts on the scrap previously cut.

The upper compartment contains a door; the others are drawers. The door has a subfront, to which the hinges are attached. Cut this from ½-inch pine. Drill a clearance hole ½ inch in diameter for the pull screw head. Drill the screw body hole ¼ inch in diameter into the front panel. Attach the front and subfront with glue and brads. Then install hinges. Use 2-inch semiconcealed nonmortise hinges, and mount as shown.

Make the drawers next. The sides, rear and subfront are ½-inch pine. The bottoms are ¼-inch plywood. Cut the pieces to size, then assemble with glue and finishing nails. Make the grooves, dadoes, and rabbets on a table saw or with a router. Drill the screw and clearance holes before assembly, as you did for the door.

Add the strip hinge next. Place both halves of the top on a flat surface, with the

160

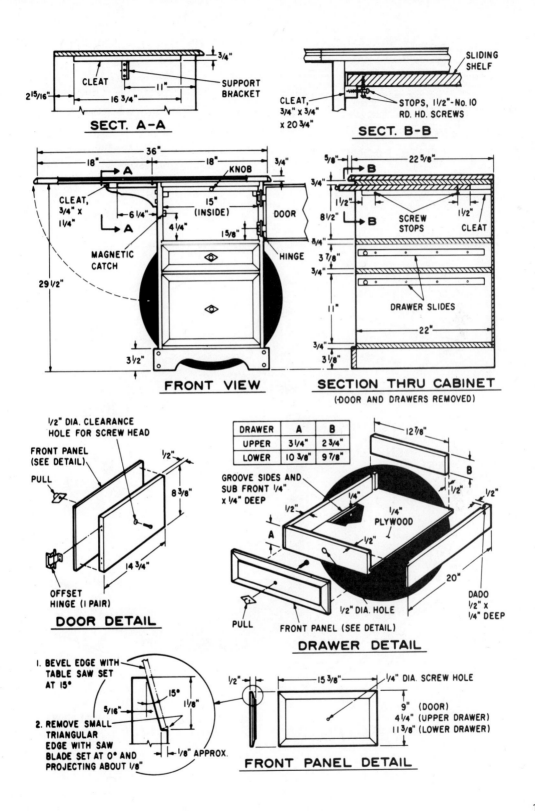

SECT. A-A

3/4"

CLEAT

SUPPORT BRACKET

2 15/16"

16 3/4"

11"

SECT. B-B

SLIDING SHELF

CLEAT, 3/4" x 3/4" x 20 3/4"

STOPS, 1 1/2"-No. 10 RD. HD. SCREWS

FRONT VIEW

36"

18"

18"

3/4"

A

KNOB

CLEAT, 3/4" x 1 1/4"

6 1/4"

4 1/4"

15" (INSIDE)

1 5/8"

DOOR

MAGNETIC CATCH

A

HINGE

29 1/2"

3 1/2"

SECTION THRU CABINET

(DOOR AND DRAWERS REMOVED)

5/8"

22 5/8"

B

3/4"

1 1/2"

8 1/2"

B

SCREW STOPS

1 1/2"

CLEAT

3/4"

3 7/8"

3/4"

DRAWER SLIDES

11"

22"

3/4"

3 1/8"

DOOR DETAIL

1/2" DIA. CLEARANCE HOLE FOR SCREW HEAD

FRONT PANEL (SEE DETAIL)

1/2"

PULL

8 3/8"

14 3/4"

OFFSET HINGE (1 PAIR)

DRAWER DETAIL

DRAWER	A	B
UPPER	3 1/4"	2 3/4"
LOWER	10 3/8"	9 7/8"

12 7/8"

B

GROOVE SIDES AND SUB FRONT 1/4" x 1/4" DEEP

1/4"

1/2"

1/2"

1/4" PLYWOOD

A

1/2"

1/2"

1/2"

20"

DADO 1/2" x 1/4" DEEP

PULL

FRONT PANEL (SEE DETAIL)

1/2" DIA. HOLE

1. BEVEL EDGE WITH TABLE SAW SET AT 15°

15°

5/16"

1 1/8"

2. REMOVE SMALL TRIANGULAR EDGE WITH SAW BLADE SET AT 0° AND PROJECTING ABOUT 1/8"

1/8" APPROX.

FRONT PANEL DETAIL

1/2"

15 3/8"

1/4" DIA. SCREW HOLE

9" (DOOR)
4 1/4" (UPPER DRAWER)
11 3/8" (LOWER DRAWER)

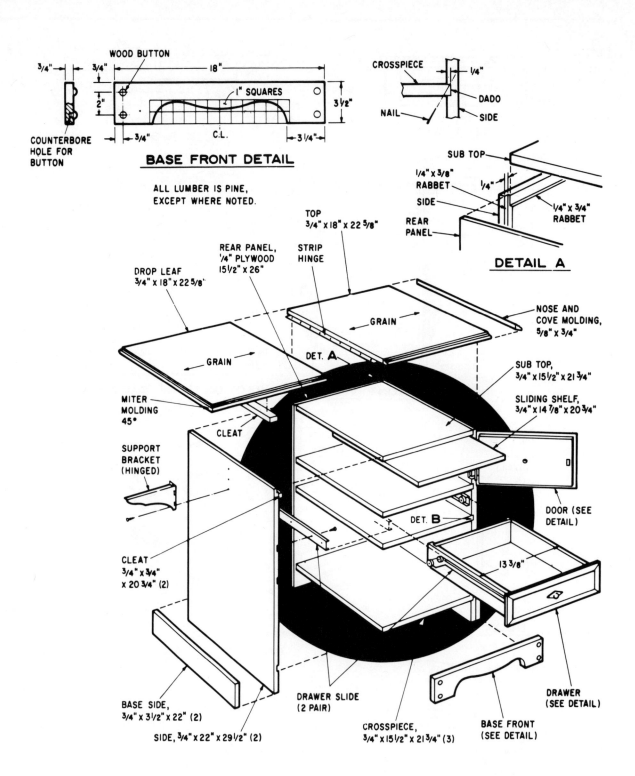

WOOD BUTTON

3/4"   3/4"   18"

2"   1" SQUARES

3 1/2"

COUNTERBORE
HOLE FOR
BUTTON

3/4"   C.L.   3 1/4"

BASE FRONT DETAIL

ALL LUMBER IS PINE,
EXCEPT WHERE NOTED.

CROSSPIECE   1/4"

DADO

NAIL   SIDE

SUB TOP

1/4" x 3/8"
RABBET

1/4"

SIDE

REAR
PANEL

1/4" x 3/4"
RABBET

DETAIL A

TOP
3/4" x 18" x 22 5/8"

REAR PANEL,
1/4" PLYWOOD
15 1/2" x 26"

STRIP
HINGE

DROP LEAF
3/4" x 18" x 22 5/8"

GRAIN

DET. A

GRAIN

NOSE AND
COVE MOLDING,
5/8" x 3/4"

SUB TOP,
3/4" x 15 1/2" x 21 3/4"

SLIDING SHELF,
3/4" x 14 7/8" x 20 3/4"

MITER
MOLDING
45°

CLEAT

SUPPORT
BRACKET
(HINGED)

DET. B

DOOR (SEE
DETAIL)

CLEAT
3/4" x 3/4"
x 20 3/4" (2)

13 3/8"

BASE SIDE,
3/4" x 3 1/2" x 22" (2)

SIDE, 3/4" x 22" x 29 1/2" (2)

DRAWER SLIDE
(2 PAIR)

CROSSPIECE,
3/4" x 15 1/2" x 21 3/4" (3)

BASE FRONT
(SEE DETAIL)

DRAWER
(SEE DETAIL)

bottom side facing up. Abut the pieces carefully, then position the hinge and mark the hole centers. Install only the four corner and two center screws. Check the fit. If the fit is all right, install the balance of the screws.

You can now join the top to the cabinet. Leave it on the flat surface and carefully place the cabinet in place on it. Center it from side to side. Mount the rear edges of the top and cabinet flush. Mount the top with glue and screws. A few nails driven first before screwing will ensure that the top will not shift during assembly.

Next mount the drop-leaf support bracket. Use three flat-head screws. The bracket will be properly positioned if you install it with the cabinet upside down on a flat surface. The bracket is made to fold flat when the leaf is down. Install a bracket support cleat on the bottom side of the lid as shown.

The shelf for the typewriter is made to slide snugly between the underside of the top and two cleats. To prevent the shelf from being pulled out too far, mount stops, consisting of round-head screws, as shown.

You must remove drawer hardware, pulls, and hinges when applying the finish. *Note:* You can leave the strip hinge on, but take care not to paint or stain it.

Seal the wood with a penetrating sealer, then apply stain as desired. We used clear Firzite diluted 50 percent to be used as a sealer, then a coat of Ethan Allen dark pine stain. When the stain has dried, follow with a coat of Sapolin dark walnut stain. This combination gives one of the finest pine stain finishes we have ever seen. Follow with two coats of Deft clear satin finish.

The drop-leaf bracket and nonmortise hinges should be available locally. If not, write to Armor Products.

Oak Server with Easy-Pull Extension

THIS ATTRACTIVE SERVER features a sturdy pull-out extension leaf, which increases the top surface almost 50 percent when fully extended. When not in use, the leaf slides back into its compartment, where it is completely concealed. A pair of magnetic latches are concealed in the compartment below the top of the server, and allows the lead to be slid in and out with an easy touch.

To use the extension leaf, just push quickly against the edge of the leaf to release the spring-loaded latches. The end of the leaf pops out several inches, and the extension can be pulled out as far as desired. The leaf is made of inexpensive plywood topped with plastic laminate for a durable, stain-resistant surface. We used black slate laminate, which contrasts handsomely with the golden oak. It is also an ideal material for trouble-free serving, since it is unaffected by water, alcohol, or other liquids.

Construction begins with the case, which consists of three frame sections: two ends and the front. They are assembled with glue and dowels to form the main part of the unit. Cut all parts to size first, as shown in the Materials List.

The lumber used was nominal 1-inch red oak, which is actually $^{13}/_{16}$ inch. If you prefer to use another wood, be sure to check the actual dressed thickness of the lumber. Most nominally 1-inch softwood, for example, are ¾ inch. Alter these plans to reflect the difference, if necessary.

The thinner of the two end stiles at the front are not the same width. Cut out the scallop at the lower edge of the bottom rails as shown, then drill the dowel holes with ⅜ inch diameter and 1¹⁄₁₆ inches deep. A doweling jig is recommended to ensure that the holes will be centered and drilled straight. After drilling the four holes in each rail, use dowel centers to transfer the hole locations to the mating stiles. Now drill the two holes in each stile, also ⅜ × 1¹⁄₁₆ inches.

Check the fit of the parts, using undersize dowels. You can make them by sanding regular dowels until they slide easily into the holes. Make sure that the parts have been drilled accurately and that the pieces will assemble properly when glue and regular dowels are used.

Disassemble the stiles and rails, then cut ¼- × -¼-inch rabbets along the inner edges to take the end panel. The rabbet cuts on the rails should run from end to end. On the stiles, however, they should extend slightly past the rabbet cut in the rails to allow the ¼-inch panel to fit in the corners.

You can now permanently assemble the end frames using glue and ⅜- × -2-inch spiral dowels. Clamp with bar or pipe clamps, protecting the edges of the work with strips of wood under the clamp jaws. Allow the glue to set as directed by the

Fig. 25-1. Groove the three frame members along the top edge on the table saw to accept the tabletop fasteners.

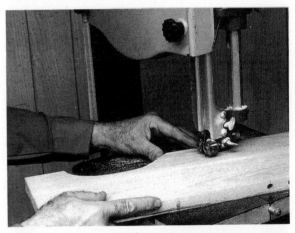

Fig. 25-2. The front rail being cut on the band saw. Save the excess wood from this operation for use in the next step.

Fig. 25-3. Assemble the subtop to the frame with tabletop fasteners. Cut grooves in the frame to accept fasteners.

Fig. 25-4. Cut glass to fit doors. Use screw-type glass holders to hold the glass and grilles on the front doors.

manufacturer—at least overnight—before removing the clamps.

The front frame consists of two rails, two stiles, and a center divider. First scallop the bottom rail as shown. Save the scrap piece to make clamping easier and to protect the wood. Following the same procedure used for the end frames, locate and drill the dowel holes. (Note that these members are not rabbeted.) Assemble the center post and rails first, after making a trial fit as described previously. Apply glue

to the mating parts, insert the dowels, then clamp securely as before. When the glue has set, remove the clamp, then add the two stiles and clamp until unit is dry. Be sure to check that pieces are square and, if necessary, adjust before the glue sets.

Now groove the three frame members along the top edge to accept the tabletop fasteners. Use a table saw for this operation. Set the fence to bring the blade ½ inch from the edge. Adjust the blade height so it protrudes ¼ inch above the table, then

Fig. 25-5. This view of the extension shows how to install the magnetic latches and strikers. Check for smooth operation.

Fig. 25-6. Miter the nose molding and attach it with glue and brads. There should be a recess in the top above the molding.

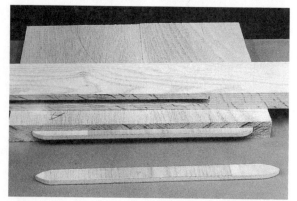

Fig. 25-7. Cut splines from ¼-inch plywood. Then shape the ends so they conform to the shape of the blind groove.

Fig. 25-8. Fit the router with an ogee cutter to shape the door cutout and all the edges at the front of the doors.

MATERIALS LIST

Purpose	Size	Description	Quantity
Top	1″ × 18″ × 35½″	Oak	1
Top frame, front	1″ × 3⅜″ × 36″	Oak	1
Top frame, rear	1″ × 2½″ × 36″	Oak	1
Top frame, left	1″ × 3½″ × 12½″	Oak	1
Leaf	¾″ × 12″ × 28¼″	Fir plywood	1
Leaf trim	⅛″ × ¹³⁄₁₆″ × 26″	Oak	2
Leaf end	1″ × 2¼″ × 12⅜″	Oak	1
Leaf stop	³⁄₁₆″ × ¹³⁄₁₆″ × 2½″	Oak	2
Frame stop	⅛″ × ¹³⁄₁₆″ × 1½″	Oak	2
Leaf laminate	1″ × 12¼″ × 28¼″	Oak	1
Leaf support	¼″ × 13⅜″ × 31½″	Plywood	1
Support cleat	¾″ × 2¼″ × 11″	Pine	1
End stile, front	1″ × 1¹¹⁄₁₆″ × 31″	Oak	2
End stile, rear	1″ × 2½″ × 31″	Oak	2
End rail, upper	1″ × 3½″ × 12½″	Oak	2
End rail, lower	7½″ × 12½″	Oak	2
End panel	13″ × 19¾″ × ¼″	Oak plywood	2
Front divider	1″ × 2½″ × 20⁵⁄₁₆″	Oak	1
Front rail, upper	1″ × 2½″ × 29³⁄₁₆″	Oak	1
Front rail, lower	1″ × 2½″ × 29³⁄₁₆″	Oak	1
Front stile	1″ × 2½″ × 31¼″	Oak	2
Magnet support	1″ × 1¾″ × 2⅞″	Oak	1
Rear rail, upper	1″ × 2½″ × 32⅝″	Oak	1
Rear rail, lower	1″ × 2½″ × 32⅝″	Oak	1
Floor frame, front/rear	¾″ × 2¼″ × 32⅝″	Pine	2
Floor frame, end	¾″ × 2¼″ × 14⅛″	Pine	4
Floor panel	¼″ × 15½″ × 32⅝″	Oak plywood	1
Shelf	1″ × 15⅞″ × 32½″	Oak	1
Rear panel	¼″ × 22″ × 33⅛″	Oak plywood	1
Door stile	1″ × 2½″ × 21″	Oak	4
Door rail, upper	1″ × 10⅞″ × 8⅞″	Oak	2
Door rail, lower	1″ × 2½″ × 8⅞″	Oak	2
Spline	¼″ × ½″ × 9″	Fir plywood	2
Door grid	⅛″ × 9½″ × 16½″	Fir plywood	2
Molding	⅝″ × ¾″	Nose and cove (NC)	15 ft.
Dowel (SD)	⅜″ × 2″		46
Table top fastener (TTF)			10
Glass holder (GH)			26
Door pull (DPE)			2
Magnetic catch (PM)			2
Non-mortise hinge (NMH)			4
Beauty Brad (BBN)			24
Screw	1½″ 8 RH		18
Screw	¾″ 6 RH		13
Nail, finishing	2″		16
Shelf support			4
Glass to fit			

Note: Items in parentheses are available from Armor Products.

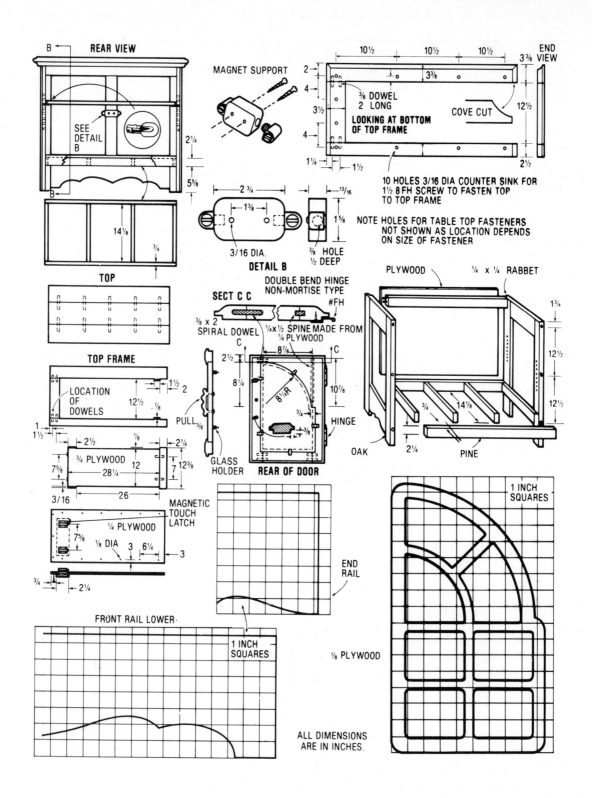

REAR VIEW

B

SEE DETAIL B

2¼

5⅝

B

TOP

14⅛

¾

MAGNET SUPPORT

10½   10½   10½   3⅜   **END VIEW**

2

4

3½   ⅜ DOWEL 2 LONG

4   **LOOKING AT BOTTOM OF TOP FRAME**   COVE CUT   12½

1¼   1½   2½

10 HOLES 3/16 DIA COUNTER SINK FOR 1½ 8 FH SCREW TO FASTEN TOP TO TOP FRAME

NOTE HOLES FOR TABLE TOP FASTENERS NOT SHOWN AS LOCATION DEPENDS ON SIZE OF FASTENER

DETAIL B

2¾   13/16

1⅜   1⅝

3/16 DIA.   ⅜ HOLE ½ DEEP

SECT C C

⅜ x 2 SPIRAL DOWEL

DOUBLE BEND HINGE NON-MORTISE TYPE

¼ x ½ SPINE MADE FROM ¼ PLYWOOD   #FH

TOP FRAME

LOCATION OF DOWELS   1½   2

12½   ⅛

1   1½

2½   ⅛   2½

¾ PLYWOOD   12   7   12⅜

7⅝   28¼

26

3/16

MAGNETIC TOUCH LATCH

¼ PLYWOOD

7⅝

⅛ DIA   3   6¼   3

¾   2¼

FRONT RAIL LOWER

1 INCH SQUARES

PULL ⅜

GLASS HOLDER

C   8⅞   C

2½

8¼   8¼R

¾   10⅞

⅜

HINGE

REAR OF DOOR

1 INCH SQUARES

END RAIL

⅛ PLYWOOD

ALL DIMENSIONS ARE IN INCHES.

PLYWOOD   ¼ x ¼ RABBET

1¾

12½

¾   14⅛   12½

OAK   2¼   PINE

1 INCH SQUARES

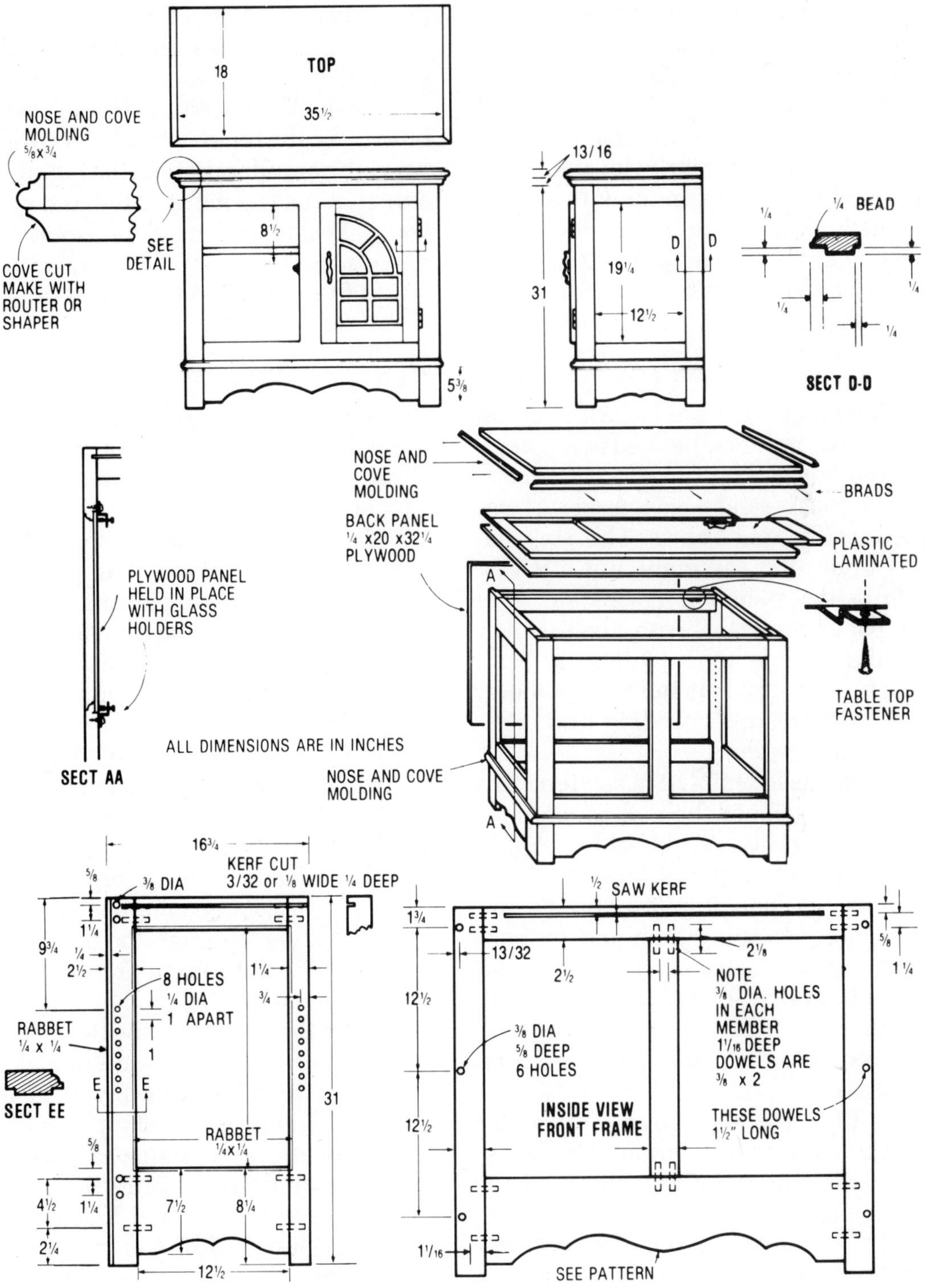
TOP
18
35½
NOSE AND COVE MOLDING
⅝ x ¾
COVE CUT MAKE WITH ROUTER OR SHAPER
SEE DETAIL
8½
5⅜
13/16
31
19¼
12½
D
D
¼ BEAD
¼
¼
¼
¼
SECT D-D
NOSE AND COVE MOLDING
BRADS
BACK PANEL
¼ x20 x32¼
PLYWOOD
PLASTIC LAMINATED
TABLE TOP FASTENER
PLYWOOD PANEL HELD IN PLACE WITH GLASS HOLDERS
SECT AA
ALL DIMENSIONS ARE IN INCHES
NOSE AND COVE MOLDING
A
A
16¾
KERF CUT
3/32 or ⅛ WIDE ¼ DEEP
⅜ DIA
⅝
9¾
1¼
¼
2½
8 HOLES
¼ DIA
1 APART
1
1¼
¾
RABBET
¼ x ¼
E
E
SECT EE
31
RABBET
¼x¼
⅝
4½
1¼
7½
8¼
2¼
12½
½ SAW KERF
1¾
13/32
2½
2⅛
NOTE
⅜ DIA. HOLES IN EACH MEMBER 1¹⁄₁₆ DEEP
DOWELS ARE ⅜ x 2
⅝
1¼
12½
⅜ DIA
⅝ DEEP
6 HOLES
INSIDE VIEW FRONT FRAME
THESE DOWELS 1½" LONG
12½
1¹⁄₁₆
SEE PATTERN

make the cut as shown. Note that the groove in the front frame starts and stops 3 inches from the ends. The groove in the end sections runs through from end to end.

The three dowel holes at the rear of the front stiles must be carefully located to ensure a good fit. Line them up with similar holes made in the edge of the side stiles, using dowel centers as described previously. Also drill the rear rails for dowel holes, using the same techniques previously described. Drill eight holes, ¼ inch in depth and diameter, 1 inch apart, into the inside surface of each end stile for adjustable shelf holders, before final assembly of the frame.

Next, rough-sand the exposed surfaces of the front and end frames. This step can also be done after assembly, but it is easier while the pieces are separate. Use 80-grit paper, preferably with a belt sander. When the surface at the joints is level, change to a 120-grit belt and sand smooth. Wait to do final finish sanding until after assembly is complete.

The case is assembled in sections. Attach the rear rails to the end frame first, again using dowels and glue. Apply clamps, then set aside until the glue sets. Then apply glue and dowels to the end and front frames, clamping each part in turn. Use bar or pipe clamps across the top and bottom and wood C-clamps at the midway area of the stiles. After the case is glued up, use the router to shape the openings in the end frames.

The floor frame consists of an outer rectangle with two intermediate crosspieces. Assemble it with glue and 2-inch finishing nails. When the glue has set, install it into the lower part of the case. Position the top surface of the floor frame ¼ inch below the top edge of the lower front and side rails. Attach firmly into the inside of the case with #8 1½-inch round-head screws.

To make the top, glue at least three boards for the required 18-inch width. Reverse the annular rings of the boards to ensure that the top remains flat and does not warp. Locate and drill the holes for the dowels, spaced as indicated. Each joint requires five dowels. Assemble as previously described.

The frame for the top consists of a front, back, and one end. The other end is left open to allow the extension leaf to pass through. Dowel and glue the end piece and allow it to set. Shape the bottom edge with a cove cutter.

Place the previously glued top upside down on a flat surface, then position the frame over it, centering it from side to side. The back edges of each piece must be flush. Fasten the top to the frame with #6 ¾-inch flat-head screws driven through the frame. Next, place the case upside down onto the top frame and check for fit. Fasten temporarily using tabletop fasteners, as shown.

Cut the extension support from a piece of ¼-inch plywood. We used scrap wall paneling, since it is hidden from view when the project is complete. Using glue and brads, nail through the plywood into the support cleat to reinforce the area under the latches.

Place the cabinet on the floor right side up, then add the nose and cove molding to the front and two ends. If you have built the top correctly, there should be a recess in the top above the frame into which the molding is fastened. Miter the moldings and attach with glue and brads.

After the molding has been installed, remove the top to expose the top frame and extension support. Set it aside while you prepare the extension. Make the leaf from a piece of ¾-inch plywood with oak trim and ends. After cutting to size, apply the plastic laminate with contact cement as directed by the manufacturer, letting it overhang slightly at the edges. Trim the excess, then add the oak strip at the outside end. Rout the bottom edge of this piece so it matches the cove cut in the top frame.

Add the leaf stops to the inside end of the extension and the frame stops to the open end of the frame, as shown in the drawing. These stops also act as spacers.

Install the two magnetic touch latches and matching strikes, then fasten the accompanying metal strikes to the end of the extension. After checking for smooth operation, refasten the top section to the case.

Because of their shape, the doors are made with two types of butt joints, using both dowels and splines. The spline is necessary to maintain the integrity of the joint where the upper door rail narrows to about ½ inch. You cannot use dowels in such a thin piece.

Locate and drill the dowel holes at the two bottom joints and inside top of each door, then cut the ¼- x -¼-inch blind grooves for the remaining joint. You can do this step with the router, shaper, or on the table saw.

Cut matching splines from ¼-inch plywood, then shape the ends so they conform to the shape of the groove.

Check for fit, then glue the door frames together. Sand the surfaces smooth, as described previously. Follow by rabbeting the interior (back) edges all around the rear

side to fit the nonmortise hinges. Use a beading cutter to shape the frame openings and all edges at the front of the doors.

Fasten the doors to the cabinet with nonmortise hinges. They are held closed with magnetic catches mounted on the magnet support, which is screwed into the back of the center divider. These adjustable magnets allow trouble-free holding and release.

Cut the grille from ⅛-inch plywood, following the pattern. Use a jigsaw or saber saw fitted with a fine-toothed blade.

The oak plywood end panels and grilles are held in place with screw-type glass holders. Cut the glass to fit the door openings, paint the panels a dark color, and install them in front of the grille. Insert shelf supports and shelf and check for fit.

Install the floor deck and rear panel and shelf with 2-inch finishing nails. Add the moldings at the lower part of the cabinet. Sand all rough surfaces smooth, then finish-sand the entire unit with 240- or 280-grit paper. You can finish the server to suit, but you should use a filler on oak or other open-grained woods.

This unit was finished with one application of golden oak paste wood filler, followed with a thin coat of shellac. Then two coats of sanding sealer were applied, followed by two coats of clear gloss lacquer.

To apply paste filler, use a brush and brush in the direction of the grain. Then, when it starts to set, rub it off across the grain. Paste wood filler is available at most paint shops.

Pool Table

A POOL TABLE is not a simple piece of work that a beginner can put together in a weekend. For someone who enjoys woodworking, however, this challenging project will provide many evenings of pleasure while it is being made, as well as after it is completed.

Start by constructing the two pedestals. Lay out the end pieces, or legs, on your stock and cut four identical pieces, as shown. Use ¾-inch stock. All wood used in the project, except the plywood, should be well seasoned or kiln-dried. Pine is suitable.

Attach the ¾- × -¾-inch pine cleats to the legs, setting each in ⅛ inch from the edge to accommodate the pedestal skin. Then attach the two horizontal crosspieces, one at the bottom and one part way up the leg, as shown. Use nails and glue for this step.

Next, attach the two gum plywood skin panels. Each front panel is ⅛- × -20- × -28½-inch gum plywood. The two back panels are ⅛- × -21- × -28½-inch gum plywood.

Hold the skin panels in place with glue and brads. When the glue is set, you can round the corners of the pedestal if you wish. Insert a T-nut leveler at each corner, as shown, so the table can be leveled precisely when it is used for play.

Fig. 26-1. A bed support frame with subrail attached. Check the fit of the pocket liners before you attach the subrail. Note that the tunnel floor stops short of the apron to allow the balls to roll into the ball box, which will lie below the hole in the foreground.

Fig. 26-2. Check the width of apron with scrap wood before you cut the 1/8-inch gum plywood skin. When attaching apron skin, be sure to coat the edges of the apron formers, subrail, and retainer groove with glue. Insert the edge of the skin into the groove, and bend over the formers.

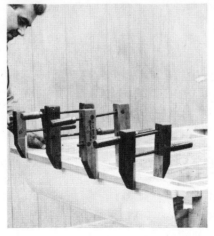

Fig. 26-3. (left) Hold the upper edge of the apron skin firmly against the subrail with a strip of scrap wood and clamps until the glue dries.

Fig. 26-4. (right) The rounded corner blocks, which have been cut in pie-shaped quarter sections, are glued in place in a stepped pattern.

Fig. 26-5. (top left) Fill in the spaces caused by the steps of the corner blocks with an auto body filler and allow it to dry thoroughly. Finally, sand the excess filler material and rough portions with garnet paper until you have achieved a smooth, rounder corner.

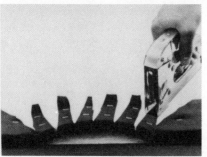

Fig. 26-6. (middle left) When you attach the table covering, slit the cloth as shown so you can work around side pockets. Note how the cloth is pulled to the under edge of the table bed and stapled.

Fig. 26-7. (middle right) The completed ball box assembly. Cut the pieces for the box from ¾-inch pine and assemble with glue and screws. Round the edges with sandpaper. Attach the ball box to the frame.

Fig. 26-8. Temporarily assemble the rail on the table to cut the pockets and the rounded outside corners. Undercut the pockets.

Fig. 26-9. Use a dado head to cut the feather strip groove in each rail. Note that the two bevels of the inside edge have been cut.

Fig. 26-10. When covering the rail, lay the cloth on the rail top, placing the feather strip on top over the groove. Press the strip and force the cloth into the groove.

When the pedestals are finished, cut out the parts for the bed support (parts A through G) from ¾-inch fir plywood, as shown.

The bed, ball tunnel and gulleys are all assembled right on the pedestal. Start by screwing part B to the tops of the legs of each pedestal. Each part B goes outside the pedestal legs.

Attach the long cleats to the inside bottom of each tunnel wall (part A). Then assemble bed support and ball tunnel and gulleys. The surest way to do this step is to assemble the structure temporarily, merely tacking the parts together lightly or holding them with clamps and scrap pieces of wood. This method will enable you to see how everything goes together and make sure all parts fit.

When you are satisfied that everything is in order, reassemble the bed support with glue, nails, and screws. Also build the gulleys.

When cutting parts C and D as well as

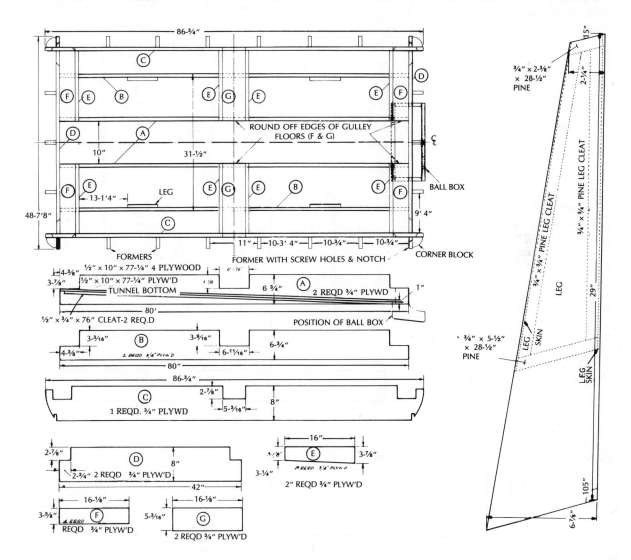

the corner apron formers, pay careful attention to the mitered notches that will accommodate the corner pockets. (See the drawings for details of how to cut these notches.) Also, be sure to check the fit of the pocket liners in place before the table bed is finally assembled.

Once the bed is constructed, cut the subrails out of ¾-inch pine stock, according to the dimensions in the drawing. Attach the end and side subrails flush with the tops of the end and sides of the apron pieces using screws and glue.

While the subrail glue is setting, cut 22 apron formers of ¾-inch pine, as shown in the drawing. Notch all of these formers at the bottom to receive the apron retainer strip. Also drill and countersink 4 or the 22 for two screws each (see drawing) and give them a mitered notch at the top to accommodate the corner pockets. Make two with right-hand notches and two with left-hand notches. The corner detail drawing and the apron former detail drawing illustrate how this should be done.

Screw and glue the apron former

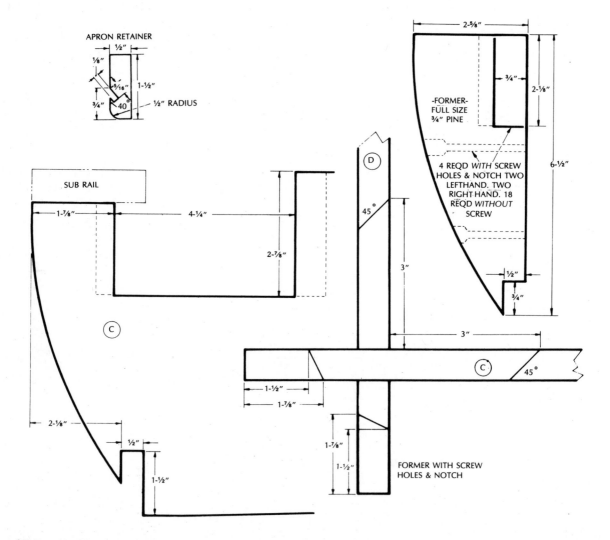

pieces to the apron side and end pieces. Screw the four corner formers to the side pieces through the drilled holes. Glue and screw the 18 other formers with screws driven from the inside through the end and side pieces and from the top through the subrail into the formers.

Shape and groove ½- × -1½-inch pine strips for the apron retainers, as shown in the profile drawing. Make two side pieces each 81½ inches long and two end pieces each 43½ inches long. Glue apron-skin retainer strips along the bottoms of the side and end pieces, fitting them into the

notches at the bottoms of the apron formers. The slanted groove should be on the outside facing upward.

Give the glue time to set. Then, use a scrap piece of ⅛-inch gum plywood to check the width of the apron skin. Cut four strips of gum plywood to this width and to the same lengths as the retainer strips.

To attach the apron skin, run a bead of glue into the groove of the apron retainer. Spread it in the groove with a brush and brush glue on the outside edges of the apron formers and the subrail. Insert one edge of the piece into the groove and bend

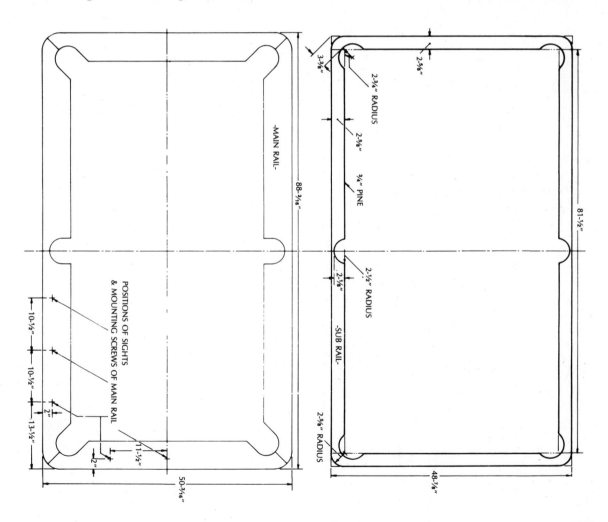

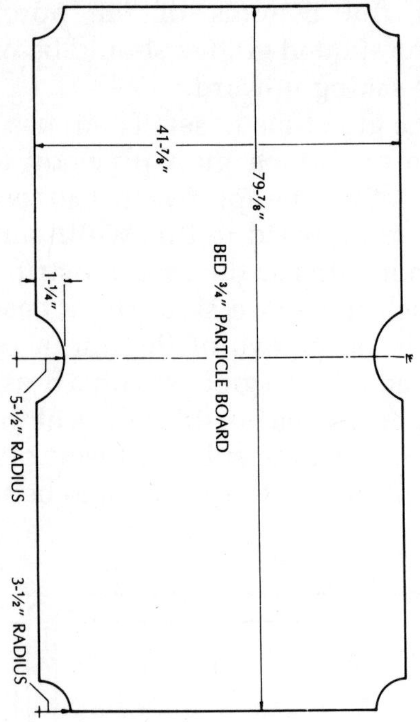
41-7/8″
79-7/8″
BED 3/4″ PARTICLE BOARD
1-1/4″
5-1/2″ RADIUS
3-1/2″ RADIUS

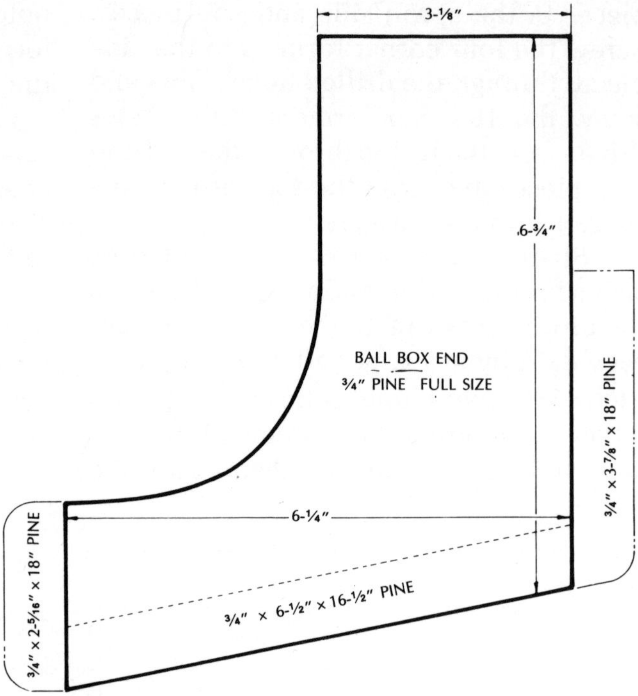
3-1/8″
6-3/4″
BALL BOX END
3/4″ PINE FULL SIZE
3/4″ × 3-7/8″ × 18″ PINE
6-1/4″
3/4″ × 2-5/16″ × 18″ PINE
3/4″ × 6-1/2″ × 16-1/2″ PINE

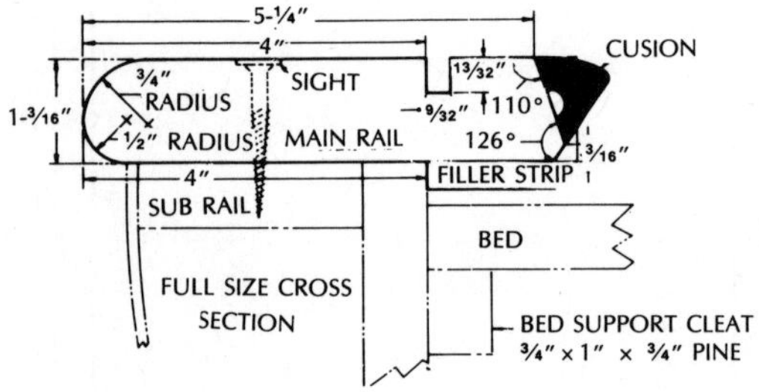
5-1/4″
4″
CUSION
1-3/16″
3/4″ RADIUS
SIGHT
13/32″
9/32″
110°
1/2″ RADIUS
MAIN RAIL
126°
3/16″
4″
FILLER STRIP
SUB RAIL
BED
FULL SIZE CROSS SECTION
BED SUPPORT CLEAT
3/4″ × 1″ × 3/4″ PINE

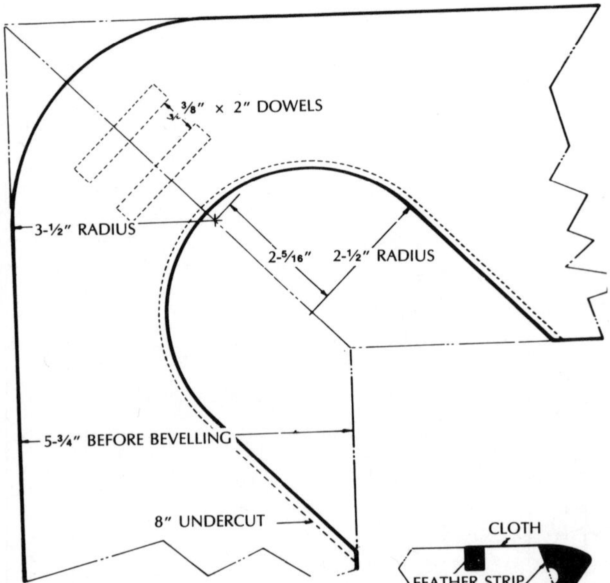
3/8″ × 2″ DOWELS
3-1/2″ RADIUS
2-5/16″
2-1/2″ RADIUS
5-3/4″ BEFORE BEVELLING
8″ UNDERCUT

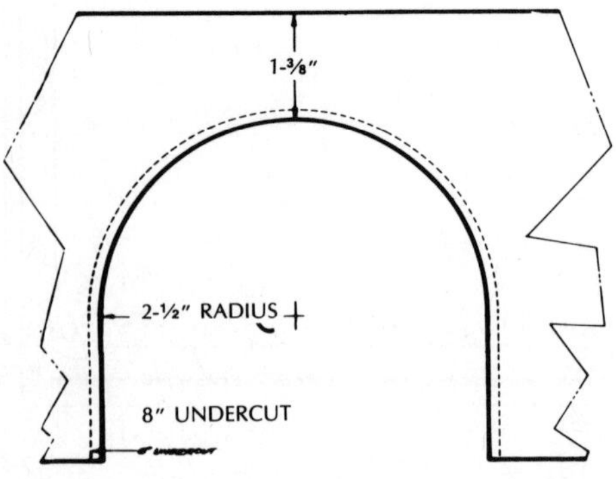
1-3/8″
2-1/2″ RADIUS
8″ UNDERCUT

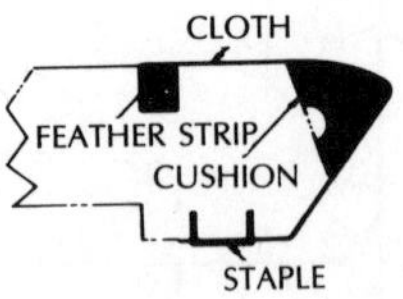
CLOTH
FEATHER STRIP
CUSHION
STAPLE

MATERIALS LIST

Purpose	Size	Description	Quantity
Main rail ends	1¼″ × 5¾″ × 50³⁄₁₆″	Pine	2
Main rail sides	1¼″ × 5¾″ × 88³⁄₁₆″	Pine	2
Main rail filler strips	⁵⁄₁₆″ × 1½″ × 34″	Pine	6
Feather strips	¼″ × ⁵⁄₁₆″ × 33″	Pine	6
Subrail ends	¾″		2
Subrail sides	¾″ × 2⅝″ × 81½″	Pine	2
Apron formers	¾″ × 2⅝″ × 6¾″	Pine	22
Apron retainer ends	½″ × 1½″ × 43½″	Pine	2
Apron retainer sides	½″ × 1½″ × 81½″	Pine	2
Apron ends	⅛″ × 8¼″ × 43½″	Gum plywood	2
Apron sides	⅛″ × 8¼″ × 81½″	Gum plywood	2
Tunnel bottom	½″ × 10″ × 77¼″	Fir plywood	1
B bed supports	¾″ × 6¾″ × 80″	Fir plywood	2
C bed supports	¾″ × 8″ × 86¾″	Fir plywood	2
D bed supports	¾″ × 8″ × 42″	Fir plywood	2
Center tunnel sides	¾″ × 6¾″ × 80″	Fir plywood	2
Tunnel bottom cleats	½″ × ¾″ × 76″	Pine	2
End bed support cleats	¾″ × 1″ × 34″	Pine	2
Side bed support cleats	¾″ × 1″ × 32″	Pine	4
Bed	¾″ × 41⅞″ × 79⅞″	Particle board	1
Leg sides	¾″ × 7″ × 31″	Pine	4
Upper leg stringers	¾″ × 5½″ × 28½″	Pine	2
Lower leg stringers	¾″ × 2⅜″ × 28½″	Pine	2
Leg cleats	¾″ × ¾″ × 19½″	Pine	8
Front leg skin	⅛″ × 20″ × 28½″	Gum plywood	2
Rear leg skin	⅛″ × 21″ × 28½″	Gum plywood	2
Gulley sides	¾″ × 3⅞″ × 16⅛″	Fir plywood	8
F gulley bottoms	¾″ × 3⅝″ × 16⅛″	Fir plywood	4
G gulley bottoms	¾″ × 5³⁄₁₆″ × 16⅛″	Fir plywood	2
Ball box ends	¾″ × 6¼″ × 8″	Pine	2
Ball box front	¾″ × 2⁵⁄₁₆″ × 18″	Pine	1
Ball box rear	¾″ × 3⅞″ × 18″	Pine	1
Ball box bottom	¾″ × 6½″ × 16½″	Pine	1
Corner pocket bottoms	¾″ × 4⅝″ Dia.	Plywood	4
Side pocket bottoms	¾″ × 3″ × 5″	Plywood	2
Corner blocks	¾″ × 3″ × 3″	Pine	32

Note: Also need rubber cement, glue, nails, screws, dowels, bed and cushion cloth, cushion rubber, pocket liners, leg levelers, body filler, sights and spots, and score markers.

it up and around the formers. Use a length of scrap wood and clamps to hold the top edge of the skin section against the edge of the subrail. After the glue is set, use a block plane to trim the top edge flush with the top of the subrail, if necessary.

Cut four sets of corner blocks from ¾-inch pine. Each set comprises progressively smaller quarter sections of a pie. Glue them in place, as shown. Next, mix a batch of auto body filler (available at any auto supply store) and apply it over the stepped corner blocks. When it is set, sand the filled corner with #80 garnet paper so it forms a smooth, rounded corner that is faired into the apron on each side. When this is done, smooth the surface with medium-grit (#120 to #150) garnet paper. *Note:* body filler sets rapidly, so don't mix more at one time than you can apply in about 3 minutes.

Cut the pieces for the ball box from ¾-inch pine and assemble the box as shown with glue and screws. Round the edges with sandpaper.

The bed of the table is made of ¾-inch particleboard. Cut it to the dimensions shown and cover it with billiard cloth. Press the cloth first with a steam iron to remove the wrinkles and fold marks. The rest is easy. Do one long edge first, pulling the cloth around to the bottom side and stapling it in place. Make slits in the cloth to fit it around the pockets, as shown. When you complete the long edge, do an end, then the other long edge, and then remaining end. Do not use a lot of tension, just enough to pull the cloth smooth.

Put the cloth-covered bed aside temporarily, but remember to put it in place on the bed-support structure before you attach the main rails permanently.

Cut the main rails to their basic shape. Miter the corners, but do not round the outside edges, bevel the inside edges, or cut the pockets.

Miter the corners and check the fit on the table. Drill holes for two dowels at each corner, as shown. The easiest, most accurate way of doing this step is with a dowel jig.

Use glue and nails to attach the filler strip to each rail section. Keep the nails away from the edge, because the filler strip and main rail will be beveled together as a unit.

Reassemble the rail sections on the table and clamp them into place. Lay out the pockets and the rounded corners, and cut them with a saber saw. Set the saber saw to undercut the pockets 8 degrees. Do not undercut the rounded outside corners of the rails.

Disassemble the railing and cut the groove for the feather strip on a table saw. Also make the two bevels for the inside edge at this time.

Apply the rubber cushion strip to the inside top beveled edge. Coat both the railing and strip with rubber cement and let the coatings dry. Press the two parts together firmly, allowing the strip of rubber to extend slightly beyond the railing at each pocket. When the strip if firmly in place, cut the ends of each piece of stripping flush with the pockets. Use a sharp knife dipped in water. The water on the blade acts as a lubricant and makes it easier to cut the rubber.

To cover a rail section with billiard cloth, place a long strip of cloth along the rail with one edge over the feather strip groove. Place the feather strip on the cloth over the groove and press it down so the cloth is forced into the groove.

Cut away the excess protruding from the groove on the inside edge. Fold the remaining cloth back over the feather strip, over the rail and cushion, and back underneath the rail. Staple it in place. Fold the cloth at the corner and side pockets so the seam is toward the bottom, and staple it on the underside of the rail. In addition, cut slits as necessary to work the cloth around the pockets as you did when covering the table bed. Trim away all excess cloth.

Put the table bed in place and attach the bed cleats to the apron sides and ends with screws and glue. When the glue is set, drive screws form the bottom through the cleats into the bed to hold it in place. Do not glue the bed or the rails in place because you might want to remove them at some time to recover the table.

With the bed in place, reassemble the rails on the table, gluing and doweling the mitered corners, and clamp it firmly in place. Drill, countersink, and screw the rail sections to the subrail. Sights and spots cover the countersunk screw holes. Use a router to round the outside edges of the rails.

Cut the pocket bottoms as shown, line them with scrap billiard cloth, and staple them in place at the bottom of the pocket liners. Staple the pocket liners to the apron or, if you have trouble getting a staple gun into the pocket, use tacks.

When finishing the table with the wood finish of your choice, be sure to protect the felt with masking tape. Insert the spots and sights after the wood is finished. If your local dealer cannot supply the bed and cushion cloth, cushion rubber, pocket liners, leg levelers, body filler, sights and spots, and score markers, write to Armor Products.

Rollabout Buffet Server

THIS HANDSOME BUFFET SERVER is mounted on casters and can be easily rolled to where the action is. This function is especially appreciated when you have a large gathering on holidays and special occasions. The double top and roomy compartment below make this a very versatile and important piece of furniture.

Make the corner posts first. Choose a close-grained hardwood, such as poplar. The stock should be fairly flat and free of defects. Unless you can obtain 2¼-inch-square stock, you will need to glue up two pieces of 1⅛-inch stock. This is commonly referred to as ⁵⁄₄ (five quarters) stock. Most lumberyards carry it, but if your local supplier doesn't, you can have him order it for you.

Cut the pieces slightly oversize, then glue them up using a suitable glue. White glue is fine and easy to use. Coat both surfaces, then slide the pieces together and clamp until the glue sets. To prevent shifting during clamping, drive a nail at each end in the waste area.

When the glue has set, trim the posts to length. Next plane the sides of the block to true them up, using a planer or joiner. If you lack these machines, you can use a block or jack plane.

Fluting the posts is done with a router fitted with a round-nose bit. With a pencil and square, draw light guidelines 1 inch from the ends. Clamp a guide block on the router base, then cut the flutes. Stop the cuts when the bit reaches the pencil lines. Note that the flutes are cut on two faces only. Also note that the inside corner does not run the length of the post. It is only 6 inches long.

The wood used for the cabinet is lumber core. Several choices are available, according to your own taste. We used red birch because it has a pleasing grain pattern and is close grained. Normally the back of a cabinet of this sort is closed off with a less expensive grade of wood and left unfinished—not so in this case. Because the buffet is mounted on casters and is portable, the rear side must be made with cabinet wood and finished accordingly.

Cut the pieces to size on a table saw. If you have a plywood blade, use it. It will produce a nice, clean cut that will require

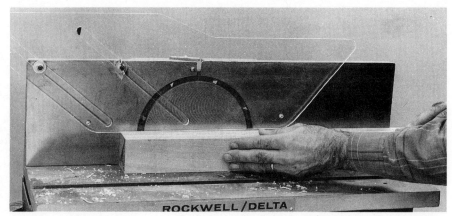

Fig. 27-1. Here the corner posts (which you can make from wood such as poplar) are glued up to form the squares, then trued up on a planer or with a block or jack plane.

Fig. 27-2. To flute the posts, use either on the shaper or with a router. If you use a router, clamp a guide to the base first. Cut the flutes on two faces.

Fig. 27-3. Use a table saw to notch the subtop. The kerf, cut on the underside, won't show or weaken the top.

Fig. 27-4. After you attach the base to the main section with screws, dress up the edges of the base with nose and cove molding. Miter the corners carefully and mount with glue and brads.

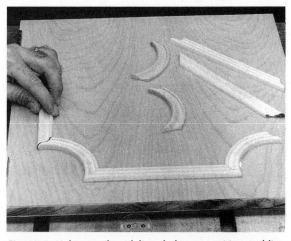

Fig. 27-5. Light pencil guidelines help you position molding on the door. Precut the corners and miter the straight sections to fit.

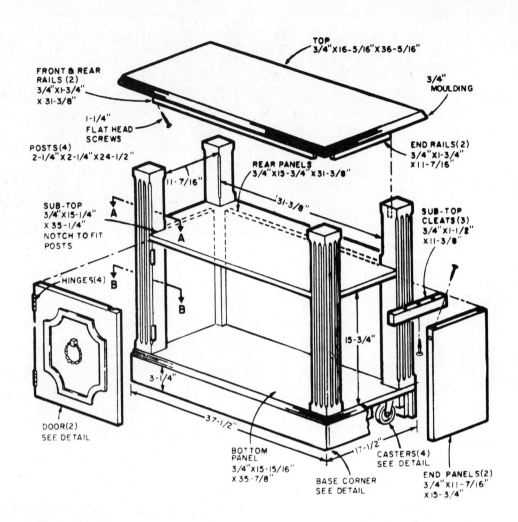

TOP
3/4"X16-5/16"X36-5/16"

FRONT & REAR
RAILS (2)
3/4"X1-3/4"
X 31-3/8"

3/4"
MOULDING

1-1/4"
FLAT HEAD
SCREWS

POSTS(4)
2-1/4"X2-1/4"X24-1/2"

11-7/16"

REAR PANELS
3/4"X13-3/4"X31-3/8"

END RAILS(2)
3/4"X1-3/4"
X11-7/16"

SUB-TOP
3/4"X15-1/4"
X 35-1/4"
NOTCH TO FIT
POSTS

31-3/8"

SUB-TOP
CLEATS(3)
3/4"X1-1/2"
X11-3/8"

HINGES(4)

15-3/4"

3-1/4"

DOOR(2)
SEE DETAIL

37-1/2"

BOTTOM
PANEL
3/4"X15-15/16"
X 35-7/8"

17-1/2"

CASTERS(4)
SEE DETAIL

BASE CORNER
SEE DETAIL

END PANELS(2)
3/4"X11-7/16"
X15-3/4"

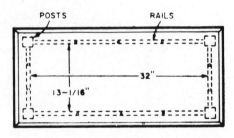

POSTS   RAILS

32"

13-1/16"

Top held on rails (dotted lines) by screws.

Decorative handles and molding trim doors.

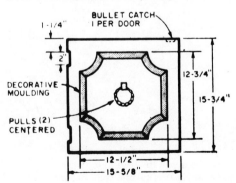

BULLET CATCH
1 PER DOOR

1-1/4"

2"

12-3/4"

15-3/4"

DECORATIVE
MOULDING

PULLS(2)
CENTERED

12-1/2"

15-5/8"

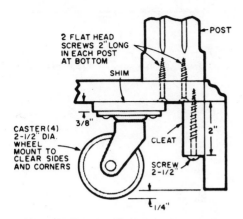

2 FLAT HEAD SCREWS 2" LONG IN EACH POST AT BOTTOM

POST

SHIM

3/8"

CASTER (4) 2-1/2" DIA. WHEEL MOUNT TO CLEAR SIDES AND CORNERS

CLEAT

2"

SCREW 2-1/2"

1/4"

Shim thickness adjusted to place casters, concealed in base, to clear carpet pile.

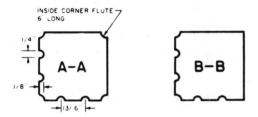

INSIDE CORNER FLUTE 6" LONG

1/4"

A-A

1/8"

13/6"

B-B

Corner post fluting as shown on 2 sides.

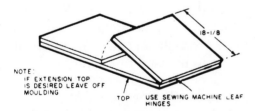

18-1/8

NOTE:
IF EXTENSION TOP IS DESIRED LEAVE OFF MOULDING

TOP   USE SEWING MACHINE LEAF HINGES

Delete molding on ends, if you add optional extension leaves to table top.

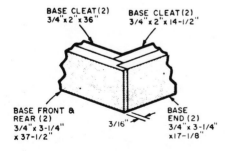

BASE CLEAT (2) 3/4" x 2" x 36"

BASE CLEAT (2) 3/4" x 2" x 14-1/2"

BASE FRONT & REAR (2) 3/4" x 3-1/4" x 37-1/2"

3/16"

BASE END (2) 3/4" x 3-1/4" x 17-1/8"

Rabbeted ends and molding help to finish base and make a professional looking job.

no further treatment. Notch the subtop to fit between the corner posts. Notches are best cut on the table saw.

After the bottom panel has been cut, mount the corner posts using glue and screws. Two screws in each corner will suffice. Next mount the end and rear panels. Hold them with screws through the bottom and top. Mount the top screws diagonally into the posts. Rather than sinking the screw heads, drill blind clearance holes on the underside of the subtop. This method will make for a stronger joint.

With end and rear panels in place, you can make up the base section. Rip the 3¼-inch width, then carefully cut the lengths to size. Rabbet the ends as indicated and join the pieces with white glue. Predrill the cleats that line the base for the screw-clearance holes, then assemble them with nails and glue. Use 1½-inch nails and drive them at a slight angle so they won't protrude from the face.

Attach the base to the main section with screws, then apply the nose and cove molding. Use 1-inch brads and glue. Sink the brads and fill with wood putty. Install the subtop using cleats. Make up the top by adding the rails before assembly. Check the location and position of the rails to make sure there is proper clearance at the corners for the posts. Diagonal screws through the rail corners into the posts hold the top firmly. Use glue. Add the molding to the outer edge of the top and check the miters carefully before assembly.

Cut the doors with matching grain. Mortise out the area for the hinges according to the drawing. Note that the gain for the hinges is cut in the door only. In other words, the gain is mortised only in the door for the full thickness of the butt hinge.

MATERIALS LIST

Purpose	Size	Description	Quantity
Top	¾″ × 16⁵⁄₁₆″ × 36⁵⁄₁₆″	Birch	1
End rails	¾″ × 1¾″ × 11⁷⁄₁₆″	Birch	2
Rails, front and rear	¾″ × 1¾″ × 31⅜″	Birch	2
Posts	2¼″ × 2¼″ × 24½″	Poplar	4
Subtop	¾″ × 15¼″ × 35¼″	Birch	1
Bottom	¾″ × 15¹⁵⁄₁₆″ × 35⅞″	Birch	1
Ends	¾″ × 11⁷⁄₁₆″ × 15¾″	Birch	2
Doors	¾″ × 15⅝″ × 15¾″	Birch	2
Rear panel	¾″ × 15¾″ × 31¾″	Birch	1
Base ends	¾″ × 3¼″ × 17⅛″	Birch	2
Base, front and rear	¾″ × 3¼″ × 37½″	Birch	2
Cleats, subtop	¾″ × 1½″ × 11⅜″	Pine	3
Cleats, base	¾″ × 2″ × 14½″	Pine	2
Cleats, base	¾″ × 2″ × 36″	Pine	2
Molding	¾″ × 28′	Nose and cove	
Decorative molding			2 sets

Misc.: Two pulls, two pair butt hinges ¾″ × 2″, two bullet catches, four swivel casters, 2½″ screws, glue, brads, nails.

Add the decorative moldings to the doors with glue. Brads are not necessary. Be careful not to use too much glue. Apply the glue only to the center of the molding and spread with a glue brush or with your finger. If necessary, wipe away any excess. Light pencil guidelines will help you position the pieces. If any glue squeezes out, wipe quickly with a damp cloth.

Mount the swivel casters so the base rests ¼ inch above the floor (more if the server is to be used in a room with a rug). Use spacer blocks to allow the wheels to protrude a sufficient amount.

Stain and finish the cabinet as desired. Add the hardware and bring on the food.

Storage Wall with Foldaway Dining Table

CRAMPED FOR SPACE? This wall unit can work well in any room and serves a dual purpose. It provides storage space and also can be transformed into an instant dining area of some elegance when needed. Its secret is a space-saving hideaway din-

ing table, which is housed in the lower center section, hidden behind two swing-away doors. The table seats four adults comfortably. The secret of successful folding is a gateleg foot and a pair of special hinges. The heavy-duty hinges not only support the two halves of the table, but, when folded, they leave a space to clear the gateleg foot, which is mounted at one end. The gateleg foot is cleverly designed so that it locks in both the folded and open positions.

The cabinet has been made with adjustable shelves in the lower sections. They are optional and need not be used, especially if you would like to install large speakers in the cabinets.

The piece is made in six sections which makes it easy to transport. The overall width is 91½ inches and the height is 77½ inches. Lumber used was 1-inch pine.

The Materials List calls for 260 spiral dowels. This is not an error. The pine boards must be edge-glued to obtain the width required. If you use wide boards, you should rip and glue them. The widest individual pieces should be about 4 inches. The annular rings must alternate up and

Fig. 28-1. A shop-built square made from 1-×-4 pine is clamped in place to guide the router when making dado cuts.

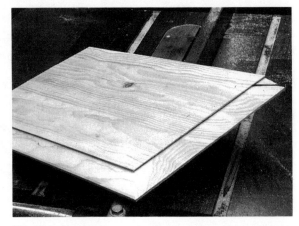

Fig. 28-2. Bevel edges on the door panel, making angle cuts on the table saw, then separate the scrap with a shallow vertical cut.

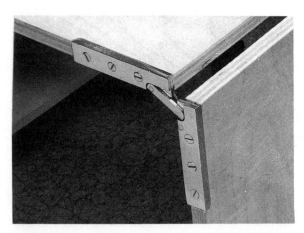

Fig. 28-3. This hinge closeup shows the action that allows the tabletop sections to move away from each other so they can fold over.

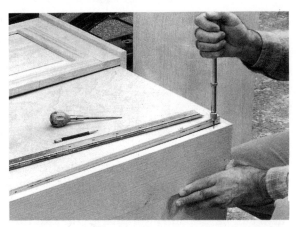

Fig. 28-4. Predrill screw holes to prevent splitting the frame when mounting the strip hinges for the table cover doors.

188

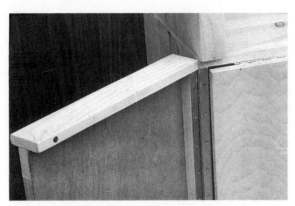

Fig. 28-5. Clearance under the front frame for the top section allows the table cover doors to close flush with the edge of the bottom shelf.

Fig. 28-6. The center support hinges to the underside of the tabletop and swings 180 degrees in the middle to lie flat when folded.

down in adjacent boards, as shown in the drawing, otherwise the boards will cup badly as the wood ages. If you have a shaper equipped with a glue-joint cutter,

you can eliminate the dowels and use the glue joint instead.

Cut the parts to size as indicated in the Materials List then, if necessary, rip the boards, reverse them, and then lay out and drill the dowel holes. A doweling jig is recommended; it will ensure accurate alignment of the dowels and a good, flat joint. Use a good grade of glue and clamp the parts securely.

When all the wide boards have been glued, sand them with a belt sander or use a jack plane. Follow with a finishing sander. When done, the boards must be flat and smooth. The cross members, or shelves as they are called in the Materials List, will be held by dadoes cut into the uprights (sides). Be sure the ends are free of any burrs, which could cause problems when you must fit them into the dadoes. Note that the shelves are cut ¼ inch narrower than the uprights to allow clearance for the rear panel.

Cut the dadoes and rabbets into the uprights using a router. A square made of ¾-inch stock simplifies cutting the dadoes. Make the square about 28 inches long so it can straddle two panels side by side, as shown. Lay out the position of each dado on the boards, then clamp the square and cut the dado ¾ inch wide and ¼ inch deep. Also cut a ¼- × -⅜-inch rabbet along the rear edge of the uprights to take the rear panel.

Each section is now ready to be assembled. Check the fit of the shelves into the dadoes and make any necessary adjustments. You might want to round the edges of the shelves before assembly. Use a router fitted with a ⅛-inch rounding bit. Do only the eight exposed shelves of the upper cabinets.

Apply glue to the dadoes and shelf

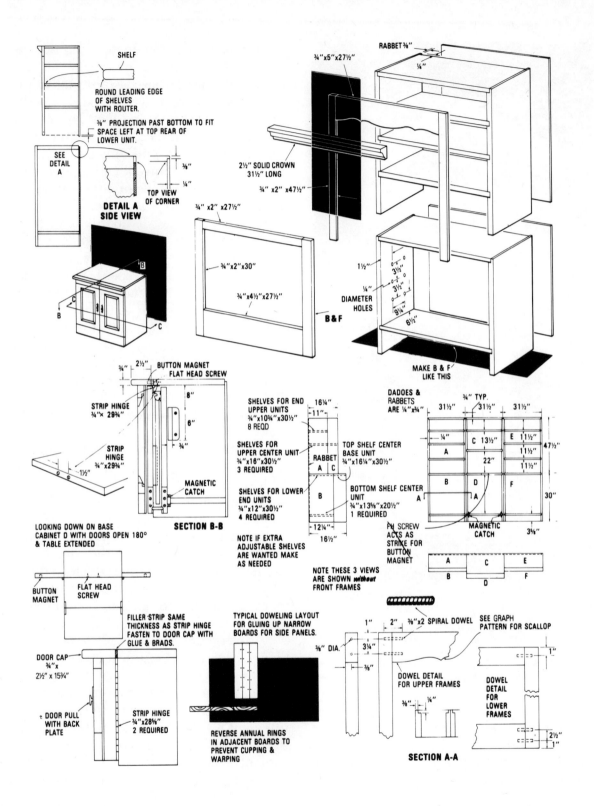

SHELF

ROUND LEADING EDGE
OF SHELVES
WITH ROUTER.

⅜" PROJECTION PAST BOTTOM TO FIT
SPACE LEFT AT TOP REAR OF
LOWER UNIT.

SEE
DETAIL
A

DETAIL A
SIDE VIEW

⅜"
¼"
TOP VIEW
OF CORNER

RABBET ⅜"
¼"

¾"x5"x27½"

2½" SOLID CROWN
31½" LONG

¾" x2" x47½"

¾" x2" x27½"

¾"x2"x30"

¾"x4½"x27½"

B & F

1½"
¼"
3½"
3½"
9¼"
6½"

DIAMETER
HOLES

MAKE B & F
LIKE THIS

BUTTON MAGNET
FLAT HEAD SCREW

¾" 2½"

STRIP HINGE
¾"x 29¾"

8"

6"

¾"

STRIP
HINGE
¾"x 29¾"

1½"

MAGNETIC
CATCH

SECTION B-B

LOOKING DOWN ON BASE
CABINET D WITH DOORS OPEN 180°
& TABLE EXTENDED

BUTTON
MAGNET

FLAT HEAD
SCREW

FILLER STRIP SAME
THICKNESS AS STRIP HINGE
FASTEN TO DOOR CAP WITH
GLUE & BRADS.

DOOR CAP
¾" x
2½" x 15¾"

τ DOOR PULL
WITH BACK
PLATE

STRIP HINGE
¾"x28⅝"
2 REQUIRED

SHELVES FOR END
UPPER UNITS
¾"x10¾"x30½"
8 REQD

SHELVES FOR
UPPER CENTER UNIT
¾"x16"x30½"
3 REQUIRED

SHELVES FOR LOWER
END UNITS
¾"x12"x30½"
4 REQUIRED

NOTE IF EXTRA
ADJUSTABLE SHELVES
ARE WANTED MAKE
AS NEEDED

16¼"
11"

RABBET
A C

B

12¼"
16½"

TOP SHELF CENTER
BASE UNIT
¾"x16¼"x30½"

BOTTOM SHELF CENTER
UNIT
¾"x13⅝"x20½"
1 REQUIRED

NOTE THESE 3 VIEWS
ARE SHOWN *without*
FRONT FRAMES

DADOES &
RABBETS
ARE ¼"x¾"

¾" TYP.

31½"   31½"   31½"

¼"
C 13½"   E 1½"
A   1½"
22"   1½"
B   D   F

FH SCREW
ACTS AS
STRIKE FOR
BUTTON
MAGNET

MAGNETIC
CATCH

47½"

30"

3⅜"

A   C   E
B   D   F

TYPICAL DOWELING LAYOUT
FOR GLUING UP NARROW
BOARDS FOR SIDE PANELS.

REVERSE ANNUAL RINGS
IN ADJACENT BOARDS TO
PREVENT CUPPING &
WARPING

⅜"x2 SPIRAL DOWEL

SEE GRAPH
PATTERN FOR SCALLOP

1"
2"
⅜" DIA.
3¾"
⅜"

DOWEL DETAIL
FOR UPPER FRAMES

⅜"   ¼"

DOWEL
DETAIL
FOR
LOWER
FRAMES

1"

2½"
1"

SECTION A-A

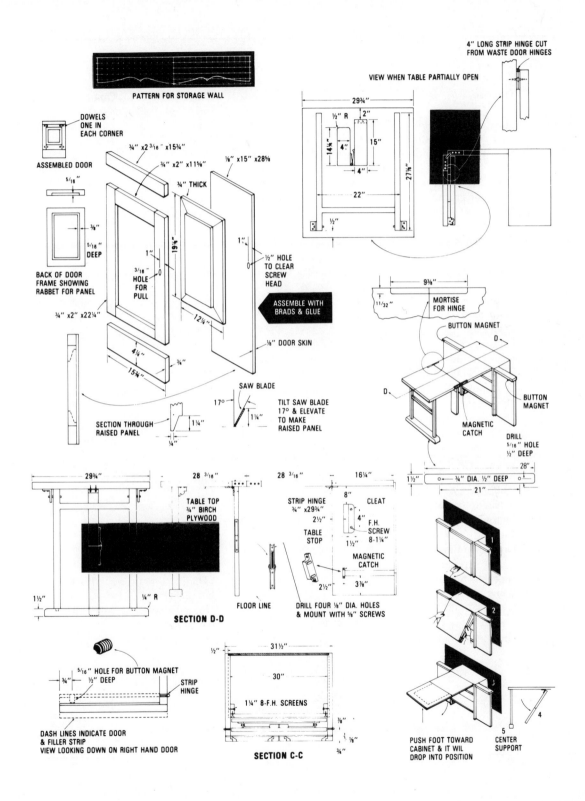

PATTERN FOR STORAGE WALL

DOWELS ONE IN EACH CORNER

ASSEMBLED DOOR

5/16"

BACK OF DOOR FRAME SHOWING RABBET FOR PANEL

3/8"
5/16" DEEP

3/4" x2 3/16" x15 3/4"
3/4" x2" x11 3/4"
3/4" THICK
1/8" x15" x28 5/8"

1"
19 3/4"
1"
1/2" HOLE TO CLEAR SCREW HEAD

3/16" HOLE FOR PULL

ASSEMBLE WITH BRADS & GLUE

3/4" x2" x22 1/4"
12 1/4"
1/8" DOOR SKIN

4 1/4"
3/4"
15 3/4"

SECTION THROUGH RAISED PANEL

1 1/4"
1/4"

SAW BLADE
17°
1 1/4"

TILT SAW BLADE 17° & ELEVATE TO MAKE RAISED PANEL

4" LONG STRIP HINGE CUT FROM WASTE DOOR HINGES

VIEW WHEN TABLE PARTIALLY OPEN

29 3/4"
1/2" R
2"
14 3/8"
4"
15
4"
27 1/8"
22"
1/2"

9 3/8"
11/32"
MORTISE FOR HINGE

BUTTON MAGNET
D
D
BUTTON MAGNET
MAGNETIC CATCH
DRILL 5/16" HOLE 1/2" DEEP

1 1/2"
3/4" DIA. 1/2" DEEP
28"
21"

29 3/4"

28 3/16"
TABLE TOP 3/4" BIRCH PLYWOOD

28 3/16"
16 1/4"
STRIP HINGE 3/4" x29 3/4"
2 1/2"
TABLE STOP
8"
CLEAT
4"
F.H. SCREW 8-1 1/4"
1 1/2"
MAGNETIC CATCH
2 1/2"
3 7/8"

1 1/2"
1/4" R

SECTION D-D

FLOOR LINE

DRILL FOUR 1/8" DIA. HOLES & MOUNT WITH 5/8" SCREWS

1
2
3
4
5 CENTER SUPPORT

PUSH FOOT TOWARD CABINET & IT WIL DROP INTO POSITION

5/16" HOLE FOR BUTTON MAGNET
3/4"
1/2" DEEP
STRIP HINGE

DASH LINES INDICATE DOOR & FILLER STRIP
VIEW LOOKING DOWN ON RIGHT HAND DOOR

1/2"
31 1/2"
30"
1 1/4" 8-F.H. SCREENS
7/8"
1/8"
3/4"

SECTION C-C

191

MATERIALS LIST

Purpose	Size	Description	Quantity
Side (end cabinet)	¾″ × 12¼″ × 30″	Pine	4
Shelf (end cabinet)	¾″ × 12¼″ × 30″	Pine	4
Side (center cabinet)	¾″ × 16½″ × 30″	Pine	2
Shelf, top (center cabinet)	¾″ × 16¼″ × 30½″	Pine	1
Shelf, lower (center cabinet)	¾″ × 13⅝″ × 30½″	Pine	1
Rear panel	¼″ × 25¾″ × 47⅞″	Plywood	3
Stile, lower	¾″ × 2″ × 30″	Pine	4
Rail, upper	¾″ × 2″ × 27½″	Pine	2
Rail, lower	¾″ × 4½″ × 27½″	Pine	2
Table stop	¾″ × 6″ × 30″	Pine	1
Cleat	¾″ × 1½″ × 6″	Pine	2
Door filler	¾″ × ⅞″ × 28⅝″	Pine	2
Door back	⅛″ × 15″ × 28⅝″	Plywood	2
Door cap	¾″ × 2½″ × 15¾″	Pine	2
Door apron	¾″ × 2³⁄₁₆″ × 15¾″	Pine	2
Door cap filler	¾″ × ³⁄₁₆″ × 15¾″	Pine	2
Raised panel	¾″ × 12¼″ × 19⅛″	Pine	2
Door rail	¾″ × 2″ × 11⅝″	Pine	4
Door stile	¾″ × 2″ × 22¼″	Pine	4
Door base	¾″ × 4¼″ × 15¾″	Pine	2
Table top	¾″ × 28⅙″ × 29¾″	Plywood	2
Center support	¾″ × 4″ × 14¼″	Pine	1
Center support	¾″ × 4″ × 15″	Pine	1
Foot base	1½″ × 1½″ × 28″	Pine	1
Pull/backplate		DP	2
Magnetic catch		MC	2
Button magnet		BM	2
Table strip hinge	¾″ × 29¾″		1
Door strip hinge	¾″ × 28⅝″		2
Center support hinge	¾″ × 4″		1
Foot and hinges		FTH	1 set
Screw	½″	No. 8 FH	2
Screw	1¼″	No. 8 FH	8
Screw	⅝″	No. 6 RH	4
Drop leaf hinge for support		DLS	1
Brad	¾″	18	48
Nail	2″	Finishing	70
Dowels, spiral	¾″ × 2″		260

Note: Specialty hardware is available from Armor Products.

ends, then mate the parts and clamp. Use a large square to make sure that the case is square and remains so after clamping.

Make the front frames next. Dowel the joints as shown in drawing. The lower frames are closed top and bottom, but the upper frames are open at the bottom. Scallop the top rails of the upper frames before assembly using a saber saw or jigsaw.

After you have assembled the top rails and the glue has set, remove the clamps and then round the edges with the ¼-inch rounding bit. When rounding the outer edges near the top, stop the router short of the end. The cut should stop at the point where the solid crown will be. Draw a stop line by laying the crown in position, then scribe a light pencil line as a guide for the router. Round the lower frames on all edges, inside and out.

Next, attach the frames to the cabinets. Apply glue to all joints and fasten with 2-inch finishing nails. Countersink the nailheads, then fill the holes with a suitable filler. Add the solid crown molding to the top, fastening it with glue and nails driven in angularly along the top edge.

If you decide to build the storage wall without the table, make a center frame and install it so it matches the end cabinets.

The table mechanism is especially designed for this application. Make the tabletop in two sections using birch plywood or other suitable finish. Place the two sections on the workbench with the ends butted, then clamp a guide to the top for the router. You need the guide to cut the mortise for the hinge. Set the guide so that the depth of the cut will be exactly $^{11}/_{32}$ inch deep and $9^{3}/_{8}$ inches long. Install the gate-leg foot at the far end of the table. Fasten the opposite end of the table to the base cabinet with a strip or piano hinge.

Note: The table hardware is imported from Spain and it is designed for a table height of less than our standard of 30 inches, with a tabletop thickness of 1½ inches, which is quite heavy. To compensate for the higher table and thinner top, we used a foot base piece, which is placed under the legs after the table is opened, and is stored in the cabinet when not in use.

The center support is hinged to the underside of the table. It drops down automatically when the table is raised. Because of its length, it is hinged at its side using a modified spring-loaded drop-leaf support. To rework the support, remove the rivets at each end by grinding the rivet head or by filing it until it drops out. Discard the rivets and end flaps. Now drill four ⅛-inch-diameter holes along the backbone, as indicated in the drawing. Mount the support to the two wood pieces using round-head screws. The spring will block one of the screw holes, but you can get a narrow screwdriver in from the edge to drive the screw.

In use, the center support hinges along its top, as well as its side. Operate it as follows. When the table is open, the folded support will dangle from the underside. Swing it toward the front of the table slightly, then open at the joint to extend the support fully. Then swing it to a vertical position, where it will stiffen and support the tabletop.

Make the two doors with raised panels. Glue up boards for the panels, then trim to size (12¼ × 19⅛ inches). Raise the panels on the table saw by elevating the blade 1¼ inches (vertical measurement) and tilting the arbor 17 degrees. Adjust the fence so there will be a ¼-inch flat at the outer edge. Hold the work securely and run it through the blade slowly. When all four

193

sides are cut, the waste should still be hanging on. Lower the blade and set the arbor to 0 degrees. Then set the fence and raise the blade as necessary to remove the waste. This operation will also square off the angular cut left by the edge of the tilted saw blade.

Make up the frame for the doors, and rabbet the rear edges to take the raised panel. You can run the rabbets off the ends of the stiles since they will be concealed when the ⅛-inch plywood is fastened to the rear of the frame. Make the plywood long enough to cover the apron and base pieces, which are assembled to make up the door. Assemble the door as shown and be sure to add the filler strip at the rear edge of the door filler cap. When the door is fastened to the cabinet, you will notice a gap at the top equal to the thickness of the strip hinges used. Cut the strip accordingly, and install with brads and glue.

Install the button magnets at the rear of the caps, and then install two flat-head screws into the edge of the cabinet. The magnets and screws keep the doors closed. At the lower part of the cabinet and just before the lower shelf, install two magnetic catches to hold the hinged tabletop secure and flat when the table is not in use.

The table stop and cleats must be installed firmly. The stop acts as a support for the table as it is being extended and also when it is being retracted. It acts as a fulcrum.

Cut the rear panels from wall paneling. Note that the upper panels are made to project ⅜ inch below the side members so the assembly will extend ⅜ inch below the top shelf of the lower cabinets, thus covering a raw edge.

After the cabinets are in place, secure the upper cabinets to the lower units at the rear with steel mending plates. These plates are available at hardware shops. Use the straight type.

Sand all exposed surfaces, then stain and finish as desired. Before you apply stain, test the product on scrap lumber. If you find the stain too dark or mottled, you might want to seal the wood lightly before staining. Use shellac thinned about 1:5 with alcohol (5 parts alcohol to 1 part shellac). Apply with a brush and allow to dry, then sand lightly with 220-grit paper. Now apply stain. You will notice the stain covers evenly without hot spots.

Sturdy Oak Bunk Bed

THESE STURDY SOLID OAK BUNK BEDS, also called *stacking beds*, are great space savers and are designed to last a lifetime. The beds are made as two separate units, and they can be stacked one over the other or used as two separate beds. Steel pins in each post ensure alignment of the beds and provide ample strength to withstand sideways loads. To provide rigidity, ⁸⁄₄-inch oak was used for the posts and ⁵⁄₈-inch oak for the rails. The struts and ladder rungs are made of ⁴⁄₄-inch material. (Lumberyards measure solid hardwoods by the ¼ inch: ⁸⁄₄-inch for example is 2-inch lumber, which has an actual thickness of 1¾ inches.)

We made wood covers to conceal the lag screw heads used in assembly. They snap into place and hold fast. They can be removed by inserting a screwdriver at the bottom for easy disassembly.

Guardrails are an important feature, especially for the upper unit. We designed our own locking mechanism, which is fully concealed. As a safety precaution, the guardrail is sturdy, locks securely, and is easily removed by an adult. To use the one designed here, locks at both ends must be depressed manually to remove the guardrail. The ladder is made with hooks at the top so it cannot slide away from the bed, but it is easily removable so it can be used at the side or ends of the bed.

The roomy drawers under the bunk bed will make any mother happy. Conventional drawers under a bed are a nuisance because it is difficult to get under the bed with a vacuum cleaner. Our drawers roll out and away from the bed. The bed posts and rails were made of solid oak, but other species may be substituted. To keep costs and weight down, we used ⁵⁄₈-inch plywood sheathing for the mattress supports.

The posts are made of ⁸⁄₄-inch stock, which actually measures 1¾ inches in thickness.

If the stock is dressed only two sides, as ours was, you will need to trim one edge to establish a straight line. This can be done in several ways: by band saw, saber saw or

Fig. 29-1. (left) When you are ready to fasten the completed posts to the rails, use masking tape on the ends of the rails to make the penciled dowel marks stand out much more clearly.

Fig. 29-2. (right) Use a spacer block to locate the ledger on the rail. First tap the screws lightly to mark the center for the screw pilot holes. Fasten the ledgers.

Fig. 29-3. (left) To make the mortise, necessary to accept the rail guard, use a ¾-inch mortising bit fit to a router. Several passes at deepening cuts might be necessary.

Fig. 29-4. (right) Use a hole-marking jig to locate the holes in the ladder sides. Install the rungs, clamping them securely to the ladder. Use one clamp per rung.

Fig. 29-5. (left) Make the covers for the lag screws, a custom safety feature, in one long strip. Then cut them apart after you have rounded the corners with a router.

Fig. 29-6. (right) The guardrails are another important safety feature. Drill the ends of the rails, kerf them, then contour them. Again, masking tape makes the lines visible.

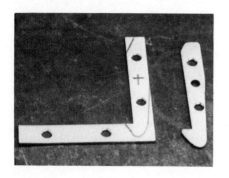

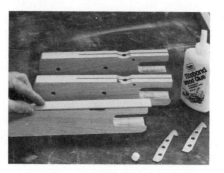

Fig. 29-7. (left) The lock, custom designed for these bunk beds, it cut from a flat steel corner. You can use a piece of solid metal if desired, but this choice will require more work.

Fig. 29-8. (right) Cover the kerfed edge of the large drawers with a ⅛-inch strip ripped from an oak board. Glue it securely, then cut away the finger slot for easy opening.

Fig. 29-9. (left) Install the lag-screw cover after the screws are tightened. To remove them, when necessary, insert a screwdriver into the opening at the bottom and pry.

Fig. 29-10. (right) The guardrail has a special locking mechanism that only adults can operate. To remove, depress the plate firmly with your finger.

table saw. If you are using a table saw, fasten a straight board to the stock then guide the board against the rip fence. To use a saber saw or band saw, draw a straight line near one edge of the stock, then saw. The sawn line will be straight enough to feed against the fence, but you will need to recut it to obtain a straight, smooth line. Therefore, set the fence to make the first cut about 3½ inches wide. Then reset the fence to 3¼ inches wide to make the final cuts. Next cut the pieces to the required length.

Make four pieces 35 inches long and the other four pieces 26½ inches long. Locate the dowel and screw holes carefully. You might want to place masking tape on the areas to be marked so the layout lines stand out clearly. Bear in mind when making your layouts that two posts for each bed have opposite faces. With regard to the short rails, two are laid out face up and two face down.

Drill the lag screw holes all the way through the piece, but the holes for the dowels and knock-down fittings are blind. Drill them to the depths shown. Note that the combined depth of the dowel holes is made a trifle deeper than the dowel length to ensure that the glue line joint will close tightly.

Drill the stacking holes into the top of the lower posts and the bottom of the upper posts. The holes in the top section are $^{13}/_{32}$ inch in diameter which allows the post to fit over the ⅜-inch steel pin in the lower section without binding. Lay out the curves at the top of the upper post, then cut and sand smooth. Round the corners of the posts with a router fitted with a ¼-inch round-over bit. Follow with sanding.

Next, make the short rails and struts. Cut the rails from ⅝ stock (actual size 1⅛ inches) and the struts from 4/4 stock (actual thickness $^{13}/_{16}$ inches). Rip the rail stock to 4½-inch widths, then trim the lengths to 29$^{5}/_{16}$ inches. Next, rip the struts to 2-inch widths and cut the lengths to match the short rails. Lay out the ⅜-inch hole locations to match those in the posts. The use of a doweling jig is recommended here to ensure accuracy of the perpendicular holes. Round the corners along the lengths of each piece using a ⅜-inch rounding bit.

Make the long rails in a similar manner, but drill the pilot holes for the lag screws with a ¼-inch drill bit. Make these holes 1¾-inches deep. Mortise the two upper long rails to accept the locking mechanism of the guardrails using a ¾-inch mortise bit. Clamp a guide strip along the lower edge of the rail and position it so the cutter will cut the mortise 1 inch from the top edge. Unless you have a heavy-duty router, you should make several passes

MATERIALS LIST

Purpose	Size	Description	Quantity
Lower post	¾" × 3¼" × 35"	Oak	4
Upper post	1¾" × 3¼" × 26½"	Oak	4
Short rail	1⅛" × 4½" × 29⁵⁄₁₆"	Oak	4
Long rail	1⅛" × 4½" × 74¾"	Oak	4
Strut	¹³⁄₁₆" × 2" × 29⁵⁄₁₆"	Oak	4
Short Ledger	¾" × ¾" × 29⁵⁄₁₆"	Oak	4
Long Ledger	¾" × ¾" × 74¾"	Oak	4
Mattress support	⅝" × 31¼" × 74¼"	Plywood	2
Ladder side	1⅛" × 2½" × 57"	Oak	2
Ladder rung	¹³⁄₁₆" × 2" × 12"	Oak	5
Lag screw cover	¹³⁄₁₆" × 1½" × 4¾"	Oak	8
Guard crosspiece	¹³⁄₁₆" × 2" × 34"	Oak	4
End guard	1⅛" × 2⁷⁄₁₆" × 11½"	Oak	4
Guard kerf cover	⅛" × 1⅛" × 11½"	Oak	4
Drawer front/rear	¾" × 7⅞" × 36⅜"	Oak plywood	4
Drawer side	¾" × 7⅞" × 31"	Oak plywood	4
Drawer cleat	1⅛" × 1⅛" × 5½"	Oak	8
Drawer bottom	¼" × 31¼" × 35⅝"	Fir plywood	2
Drawer edging	⅛" × ¾" × 32'	Oak	
Glue block	¾" × ¾" × 1⅝"	Oak	28
Steel dowel	⅜" × 2"	C.R.S.	4
Hardwood dowel	⅜" × 2"		60
Lag screw	⅜" × 3½"		16
Washer	⅞"	OD	16
Pan head screw	1½"	10	64
Screw	1½"	12 FH	4
Brad	1" × 18"		48
Ladder hood	⅛" × 1" × 7⅜3/8"	C.R.S.	2
Guard latch	¹⁄₁₆" × ⅝" × 4"	C.R.S.	4
Spring	⁵⁄₁₆" × 1⅛"		4
Screw set	14 - 20" × ⅜"		4
Concealed casters		#76000*	4
Drawer pull		#70005*	2
Knockdown fitting		#78016*	8
Paste wood filler		#85002*	3 lbs.

Note: Items with asterisk are available from Armor Products.

with the router, increasing the depth of the cut until you reach the full depth.

Two kinds of glue were used for this project: yellow glue (aliphatic resin) and hide glue. The hide glue was used for the ladder. Glue-size the ends of the short rails and struts beforehand by diluting the yellow glue with water. Brush it onto the end grain and allow it to dry. It will be absorbed by the porous end grain and will dry quickly.

Next, dry-sand lightly, then reapply

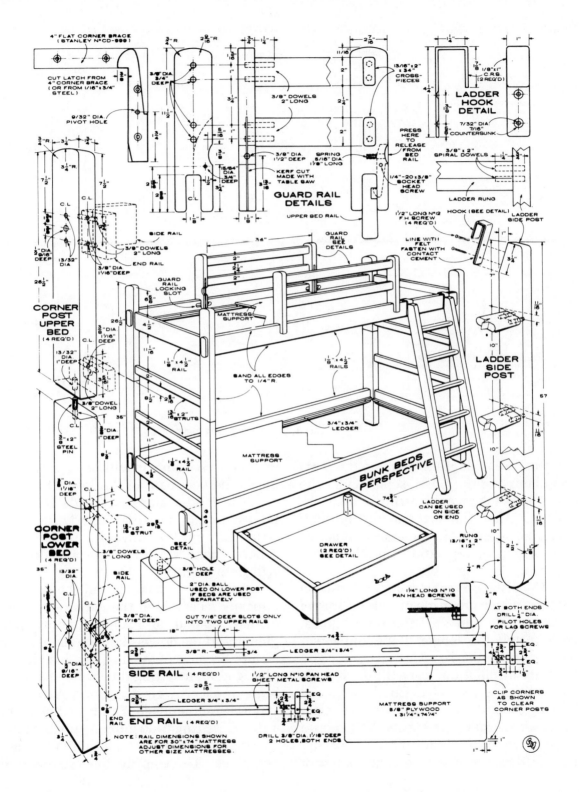

4" FLAT CORNER BRACE
(STANLEY N°CD-999)

CUT LATCH FROM
4" CORNER BRACE
(OR FROM 1/16"x 3/4"
STEEL)

9/32" DIA.
PIVOT HOLE

3/8" DIA.
3/4"
DEEP

3/8" DOWELS
2" LONG

KERF CUT
MADE WITH
TABLE SAW

3/8" DIA
1/2" DEEP

SPRING
5/16" DIA.
1/8" LONG

1/4"-20 x 3/8"
SOCKET
HEAD
SCREW

PRESS
HERE
TO
RELEASE
FROM
BED
RAIL

13/16"x 2"
x 34"
CROSS-
PIECES

**LADDER
HOOK
DETAIL**

7/32" DIA
7/16"
COUNTERSUNK

1/8"x 1"
C.R.S.
(2 REQ'D)

**GUARD RAIL
DETAILS**

UPPER BED RAIL

GUARD
SEE
DETAILS

3/8" x 2"
SPIRAL DOWELS

LADDER RUNG

HOOK (SEE DETAIL)

LADDER
SIDE
POST

LINE WITH
FELT
FASTEN WITH
CONTACT
CEMENT

1/2" LONG N°12
F.H. SCREW
(4 REQ'D)

**CORNER
POST
UPPER
BED**
(4 REQ'D)

3/8" DOWELS
2" LONG

SIDE RAIL

END RAIL

3/8" DIA
1 1/16" DEEP

GUARD
RAIL
LOCKING
SLOT

MATTRESS
SUPPORT

1 1/2"x 4 1/2"
RAIL

SAND ALL EDGES
TO 1/4" R.

1 1/2"x 4 1/2"
RAILS

**LADDER
SIDE
POST**

57

**CORNER
POST
LOWER
BED**
(4 REQ'D)

3/8" DOWEL
2" LONG

3/8" x 2"
STEEL PIN

1 1/2"x 2"
STRUTS

3/4"x 3/4"
LEDGER

MATTRESS
SUPPORT

**BUNK BEDS
PERSPECTIVE**

74 1/4"

LADDER
CAN BE USED
ON SIDE
OR END

RUNG
13/16"x 2"
x 12"

3/8" HOLE
1" DEEP

2" DIA BALL
USED ON LOWER POST
IF BEDS ARE USED
SEPARATELY

DRAWER
(2 REQ'D)
SEE DETAIL

1/4" LONG N° 10
PAN HEAD SCREWS

AT BOTH ENDS
DRILL 1/4" DIA.
PILOT HOLES
FOR LAG SCREWS

CUT 7/16" DEEP SLOTS ONLY
INTO TWO UPPER RAILS

LEDGER 3/4"x 3/4"

SIDE RAIL (4 REQ'D)

1 1/2" LONG N°10 PAN HEAD
SHEET METAL SCREWS

LEDGER 3/4" x 3/4"

END RAIL (4 REQ'D)

DRILL 3/8" DIA. 1 1/16" DEEP
2 HOLES, BOTH ENDS

CLIP CORNERS
AS SHOWN
TO CLEAR
CORNER POSTS

MATTRESS SUPPORT
5/8" PLYWOOD
x 31 1/4"x 74 1/4"

NOTE: RAIL DIMENSIONS SHOWN
ARE FOR 30"x74" MATTRESS
ADJUST DIMENSIONS FOR
OTHER SIZE MATTRESSES.

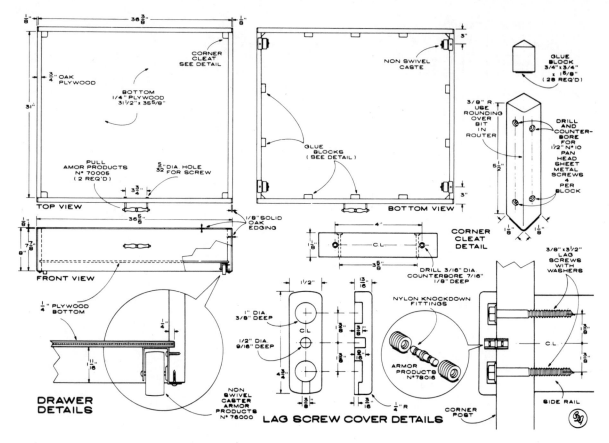

the glue full strength. Assemble the parts and clamp securely. Use scrap under the clamp jaws to prevent marring of the work surface. After the clamps are applied, check the assembly for squareness. If necessary, adjust or reposition the clamps to square up the assembly.

The plywood mattress support rests on ledgers, which are made of ¾-inch-square stock. Locate and drill the screw holes, then install the ledger along the lower edges of the rails. To ensure accuracy and simplify installation, use a 2¾-inch-wide spacer block as indicated. Cut the plywood boards to size then clip the corners to clear the inside corner of the posts. You should either paint the underside of the upper support or decorate it with contact paper or

wallpaper because it will be clearly visible to the occupant of the lower bunk.

The ladder sides are made from 5/4-inch stock and the rungs from 4/4-inch material. Lay out the dowel holes carefully. A bevel square set to an angle of 15 degrees will help greatly.

As for the posts, lay out the sides in opposite faces. After the parts have been drilled, shaped, and sanded, apply hide glue, insert the dowels into the rungs, then clamp. Because of the time involved in applying glue, inserting dowels, and assembling, the use of a fast-setting yellow glue is not recommended. We advise the use of a slower setting hide glue. Apply the glue sparingly to the rung ends and to the ladder sides. Then apply the clamps and check the assembly for squareness.

The ladder hooks are bent from a piece of ⅛- × -1-inch cold rolled steel (CRS). Drill and countersink the screw holes, then bend the steel as shown. If there is an iron shop in your town, you can probably get the pieces bent for a couple of dollars. Install the hooks with flat-head screws, then line the underside of the hook with felt to avoid scratching the bed rails.

The guardrails are made with spring-loaded locks, which must be depressed manually before the rail can be removed. As an added safety feature, both locks must be depressed in order to remove the guard. Cut the locks from 4-inch flat corners. We used Stanley #999 corners. Add the pivot hole as shown in the drawing.

Cut the wood parts as indicated. Make the kerf cut ⅛ inch wide and stop short of the end, as shown. Drill the blind ¼-inch set screw hole ¾ inch deep. Again, drill one piece face up and one face down.

Note: if the bed is to be used against the wall, only one guardrail is needed. Two are used if the bed is to be set up away from the wall.

To close the kerfed edge, add the ⅛-inch strip of wood. Glue it as one long strip, then cut away the ''bridge'' over the finger hole after the glue has set.

You can install the lock and spring after you have stained the piece and applied the finish coats. Insert the spring and depress it with a small stick as you insert the lock up from the kerf opening at the bottom. Line up the pivot hole with the opening in the wood, then insert the set screw. When properly installed, the hooked strike of the lock should disappear fully into the kerf when the finger plate is depressed. If the strike doesn't fully depress, file away more metal at the rear of the lock.

Cut and drill the lag screw covers as shown. After the finish coats have been applied, install the female socket into the ½-inch hole at the center of the piece. Install a similar female socket into the appropriate hole in the bed post. Insert the male section into one of the sockets and drive the cover in by striking with a hammer and soft block of wood. To remove the cover, insert a screwdriver up through the opening at the bottom and pry away from the post.

The drawers are of simple construction, but sturdy. Make the sides, front, and rear of oak plywood, and fasten them with hard wood corner blocks. Before assembly, edge the ends of the front and rear plywood panels with ⅛-inch solid oak strips which are glued and nailed. The brads are used mainly to hold the edging in place while clamps are applied. Apply the top edging after the drawers are assembled.

Install the bottom ¼-inch plywood panels after you have assembled three sides of the drawer. Install the fourth or rear panel last, thus locking in the bottom panel. Install glue blocks at each bottom corner and along each of the panels. Fit the drawers with the special nonswivel casters, which permit the drawers to roll in and out effortlessly without tracking off.

Oak is an open-grained wood and can be finished with an application of stain and a topcoat of lacquer, varnish, or other clear finish. For a smooth professional finish, however, give the open grain an application of paste wood filler. This is available with stain already mixed in so the wood can be stained and filled in one operation. Apply the filler with a brush in the direction of the grain. After it sets—about 15 minutes—wipe it off with burlap or excelsior, rubbing across the grain. This will pack the filler into the pores of the wood. After the filler has dried overnight, brush or spray on a sealer coat. When the sealer has dried, apply several topcoats of lacquer. For a truly professional finish, rub the lacquer with a good-quality compound.

If the beds are later to be used separately, use ball finials on the posts of the lower bed. Simply drill $\frac{3}{8}$-inch-diameter holes 1 inch deep into 2-inch balls. The balls will fit over the protruding steel pins.

Wall Unit with Foldaway Bed

COLOR TV, DISC PLAYERS, and related electronic gear, are a dilemma for both homeowner and apartment dweller. Although adding greatly to the enjoyment of our leisure and working hours, they are also gradually encroaching on our living quarters, which are being made smaller than ever before. In essence, we are cramped for living space.

That's where this hideaway bed/electronics storage unit comes in. The average twin bed occupies a floor space of about 30 square feet. If we can eliminate the bed, we can gain that space. Of course we cannot eliminate the bed, but we can put it into the wall—and that's just what we have done. We placed the bed and all our favorite electronic equipment into the wall in

Fig. 30-1. Veneer tape is one way to cover plywood edges. It bonds when heat is applied. Putting tape on a roller makes it easier to use.

Fig. 30-2. You can smooth the edges of the tape with sandpaper, but a hand-held router works well. Check the edges for

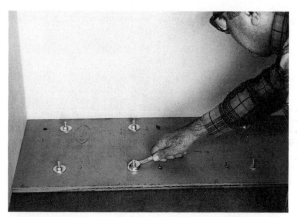

Fig. 30-3. Use carriage bolts on a baseplate. Draw them up tightly with a wrench. Later, the nuts and washers will be replaced.

Fig. 30-4. Here, the left hinge frame member has been installed and bolted securely in place. The spring and the tube are shown also.

a neat and orderly fashion. The "secret" making it possible is the Sico wall bed, which comes complete with box spring and mattress and requires only 18 inches of space stored.

The heart of the bed is the patented Power Pak unit, which is spring-loaded and requires only 12 lbs. of pressure to raise or lower bed, box spring, and mattress. The bed is available in twin, double, or queen sizes. All have an ingenious padded head rest, which is slanted in the bed position and folds neatly to cradle the pillows in the stored position. The bottom panel, which is the frame of the bed, is designed to take a wood panel of your choice.

Fig. 30-5. Raise the bed frame and check it for alignment with the edge of the recess. You can use shims to bring the unit square.

Fig. 30-7. You can finish the surface of the bed as you like. Wallpaper was used here. The small surface makes it easier to get the material smooth.

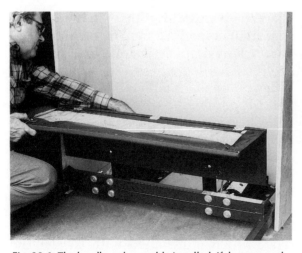

Fig. 30-6. The headboard assembly installed. If done properly, it should fold into the bottom corner when the bed frame is in the raised position.

Fig. 30-8. In the lowered position, the headboard raises automatically. Note how the head of the bed opens away from the wall.

It can be decorated with paper, paint, cork, or whatever is desired. When stored, it becomes a wall decoration.

Our wall system was designed to be compatible with the convertible wall bed, thus all units were made 18 inches deep. The bed compartment size will vary in height and width, depending on the bed size chosen, ranging from twin regular through queen. Write to the company for details. Ours is a twin regular, which requires a recess opening width of 41 inches and a height of 83 ½ inches.

Many people interested in building this wall unit will have limited access to a woodworking shop, especially apartment dwellers. With this in mind, we have designed the system so that it can be built with nothing more than a hammer and square. Many lumberyards will cut your lumber to size if you furnish them with a Materials List. The charge is nominal and with all the pieces precut, the job is greatly eased. If you have power tools, you can save the cutting costs.

Note: These units are quite large and if you build them in the shop, be sure that you will be able to get them upstairs. We built ours in a garage.

Because of the 18-inch depth, plywood panels are recommended because they eliminate gluing of narrow boards. We chose birch, but other species such as oak, pine, etc. will serve equally well. If you plan to paint the cabinets, rather than stain them, you can use fir plywood and cut costs considerably.

As mentioned earlier, we have simplified the construction so that anyone can build the cabinets with ease. Butt joints, glue, and nails are used in assembly. For the craftsman who would like more of a challenge, dadoed and rabbeted construc-tion is recommended. See the optional detail drawing. If you are using dadoes and rabbets, be sure to increase the horizontal width measurements accordingly.

For the strongest possible joints, we suggest that all edges to be glued should be glue-sized. Allow to dry, then apply the glue in the usual manner. The sizing will seal the porous edges, resulting in a good, strong joint that will not be starved for glue.

Another suggestion to consider is the use of galvanized finishing nails. These are similar to regular finishing nails except that their surface is rough as a result of the galvanizing. This roughness increases their holding power tremendously. (You can check holding power by driving one of each type of nails into a piece of scrap wood. Leave the heads slightly extended. Then use the hammer claw to remove the nails. You will be surprised at how well the galvanized nail resists removal.)

The spacing of the shelves was determined by the Radio Shack components we used. You should space the shelves to fit your equipment.

When installing the shelving, use spacers clamped as shown to ensure accuracy and simplify installation. As each shelf is installed, check it for squareness. When nailing is completed, sink nailheads and fill depressions.

The exposed front edges of the plywood can be covered in several ways. You can use solid lumber, wood tape, or plastic shelf edging. If you plan to use shelf edging, you should slot the edges of all stock before assembling the boards.

We used heat-sensitive birch veneer tape, which is installed with an electric iron. The tape comes coated with a hot melt adhesive, which becomes activated when

MATERIALS LIST

Purpose	Size	Description	Quantity
Unit A			
Side	¾″ × 18″ × 84¼″	Birch plywood	2
Top	¾″ × 18″ × 14⅛″	Birch plywood	1
Bottom	¾″ × 18″ × 14⅛″	Birch plywood	1
Back	¼″ × 15⅝″ × 84¼″	Plywood	1
Header	¾″ × 2½″ × 14⅛″	Birch plywood	1
Door	1⅜″ × 14″ × 80″	Birch plywood	1
Hinge	3″	Nonmortise	2
Door knob			1
Wood tape veneer			17′
Unit B			
Side	¾″ × 18″ × 84¼	Birch plywood	2
Shelves	¾″ × 18″ × 31″	Birch plywood	2
Top	¾″ × 18″ × 31″	Birch plywood	1
Bottom	¾″ × 18″ × 31″	Birch plywood	1
Desk top	¾″ × 24″ × 31″	Birch plywood	1
Shelf	¾″ × 12″ × 31″	Birch plywood	1
Door	¾″ × 16¾″ × 25⅛″	Birch plywood	2
Back	¼″ × 32½″ × 84¼″	Plywood	1
Door track	¾″	Stanley	1 set
Finger pull	2″ Dia.		2
Wood tape veneer			32′
Unit C			
Side	¾″ × 18″ × 84¼″	Birch plywood	2
Top	¾″ × 18″ × 41″	Birch plywood	1
Bottom	¾″ × 15″ × 41″	Birch plywood	1
Back	¼″ × 42½″ × 84¼″	Fir plywood	1
Bed face	⅜″ × 38⅜″ × 79¾″	Birch plywood	1
Wallpaper	Double roll		2
Wall bed		Sico 1900 Series	1
Wood tape veneer			18′
Unit D			
Side	¾″ × 18″ × 84¼″	Birch plywood	2
Top	¾″ × 18″ × 31″	Birch plywood	1
Bottom	¾″ × 18″ × 31″	Birch plywood	1
Shelf	¾″ × 18″ × 31″	Birch plywood	4
Divider	¾″ × 18″ × 25½″	Birch plywood	2
Shelf	¾″ × 13″ × 18″	Birch plywood	2
Door	¾″ × 8⅞″ × 25⅜″	Birch plywood	2
Back	¼″ × 32½″ × 84¼″	Plywood	1
Hinge	2″	Nonmortise	4
Pull			2
Wood tape veneer			32′

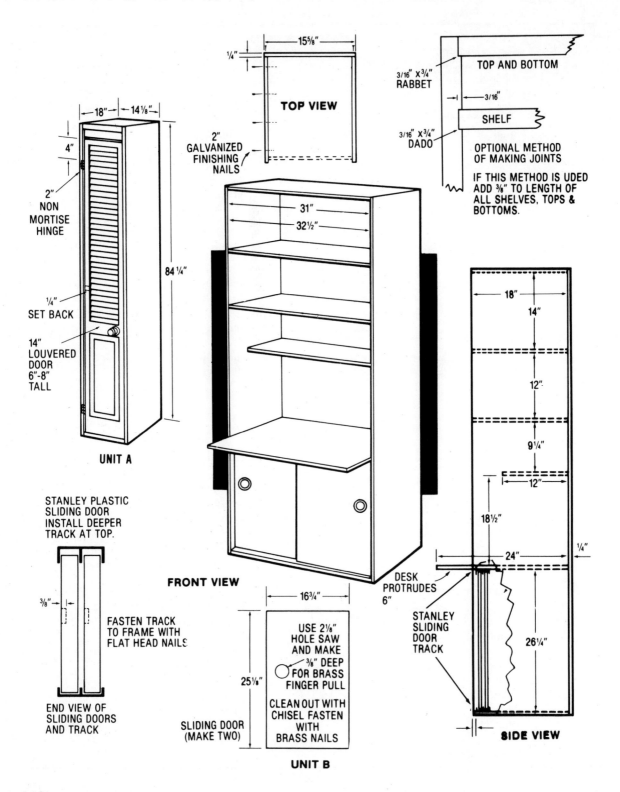

15⅝"

¼"

TOP VIEW

2"
GALVANIZED
FINISHING
NAILS

3/16" X ¾"
RABBET

TOP AND BOTTOM

3/16"

SHELF

3/16" X ¾"
DADO

OPTIONAL METHOD
OF MAKING JOINTS

IF THIS METHOD IS UDED
ADD ⅜" TO LENGTH OF
ALL SHELVES, TOPS &
BOTTOMS.

18"   14⅛"

4"

2"
NON
MORTISE
HINGE

84 ¼"

¼"
SET BACK

14"
LOUVERED
DOOR
6"-8"
TALL

31"

32½"

UNIT A

18"

14"

12"

9¼"

12"

18½"

24"

¼"

STANLEY PLASTIC
SLIDING DOOR
INSTALL DEEPER
TRACK AT TOP.

DESK
PROTRUDES
6"

STANLEY
SLIDING
DOOR
TRACK

26¼"

⅜"

FASTEN TRACK
TO FRAME WITH
FLAT HEAD NAILS

FRONT VIEW

16¾"

END VIEW OF
SLIDING DOORS
AND TRACK

25⅛"

SLIDING DOOR
(MAKE TWO)

USE 2⅛"
HOLE SAW
AND MAKE
⅜" DEEP
FOR BRASS
FINGER PULL

CLEAN OUT WITH
CHISEL FASTEN
WITH
BRASS NAILS

UNIT B

SIDE VIEW

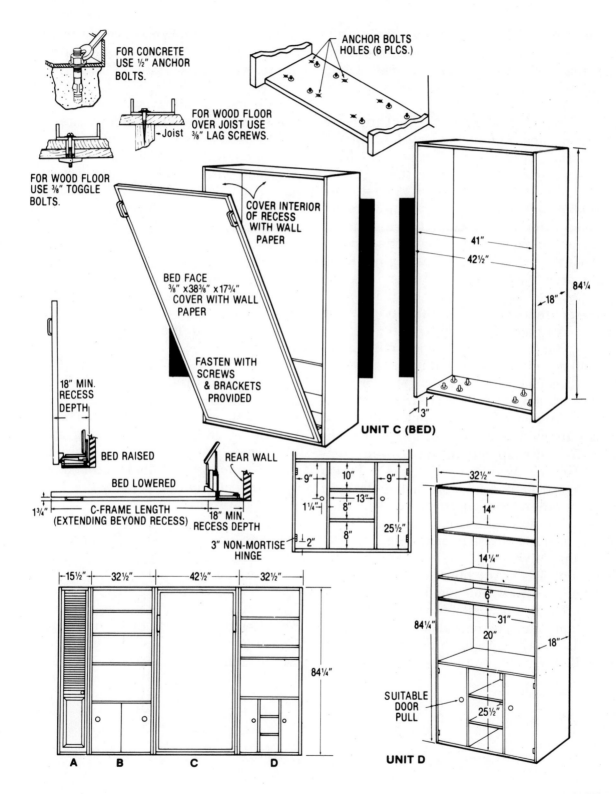

FOR CONCRETE USE ½" ANCHOR BOLTS.

FOR WOOD FLOOR OVER JOIST USE ⅜" LAG SCREWS.

Joist

FOR WOOD FLOOR USE ⅜" TOGGLE BOLTS.

ANCHOR BOLTS HOLES (6 PLCS.)

COVER INTERIOR OF RECESS WITH WALL PAPER

BED FACE
⅜" x38⅜" x17¾"
COVER WITH WALL PAPER

FASTEN WITH SCREWS & BRACKETS PROVIDED

41"

42½"

18"

84¼"

3"

UNIT C (BED)

18" MIN. RECESS DEPTH

BED RAISED

REAR WALL

BED LOWERED

1¾"

C-FRAME LENGTH
(EXTENDING BEYOND RECESS)

18" MIN. RECESS DEPTH

3" NON-MORTISE HINGE

9"   10"   9"
1¼"   13"
8"
25½"
2"   8"

32½"

14"

14¼"

6"

31"

20"

84¼"

18"

SUITABLE DOOR PULL

25½"

UNIT D

15½"   32½"   42½"   32½"

84¼"

A   B   C   D

209

the iron is applied. The tape veneer is available in many species and is easily applied. Nonadhesive veneer tape is also available; this type must be installed with contact cement.

There are several methods of applying veneer tape. The method we found most practical is to cut the horizontal (shelf) strips to exact size using a sharp single-edged razor blade. Apply them to the shelves and to the top and bottom members. After the horizontal strips are in place, follow with the long vertical sides. Abut the pieces tightly at each joint. Keep the iron moving to avoid scorching the wood. After all the strips are in place, sand the corners to break the sharp edges. Use 120-grit paper followed by 220-grit.

The back of the cabinets consists of wall paneling fastened with paneling nails. Space all nails 6 inches apart at intermediate locations, as well as around the perimeter. To simplify the application of stain and finishing coats, do not apply the backs until these operations have been completed. We used Deftco Danish Oil Finish with excellent results. Brush it on, let it set 10 minutes, then wipe with a cloth. When dry, follow with a clear topcoat.

The step-by-step instruction booklet accompanying the Sico In-Wall Bed is excellent. The instructions are easy to understand and well illustrated.

The bed is available with a baseplate or template. The baseplate has mounting bolts for the special hinges already installed. Anchor bolt holes are also drilled on the board. The front edge of the board is set back from the recessed sides to allow the installation of a rug under the bed.

Regardless of the system used, you must install the hinges with great care because they exert trememdous pressure, counterbalancing the weight of the bed. The mounting plate for the springs is provided with slotted holes to permit adjustment of the bed frame within the recess.

If you will install the bed on a hard concrete slab floor, you should anchor the baseplate with the ½-inch-diameter expanding anchor bolts provided. Do not use power-driven or nonexpanding type anchors because they can work loose. For installation over wood floors, use ⅜-inch toggle bolts and, if over joists, ⅜-inch lag screws.

Cut the bed face material of your choice to fit the frame with ¹⁄₁₆-inch clearance all around. We used ⅜-inch plywood faced with wallpaper. Fasten the board to the frame cross members using special clips and ⅜ pan-head screws provided. When properly installed, the bed frame should center in the recess with a ¼-inch gap at the sides.

The bed frame is designed to take a standard-size mattress and box spring. You can purchase them with the frame, or you can use your own if desired.

The convertible wall bed is available in various options. For further information and literature write to Sico, Incorporated, The Room Makers Division, P.O. Box 1169, Minneapolis, MN 55440.

Index

Other Bestsellers From TAB

☐ **FRAMES AND FRAMING: THE ULTIMATE ILLUS-TRATED HOW-TO-DO-IT GUIDE—Gerald F. Laird and Louise Meière Dunn, CPF**

This illustrated step-by-step guide gives complete instructions and helpful illustrations on how to cut mats, choose materials, and achieve attractively framed art. Filled with photographs and eight pages of full color, this book shows why a frame's purpose is to enhance, support, and protect the artwork, and never call attention to itself. You can learn how to make a beautiful frame that complements artwork. 208 pp., 264 illus., 8 pages full color.
Paper $15.95   **Book No. 2909**

☐ **PROJECTS FROM PINE—33 Plans for the Beginning Woodworker—James A. Jacobson**

Easy-to-understand instructions and detailed drawings and photographs make this the perfect guide for beginning woodworkers! You'll find plans for cutting boards, a flower pot drop, a candle box, wood ornaments, a wine rack, shaker items, bookends, and shelves—all ideal gift ideas and many that you may want to produce in quantity and sell at craft shows. The author takes you from selecting suitable pine lumber for your project to a detailed discussion of the finishing process. 192 pp., 147 illus., 7″ × 10″.
Paper $13.95   **Hard $17.95**
Book No. 2871

☐ **BUILDING A LOG HOME FROM SCRATCH OR KIT—2nd Edition—Dan Ramsey**

This up-to-the-minute guide to log home building takes you from initial planning and design stages right through the final interior finishing of your new house. There's advice on selecting a construction site, choosing a home that's right for your needs and budget, estimating construction costs, obtaining financing, locating suppliers and contractors, and deciding whether to use a kit or build from scratch. 302 pp., 311 illus., Paperback.
Paper $12.95   **Hard $14.95**
Book No. 2858

☐ **33 USEFUL PROJECTS FOR THE WOODWORKER—Editors of *School Shop* Magazine**

A wealth of information for beginning and advanced hobbyists . . . tools, techniques, and dozens of exciting projects. Here's a handbook that deserves a permanent spot on every woodworker's tool bench. Packed with show-how illustrations and material lists, this invaluable guide provides you with a wide variety of useful, and fun-to-make woodworking projects: a spice rack, a wall clock, a plant stand, a cutting board, a wooden chest, a magazine rack, a serving cart, a child's playhouse, and more! 160 pp., 122 illus., Paperback.
Paper 10.95   **Hard $12.95**
Book No. 2783

☐ **101 KITCHEN PROJECTS FOR THE WOODWORKER—Percy W. Blandford**

These 101 practical as well as decorative projects for every level of woodworking ability are sure to provide pleasure and satisfaction for builder and cook alike! Included are bread and cheese boards, carving boards and butcher blocks, trays, cookbook stand and stacking vegetable bin, spatulas, forks, spring tongs, mug racks, pivoting and parallel towel rails, spice racks, tables, a hutch, and much, much more! 270 pp., 214 illus.
Paper 17.95   **Hard $23.95**
Book No. 2884

☐ **WOODCRAFTING HERITAGE TOYS: A TREASURY OF CLASSIC PROJECTS—H. LeRoy Marlow**

This classic treasury is for the woodworker who wants projects demanding more skill and artistry than the ordinary quick-and-easy plans found in most books. It is a collection of 17 delightful and *original* keepsake-quality wooden toys. All the toys presented are made entirely of wood fastened by glue—no nails, screws, staples, plastic, or other materials are used. Full-scale patterns for the toys need only to be traced—no enlargements or other calculations are necessary. 192 pp., 167 illus., plus 8 full-color pages.
Paper $19.95   **Hard $24.95**
Book No. 2863

☐ **40 EASY-TO-BUILD HOME FURNISHINGS—The Editors of *School Shop* Magazine**

A treasure of decorative, practical, and money-saving projects. Here's an intriguing collection of 40 easy-to-build, functional and decorative projects that you can make quickly and easily with a minimum supply of tools. From home furnishings and accessories, storage units, and office supplies to projects that will add to your indoor and outdoor hobby and sports fun, each project has been carefully selected for ease of construction practicability. 144 pp., 67 illus.
Paper $12.95   **Hard $16.95**
Book No. 2788

☐ **77 ONE-WEEKEND WOODWORKING PROJECTS—Percy W. Blandford**

Let this guide put the fun back into your hobby! Overflowing with step-by-step instructions, easy-to-follow illustrations, dimensioned drawings, and material lists, this indispensable guide includes plans for 77 projects: tables, racks and shelves, take-down book rack, low bookcase, corner shelves, magazine rack, portable magazine bin, shoe rack, vase stand, beds and cabinets, yard and garden projects, toys, games and puzzles, tools, and more. 304 pp., 226 illus.
Paper $17.95   **Hard $23.95**
Book No. 2774

Other Bestsellers From TAB